Book
Yourself
Solid

Book Yourself Solid

The Fastest, Easiest, and
Most Reliable System for
Getting *More Clients*
Than You Can Handle
*Even if You Hate
Marketing and Selling*

SECOND EDITION, REVISED & EXPANDED

Michael Port

WILEY

John Wiley & Sons, Inc.

Published by John Wiley & Sons, Inc., Hoboken, New Jersey.
Published simultaneously in Canada.

For general information on our other products and services or for technical support, please contact our Customer Care Department within the United States at (800) 762-2974, outside the United States at (317) 572-3993 or fax (317) 572-4002.

Wiley also publishes its books in a variety of electronic formats. Some content that appears in print may not be available in electronic books. For more information about Wiley products, visit our web site at www.wiley.com.

Library of Congress Cataloging-in-Publication Data:

Port, Michael, 1970–
    Book yourself solid : the fastest, easiest, and most reliable system for getting more clients than you can handle even if you hate marketing and selling / Michael Port—2nd ed.
        p. cm.
    ISBN 978-0-470-64347-1 (pbk.), ISBN 978-0-470-92544-7 (ebk); 978-0-470-92546-1 (ebk); 978-0-470-92685-7 (ebk)
        1. Selling. 2. Marketing. 3. Strategic planning. I. Title.
HF5438.25.P67 2010
658.8—dc22

2010024728

Printed in the United States of America

10 9 8 7 6 5 4 3

This book is a love story disguised as a business book,
a love story between you
and all the inspiring clients you will serve.

Contents

Foreword

Face it—you'd rather be doing your life's work than filling the sales funnel or getting the word out. Every day that you aren't on a project is like an airplane seat that goes unsold. You picked up this book because you know that you can do better and grow stronger in your business acumen.

You will get out of this book only what you put into it. Don't just skim the pages to pick up pointers. Take the time to do each exercise. Take a few weeks to move through this book. Pretend you are in school and striving to be at the top of your class. *Because you are.* When you look at your calendar next year and you aren't happy with all the white space, pick this book up and go through it again more slowly.

Readers are leaders, and I believe this is true with you. Read this book as a business owner and think about the suggestions as you build a culture for your company. Who knows how big your enterprise might get? You might be hatching the next Big Blue, and you will need a common set of values to guide your vision into the future.

I resonate with this book's technology and its spirit. Most of Michael's advice comes from a point of view that can be summed up in two statements:

- Make yourself emotionally attractive.
- Live on the right side of the Law of Reciprocity.

Emotionally attractive people win the popularity contests that make up your life. Yes, you have experience, work ethic, and talent. But you still lose the business and see it floating to a competitor, and you *know* you are better than that competitor. Why? The emotional brain is two dozen times more powerful than the logical brain. The customer wants a great experience, not just good consulting or an effective process. The attention you pay to the emotional experience of working with your customers may be the best way to differentiate yourself and build a contagious brand.

Book Yourself Solid outlines practical ways to improve your ability to produce positive emotions in other people—from how you serve them to how you network with them. Above all, the book gives you advice on building a consistent process in your business. And process is very *likable* to a customer.

The Law of Reciprocity must be respected to build a sustainable business of any kind. This law postulates that in almost every case people reciprocate, especially when it comes to energy or generosity. If your customers receive added value from you, they will add energy to your relationship. If you give them enough (either intangible or tangible), you will reach a tipping point at which they become loyal to you and start to market you to their sphere of influence.

Conversely, when you create an I-win-you-lose scenario for the customer, your business is cyclical. You get a job, finish it, and return to selling yourself. You have to slug out every business win. This is true even when you are the excellent provider who behaves like the Soup Nazi on the *Seinfeld* TV show.

Either you build a business that obeys this law or you don't. There is probably no in-between. Greed is too powerful and faith is too fragile. This book will guide you into a set of practices that always give your customer a reason to give back and wish you the best.

As I finished reading this book, I was reminded of an old saying that should send you deep between the lines as you read it:

Long after people forget what you said or did, they will remember how you made them feel.

—Tim Sanders
Author of *The Likeability Factor: How to Boost Your L-Factor and Achieve Your Life's Dreams*
(Crown Publishing)

Acknowledgments

The first line of the acknowledgments section in virtually every book goes something like this: To list everyone I want to thank for their contributions to this book would be a book in itself. You really don't know how true that is until you write your own book.

So, to all the people who have shaped this book and have made my life and work as spectacular as it is today . . . thank you.

And, to my son Jake . . . the goodness in you is the fire that fuels me.

Author's Note

An unfulfilled vocation drains the color from a man's entire existence.

—Honoré de Balzac

In early 2000 I was utterly dissatisfied and completely disillusioned with my work as the vice president of programming at an entertainment company. The environment felt like a prison—long hours, unresponsive colleagues, and no personal engagement. Sound familiar? I decided to embark on a new career path as a professional business coach and consultant: a service professional. I secretly passed the time reading, researching, studying, and honing my coaching skills. After much planning, my freedom date was marked on every calendar in my apartment with a huge victorious smiley face. My resignation letter was signed, sealed, and ready for delivery. I could hardly keep my legs from sprinting out the door to follow my heart and head (both of which had checked out long ago).

On that auspicious day, I received the envelope with my bonus inside, ran to the bank, cleared the check, and proudly delivered my letter of resignation. The joy, pride, and satisfaction that I felt at that moment was incredible. I floated home and woke up the next day to plunge into my career as a business owner serving others.

I didn't bask for long in the glory, however, before I realized I was in for trouble.

Call me crazy, but I really thought clients were just going to fall into my lap. I expected them to meet me, fall in love with me, and trade their money for my services. Instead, I moped about my very costly New York City apartment, panicking, feeling sorry for myself, and doing trivial busy work that wasn't going to generate a dime of income.

Within six months I was desperate, which heralded a new phase of my life. I was fed up. I'd reached my limit. I was not going to throw in the towel and give up on my career as a business owner. My innate need to support and provide, to serve the people I was meant to serve, kicked into high gear one chilly New York morning. Rather than dwelling on the cold reality of my financial struggle and the bitter temperature outside, I worked every single day for no less than 16 hours to succeed and pay the bills. I poured myself into more resources and studied everything I could get my hands on about how to attract clients, communicate effectively, sell, market, and promote my services. First and foremost, I wanted to learn how to love marketing and selling by turning it into a meaningful spiritual pursuit.

It worked. Within 10 months I was booked solid with more clients than I could handle. But the personal checks I cashed were not the most valuable part of my business. The real heart of what I was creating was the turnkey system that propelled my business and income every month. I started sharing my success secrets with a small group of trusted clients, and I watched their success unfold before my eyes. I could hear confidence, pride, and accomplishment in their voices. Their businesses boomed!

My clients, who were service professionals of all kinds, started to get booked solid: massage therapists, mortgage brokers, accountants, therapists, acupuncturists, dentists, hair salon and spa owners, bookkeepers, web and graphic designers, business consultants, chiropractors, professional organizers, financial planners, virtual assistants, health care providers, insurance brokers, attorneys, personal trainers, travel agents, photographers, physiotherapists, Pilates and yoga instructors, coaches, Realtors, reflexologists, sales professionals, naturopaths, and others were getting more clients than they could handle.

I immediately began to engineer a completely replicable system that I could pass on to you. That system is the Book Yourself Solid system, and you're holding it in your hands, the same system I've been teaching to thousands of other service professionals around the world in my live seminars and Book Yourself Solid Intensive Coaching Programs. The results are powerful.

Over 93 percent of clients who have used the Book Yourself Solid system have increased the number of clients they serve by more than 34 percent and increased their revenue by more than 42 percent within the first year.

And that was before I published the book. When the book released in April of 2006, *Book Yourself Solid* was the Number 2 best-selling book on Amazon.com. It has since become an evergreen resource for professional service providers all over the United States, the United Kingdom, and Canada. It's been translated into Spanish, Vietnamese, Bulgarian, Polish, Bahasa Indonesian, Orthodox Chinese, and Korean. It's included in curriculums at graduate-level business schools and is touted as recommended reading by professional associations like the National Association of Realtors, which called *Book Yourself Solid* a "must read."

The thing about a published book is that once it's printed, it's done. Yet, over the years, in my speeches and coaching programs, I've changed important parts of the system, fine tuned others, and added new, up-to-date material. Enter the second edition. It keeps the best of the Book Yourself Solid system, clarifies essential parts, and trims the fat, doing away with anything that you don't absolutely need to know. I've even added an entirely new chapter on pricing and another one on the most up-to-date social media marketing. I believe this new edition of the book should make for even easier reading, faster and more effective consumption, and bigger, more impressive, and profitable results.

I'd like to impress upon you right now how realistic it is for you to become a successful self-employed professional. According to Daniel Pink (*Free Agent Nation*—citing a study by Anne E. Polvika, "Into Contingent and Alternative Employment: By Choice?," reported in the October 1996 issue of *Monthly Labor Review*), "Full-time independent contractors earn an average of 15 percent more than their employee counterparts." Daniel Pink also shows (from a study by Aquent Partners) that, "independent professionals are twice as likely as W-2 workers to have personal incomes above $75,000 per year." In fact the Aquent Partners study shows that one in four Americans is now an independent professional.

That's great news, isn't it? It proves that you've made the right choice to go out on your own. But I'd like for us to think even bigger. What if you could do more? Just imagine how different your life would be if you were earning $10,000 each and every month. How about $20,000, $30,000, or $40,000 each month? How about $100,000 each and every month? Amazingly different. I can tell you from personal experience that it opens up a world of possibilities. And you can do it too! Because the Book Yourself Solid system will get you up and out into the world in the biggest and most profitable way.

You need to learn the skills necessary to promote your work and become the go-to person in your field before it's too late. I don't want you to start working through this book two years from now. I want you to reap all of the rewards that you deserve now. If you haven't yet reached the level of success you expected or wanted in your business, there is only one small change you need to make. Put yourself smack-dab in the middle of my Book Yourself Solid system. This one move will get you sprinting (not walking . . . not running . . . but sprinting!) to monthly income and personal satisfaction that will change your business—and your life. Think of all the freedom, abundance, profitability, and joy you can create for yourself.

There is no question that the Book Yourself Solid system can change your business and your life. Of course, it's up to you whether you'll take advantage of it.

You love what you do. You're great at what you do. You stand in the service of others, and you are a remarkable human being for doing so— now it's time to get booked solid.

I will show you the way to a profitable, meaningful, and absolutely booked-solid business, overflowing with as many clients as your heart desires, clients who energize and inspire you, clients with whom you do your best work, clients who will pay you handsomely.

I hope you feel the same exhilaration in building your independent business as I do every day. I expect that the Book Yourself Solid system will not only inspire you but will keep you keenly focused on learning and relearning, experimenting and honing all that is within you. I am certain the secret to your success isn't just in the work that we do together. It lies within you. *Book Yourself Solid* will help facilitate your greatness.

We are all on this path together, learning from one another. We are all seeking joy, love, success, and happiness. I urge you to continue to trust that you are making a huge difference in the lives of your clients, yourself, and society as a whole.

Here's to you—to focusing on getting as many clients as your heart desires. It is my wish that you come to the Book Yourself Solid system with an open heart and mind. Completely remove, or at least set aside, any preconceived ideas fluttering in your head. Let this powerful process be revealed to you step by step.

The Book Yourself Solid way is one of abundance, joy, and meaning. It's my deep honor to hold your hand and walk you down this path. I've had the pleasure and fortune to serve thousands of other professionals just like you who want to build a service business based on their gifts, talents, and skills. And just like them, you inspire and energize me because you have dedicated your work to serving others. I know your successful breakthrough is near and will continue to be sustained by your faith, inner strength, and confidence.

As any silly, serious, significant, strategic, personal, or professional questions come up, please give me a shout. I'm always delighted to hear from you. Fire off any and all questions to me and my team at questions@michaelport.com. If there is anything I can do to serve you, please just ask.

Now, let's get to booking you solid!

Think Big,
Michael Port

Preface

The Book Yourself Solid system is supported by both practical and spiritual principles.

From a practical perspective there may be two simple reasons why you don't serve as many clients as you'd like to today. Either you don't know what to do to attract and secure more clients or you know what to do but you're not actually doing it. The Book Yourself Solid system is designed to help you solve both of these problems. I will give you all the information you need to book even more clients than you can handle; I will give you the strategies, techniques, and tips. If you already know what to do but aren't doing it, I'll inspire you into action and help you stay accountable so you build the business of your dreams.

From a spiritual perspective I believe that if you have something to say, if you have a message to deliver, and if there are people you want to serve, then there are people in this world whom you are *meant* to serve. Not kinda, sorta, because they're in your target market . . . but *meant* to—that's the way the universe is set up if you're in the business of serving others. If you don't understand this now, you will when you have read this book and begun to follow the Book Yourself Solid way.

The system is organized into four modules:

1. Your Foundation.
2. Building Trust and Credibility.

3. Simple Selling and Perfect Pricing.
4. The Book Yourself Solid 7 Core Self-Promotion Strategies.

We will begin by building a foundation for your service business that is unshakable. If you are truly serious about becoming a super-successful service professional, you must have a steadfast foundation on which to stand. You will then be ready to create and implement a strategy for building trust and credibility. You'll be considered a credible expert in your field and you'll start to earn the trust of the people you'd like to serve. You'll price your offerings in the sweet spot of the customer's desires and you'll know how to have sales conversations of the highest integrity that work. Then, and only then, will you execute the seven core self-promotion strategies, thereby creating awareness for the valuable services you offer by using promotional strategies that are based on your talents—strategies that feel authentic and honest.

To help you design a service business overflowing with clients who inspire and energize you, this book includes written exercises and Booked Solid Action Steps that will support you in thinking bigger about your business. Step-by-step I walk you through the actions you need to complete on the path to serving as many clients as your heart desires.

As a reader of *Book Yourself Solid*, you will want to retain your responses to the written exercises for regular review. I have prepared a complimentary downloadable workbook that includes all of the written exercises and Booked Solid Action Steps contained in this book. Simply visit my web site and download the workbook so that you may begin today to take the necessary steps to get more clients than you can handle.

Go to www.bookyourselfsolid.com/workbook.htm right now and download your free copy of the workbook so you have it in your hands before you turn another page. So, your first Action Step is to get your workbook. Go head . . . I'll wait. . . .

While you'll no doubt get great value just from reading this book, the true value—and your success—lies in your decision to take an active role and to participate fully by doing the exercises and taking the Booked Solid Action Steps I've outlined. In doing so, you will begin an evolutionary journey of personal and business development that will empower you to achieve the success you know you're capable of.

If you follow the system, it *will* work for you. No skipping, jumping, or moving ahead—the Book Yourself Solid 7 Core Self-Promotion Strategies are effectively implemented only after your foundation, credibility-building, pricing, and sales strategies are in place. One of the main reasons that service professionals say they hate marketing and selling is that they're trying to market without these essential elements, which is like eating an egg before it's cooked—of course, you'll hate it. So no matter how compelled you are to skip ahead, I urge you to *please* follow the system and watch the process unfold.

So many talented and inspired service professionals like you run from marketing and sales because they have come to believe that the marketing and selling process is pushy and self-centered and borders on sleazy. This old-school paradigm is not the Book Yourself Solid way; it is the typical client-snagging mentality. And you must *never* fall into this way of thinking and being. If you do, you'll operate in a mentality of scarcity and shame as opposed to one of abundance and integrity.

Ask yourself these questions:

- How can I be fully self-expressed in my work to create meaning for me and those I serve?
- How can I work only in the areas of my greatest strengths and talents so that I can shine?
- How many relationships with people of purpose did I make and deepen?
- How can I better listen to and serve my ideal clients?
- How can I wow people with substance?
- How can I overdeliver on my promises to my clients?
- How can I cooperate with other professionals to create more abundance?

If you keep asking yourself these questions, set a solid foundation for your business, build trust and credibility within your marketplace, learn how to price and sell your offerings, and use the seven core self-promotion strategies, you'll be booked solid in no time.

Ready to get started? Let's do it!

Your Foundation

To be booked solid requires that you have a solid foundation. That foundation begins like this:

- Choose your ideal clients so you work only with people who inspire and energize you.
- Understand why people buy what you are selling.
- Develop a personal brand so you're memorable and unique.
- Talk about what you do without sounding confusing or bland.

Over the course of Module One, I'll step you through the process of building your foundation so that you have a platform on which to stand, a perfectly engineered structure that will support all of your business development and marketing, and—dare I add—personal growth. That's because being in business for yourself, especially as someone who stands in the service of others, requires constant personal reflection and spiritual growth.

Building your foundation is a bit like putting a puzzle together. We're going to take it one piece at a time, and when we're done you'll have laid the foundation for booking yourself solid.

CHAPTER 1

The Red Velvet Rope Policy

He who trims himself to suit everyone will soon whittle himself away.

—Raymond Hull

Imagine that a friend has invited you to accompany her to an invitation-only special event. You arrive and approach the door, surprised to find a red velvet rope stretched between two shiny brass poles. A nicely dressed man asks your name, checking his invitation list. Finding your name there, he flashes a wide grin and drops one end of the rope, allowing you to pass through and enter the party. You feel like a star.

Do you have your own red velvet rope policy that allows in only the most ideal clients, the ones who energize and inspire you? If you don't, you will shortly. Why?

First, because when you work with clients you love, you'll truly enjoy the work you're doing; you'll love every minute of it. And when you love every minute of the work you do, you'll do your *best* work, which is essential to book yourself solid.

Second, because you *are* your clients. They are an expression and an extension of you. Do you remember when you were a teenager and your mother or father would give you a hard time about someone you were hanging out with? Your parents may have said that a particular kid reflected badly on you and was a bad influence. As a teen you may have thought about how unfair that felt, but the truth is that you are the company you keep. Let this be the imperative of your business: Choose your clients as carefully as you choose your friends.

The first step in building your foundation is to choose your ideal clients, the individuals or businesses with whom you do your best work, the people or environments that energize and inspire you. I'm going to help you identify specific characteristics of individuals or organizations that would make them ideal to work with. You will then develop a rigorous screening process to find more of them. I'm also going to help you prune your current client list of less-than-ideal clients.

When I began my business I would work with anyone who had a pulse and a checkbook. Then I began to consider what it would mean to choose my clients. What it would mean to work only with clients that were ideal for me. And thank goodness I did. Now I live by what I call the red velvet rope policy of ideal clients. It increases my productivity and my happiness, it allows me to do my best work, and I have more clients and referrals than I can handle by myself. And so will you.

For maximum joy, prosperity, and abundance, think about the person you are when you are performing optimally, when you are with all the people who inspire and energize you. Now think about all of the frustration, tension, and anxiety you feel when you work with clients who are less than ideal—not so good, right?

Wouldn't it be great to spend every day working with clients who are ideal for you, clients whom you can hardly believe you get paid to work with? This ideal is completely possible once you identify who you want to work with and determine with certainty that you will settle for nothing less. Once you do that, it's just a matter of knowing which of your existing clients qualify and how to acquire more just like them.

Dump the Duds

Author and business guru Tom Peters takes us a step further. In *Reinventing Work: The Professional Service Firm 50*, he challenges us to dump our dud clients. "Dump my clients?!" you exclaim. I can just hear your shocked protestations and exclamations. "I thought this was a book about getting clients, not dumping them!" But Peters is referring to the *dud* clients—not all of your clients. It sounds harsh, but think about it. Your dud clients are those you dread interacting with, who drain the life out of you, bore you to tears, frustrate you, or worse, instill in you the desire to do them—or yourself—bodily harm, despite your loving nature.

I'm well aware of the many reasons you *think* you can't dump your dud clients, and I know this can seem really scary early on, but hang in there with me. Embrace the concept and trust that this is sound advice from a loving teacher and a necessary step on the path to booking yourself solid.

Why have clients, or anyone for that matter, in your life who zap your energy and leave you feeling empty? In the first year of being in business on my own, I cut 10 clients in one week. It wasn't easy. It required a major leap of faith, but the emotional and financial rewards were astonishing. Within three months, I had replaced all 10 and added 6 more. Not only did I increase my revenue, I felt more peaceful and calm than I ever had before, and I enjoyed my clients and my work more.

When I asked myself the question, "Would I rather spend my days working with incredibly amazing, exciting, super cool, awesome people who are both clients and friends, or spend one more agonizing, excruciating minute working with barely tolerable clients who suck the life out me?" I had no choice. I knew the temporary financial loss would be worth the payoff.

1.1.1 Written Exercise: To begin to identify the types of clients you don't want, consider which characteristics or behaviors you refuse to tolerate. What turns you off or shuts you down? What kinds of people should *not* be getting past the red velvet rope that protects you and your business?

1.1.2 Written Exercise: Now take a good, hard look at your current clients. Be absolutely honest with yourself. Who among your current clients fits the profile you've just created of people who should *not* have gotten past the red velvet rope that protects you and your business?

1.1.3 Booked Solid Action Step: Dump the dud clients you've just listed in the preceding exercise. It may be just one client, or you may need another two pages to write them all down. (Did I warn you that I'd push you to step out of your comfort zone? If I didn't before, I am now.) Is your heart pounding? Is your stomach churning at just the thought? Have you broken out in a cold sweat? Or are you jumping up and down with excitement now that you've been given permission to dump your duds? Maybe you're experiencing both sensations at the same time; that's totally normal.

Taking a Booked Solid Action Step is a bold action and requires courage. And courage is not about being fearless—it's about owning your fear and using it to move you forward, to give you strength. There is no more rewarding feeling than the pride you'll feel once you've moved past the fear to do what you set out to do. Maybe you'll find it easier to take it one step at a time. Start by referring out just one of those dud clients. The feeling of empowerment you'll have once you've done it will motivate you to continue pruning your list of clients until the duds have all been removed.

What to Do When You Don't (Yet) Have Clients

But, Michael, what if I just started my business and don't yet have clients, let alone dud clients? Ah, yes, excellent point, my new friend. Consider yourself lucky! You'll never have to worry about dud clients because you'll put your Red Velvet Rope Policy in place on Day One.

In just a moment, you'll begin to create your Red Velvet Rope Policy. If you're starting a new business, and don't yet have many, or any, clients to speak of at this point, as you're working through the exercises, think about current or former co-workers, friends, or even service providers that you've hired in the past. To create your future Red Velvet Rope Policy you'll be able to draw on your past experiences—who inspired you and who made you want to do them bodily harm. Refrain. Rewind. Remember: love and kindness. Love and kindness.

Pruning Your Client List

If you're struggling with the idea of pruning your client list, keep in mind that it's for your client's benefit as much as it is for yours. If you're feeling empty and drained, or frustrated and dreading the interaction with the client, you're giving that client far less than your best, and it's both of you who are suffering for it. You owe it to these clients to refer them to someone who can, and will, do their best work with them. If you are working with people with whom you do not do your best work, you are out of integrity. And as we discussed earlier, you *are* your clients. When your clients go out into the world and speak of you to others, they are representing you.

With whom do you want to be associated—the duds or the ideal clients? It's also the ideal clients, those who are wildly happy with you and your services, who are most likely to go out and talk about you to others, to refer other clients like themselves, more ideal clients. The fewer duds you allow to hang around, the more ideal clients you have room for, the more referrals you'll get, and so on.

Clients are like family to me, so I know this can be hard. I lived through a period of intense and painful negative energy worrying about those challenging client relationships. It exhausted me and took me away from accomplishing the highest good for my clients. It was impossible for me to be productive, effective, or successful when working with less-than-ideal clients.

Let me share a story with you about myself and my former land-scaper, when *I* was the less-than-ideal client. For a variety of reasons, my landscaper and I were just not a good fit for each other. One of them being that every so often I'd cut the grass on a whim and then his guys would show up with nothing to mow. Instead, I'd ask them to do other projects on the property, which I thought was reasonable. Anyhow, the point is, he had issues with me; he knew I wasn't his ideal client, but rather than tell me so, he stayed with me while getting more and more annoyed until he blew up and acted like a jerk, forcing me to let him go. More than likely, he didn't feel comfortable dumping his dud clients, or the idea had never even crossed his mind. Granted, pruning his dud clients wouldn't have been as easy as pruning his clients' trees, but had he not allowed the situation to deteriorate and end on such a bad note, I might have been able to refer other clients to him who would have been ideal for him. His inability to take the booked solid action step of letting his less-than-ideal clients go left both of us dissatisfied with the situation and jeopardized his reputation.

This is what can happen when you work with clients who are not ideal for you. At some point, you're going to create a conflict, whether intentionally or not, because you're going to be frustrated with those clients. Those clients will think you're not providing them with good service, and they'll be right. It doesn't serve you or the client when you stay in a less-than-ideal situation. Please don't make the same mistake my landscaper did. If you do, you'll have former clients going out into the world telling anyone who will listen that you're the worst person to work with.

There's nothing *wrong* with your dud clients, of course. They're just not right for you. Clients who are not ideal for you could be ideal for someone else. So keep in mind that you don't need to fire clients; you just need to help them find a better fit. You can be tactful, diplomatic, and loving. You can even attempt, when appropriate, to refer them to a colleague who might be a better fit. Whenever possible, keep it simple. Try, "I'm not the best person to serve you." Or "I don't think we'd be a good fit."

Are you always going to get a positive response when dumping your dud clients? Probably not. If the first thing that comes to mind is, "I don't want anyone out there thinking badly of me," I'm with you. I want everyone to love me, too. But living life fully requires difficult conversations and you can never please everyone. To even try is an exercise in futility, as the following fable demonstrates.

The Old Man, the Boy, and the Donkey

An old man, a boy, and a donkey were going to town. The boy rode on the donkey and the old man walked beside him. As they went along they passed some people who remarked it was a shame the old man was walking and the boy was riding. The man and boy thought maybe the critics were right, so they changed positions.

Later, they passed some people who remarked, "What a shame! He makes that little boy walk." They then decided they both would walk.

Soon they passed some more people who thought they were stupid to walk when they had a decent donkey to ride. So they both rode the donkey.

Later, they passed some people who shamed them by saying how awful to put such a load on a poor donkey. The boy and man said they were probably right, so they decided to carry the donkey. As they crossed the bridge, they lost their grip on the animal, and he fell into the river and drowned.

The moral of the story? *If you try to please everyone, you might as well kiss your ass goodbye.*

The point is that you are looking for qualities in a person that you resonate with, so don't limit yourself to just thinking about the clients that you don't yet have. Your Red Velvet Rope Policy is a filtration system that lets in ideal clients. However, you can choose to loosen or tighten the rope at will. I'm not (necessarily) asking you to turn away your very first clients. I understand what you're up against. When you start your business, if you feel that you'd like to keep your red velvet rope a little looser so you can work with more clients, go ahead. Just make sure you know what is ideal and what isn't ideal about the people you're letting into the VIP room. As you become booked solid, you'll tighten your red velvet rope and become even more exclusive so as to work only with those that energize and inspire you—and most important—allow you to do your best work.

Creating Your Red Velvet Rope Policy

The benefits of working with ideal clients are many and meaningful:

- You'll have clean energy to do your best work.
- You'll feel invigorated and inspired.
- You'll connect with clients on a deeper level.
- You'll feel successful and confident.
- You'll know your work matters and is changing lives.
- The magic of you will come to life.

My ideal clients have these qualities:

- Bright (full of light and easily excitable).
- Resilient (keep coming back).
- Courageous (face their fears).
- Think big (their projects benefit large groups of people).
- Value-oriented (they gain value from relationships with me and others).
- Naturally collaborative (they contribute to and focus on their solutions).
- Rapid responders (talk today, done tomorrow).
- Positive (naturally optimistic).

Your list might look completely different. Maybe you only want to work with certain types of clients. Maybe reliability or long-term goals are important to you. Maybe your top priority is how often a client works with you or how many projects they do with you. The economic status of a client may be one factor, but remember—it's only one of many. In fact, it's often a primary consideration for many service professionals who wind up working with clients who are less than ideal. So take heed—the economic status of a potential client should be only one of many considerations. Notice that my list considers the *quality* of my ideal clients first—who they *are* rather than what they *have* or the circumstances they're in.

1.1.4 Written Exercise: Define your ideal client. What type of people do you love being around? What do they like to do? What do they talk about? With whom do they associate? What ethical standards do they follow? How do they learn? How do they contribute to society? Are they smiling, outgoing, creative? What kind of environment do you want to create in your life? And who will get past the Red Velvet Rope Policy that protects you? List the *qualities, values,* or *personal characteristics* you'd like your ideal clients to possess.

1.1.5 Written Exercise: Now let's look at your current client base. Whom do you love interacting with the most? Who do you look forward to seeing? Who are the clients who don't feel like work to you? *Who is it you sometimes just can't believe you get paid to work with?* Write down the names of clients, or people you've worked with, whom you love to be around.

1.1.6 Written Exercise: Get a clear picture of these people in your head. Write down the top five reasons that you love working with them. What about working with them turns you on?

1.1.7 Written Exercise: Now go deeper. If you were working only with ideal clients, what qualities would they absolutely *need* to possess in order for you to do your *best* work with them? Be honest and don't worry about excluding people. Be selfish. Think about yourself. For this exercise, assume you will work only with the best of the best. Be brave and bold and write without thinking or filtering your thoughts.

How different were the last two lists? You may have nailed it the first time. Maybe you're right on track, or maybe you have some perfect client opportunities to uncover.

By knowing who your ideal clients are and selecting only those who have at least 75 percent of the qualities you identified, you will have more fun, accomplish greater results, and experience incredible joy and fulfillment in your business.

This is beneficial because you'll be able to identify other ideal clients you'd love to work with. People enjoy knowing how important they are to you, and if they know you do your best work with, and for, people like them, they are much more inclined to work with you. It raises the stakes for them.

Look at these requirements and think about how you can start to turn them into filters. As for me, I'm like a giant generator—the more gas (meaning projects or clients) I take in, the more power I create. But the wrong kind of fuel causes me to sputter and conk out. Think about a hot sports car running on diesel fuel—not pretty. Neither is this roadster when he gets the wrong kind of energy. Every engine needs a filtration system to keep the system running smoothly and cleanly, just as you need to create a clean system of clients that will filter out the imperfections.

My client filters include these:

- I feel more energized and excited after working with my clients.
- My clients seek open feedback, and better yet, they take action when they get it.

- My clients have faith that leaves some people bewildered and some astonished.
- My clients are not victims; they hold themselves accountable and think about the betterment of others.
- My clients continually seek out and develop valuable personal and professional relationships.
- My clients feel stimulated and energized by the input and collaborative efforts of others.
- My clients use anecdotes and colorful speech, and they share personal stories.
- My clients do not procrastinate; they respond quickly to new opportunities.
- My clients are naturally optimistic and do not complain.

1.1.8 Written Exercise: What filters do you want to run your perfect clients through?

Ideal Clients, the Duds, and Everyone Else

As you eliminate the duds, you'll open up room for ideal clients. As you use the Book Yourself Solid system to attract more and more ideal clients, you'll discover that you're happier, more vibrant, more energetic, and more productive. You'll be on fire. You'll be giving your clients the best of yourself and your services, and you'll love every minute of it.

1.1.9 Written Exercise: Draw a simple table with three columns: Label the first column "Ideal Clients," the second "Duds," and the third "Everyone Else." Now divide your clients into these three groups. Don't hold back or leave anyone out.

As if that weren't enough, you may begin to notice that many of your mid-range clients, those who made neither the ideal client nor the dud list, are undergoing a transformation. Why? While you were working with dud clients, you weren't performing at your best. If you think that that wasn't affecting your other clients, think again. The renewed energy and the more positive environment you'll create as a result of letting go of the duds will most likely rejuvenate the relationships between you and some of your mid-range clients, turning many of them into ideal clients.

1.1.10 Written Exercise: Brainstorm your own ideas for reigniting these mid-range clients. Contemplate the ways in which you may, even inadvertently, have contributed to some of your clients being less than ideal clients. Are there ways in which you can light a new fire or elicit greater passion for the work you do together? Do you need to set and manage expectations more clearly right from the beginning? Can you enrich the dynamics between you by challenging or inspiring your clients in new ways? Go ahead—turn off your left-brain logical mind for a moment and let your right-brain creativity go wild.

Observe carefully the ways in which your relationships with your clients begin to shift as you embrace the Book Yourself Solid way. Some of your mid-range clients may fall away. Others may step up their game and slide into the ideal client category.

When you're fully self-expressed, fully demonstrating your values and your views, you'll naturally attract and draw to yourself those you're best suited to work with, and you'll push away those you're not meant to work with.

A Perpetual Process

The process we've just worked through is one that you must do on a regular basis. Pruning your client list is a perpetual process because all relationships naturally cycle. The positive and dynamic relationships you have now with your ideal clients may at some point reach a plateau, and the time may come to go your separate ways. You'll get more comfortable with the process over time. It's one that has so many rewards that it's well worth the effort.

Let Tom Peters sum it up for us: "This is your life. You *are* your clients. It is fair, sensible, and imperative to make these judgments. To dodge doing so shows a lack of integrity."

I'll go one step further and say that doing so is one of the best and smartest business and life decisions you can make. It's crucial to your success and your happiness. Prune regularly and before you know it, you'll be booked solid with clients you love working with.

2

Why People Buy What You're Selling

Before everything else, getting ready is the secret of success.
—Henry Ford

The next few steps we take down the Book Yourself Solid path will either feel like you're skipping over stepping-stones or like you're taking giant leaps of faith. Either way, these few steps will be well worth the time spent. The most important thing is to submit to the process. Stay by my side as we walk and work together on getting you booked solid.

Taking the following four steps will help you keenly understand why people buy what you're selling, an essential component in creating relentless demand for your services.

Step 1: Identify your target market
Step 2: Understand the urgent needs and compelling desires of your target market

Step 3: Determine the Number One biggest result your clients get

Step 4: Uncover and demonstrate the benefits of your investable opportunities

Step 1: Identify Your Target Market

Now that you've looked at the qualities of the people you want to work with, it's time to identify your target market, that is—the specific group of people or businesses you serve. For example, your target market might be seniors in Vancouver, BC, or mothers who have their own home-based networking marketing business or orthopedic surgeons. Your ideal clients are a small subset of the target market you choose to serve. Remember, your ideal clients are those individuals who energize and inspire you; your target market is the demographics of the group you're most passionate about serving. It is just as important to identify the right target market, as it is to identify the ideal clients.

It's also important to understand the difference between your target market and your niche. If you've done other research or reading on the subject of building your business, you may have heard both of these terms before, and you may have heard them used interchangeably. However, in the Book Yourself Solid system, they are *not* synonymous. There's an important distinction between the two: Your target market is the group of people you serve, and your niche is the service you specialize in offering to your target market. For example, you and I may both serve the same target market, say, service professionals, but offer them different services. I might specialize in getting clients and you might help them create systems for their business. We'll get to your niche in Chapter 3. Before we can talk more about the services you offer, you've got to identify your target market.

Even if you believe you have identified and chosen a target market, please don't skip this section. I often see service professionals who are struggling because either they've chosen a target market that isn't as specific as it needs to be, or they've chosen a target market based on what they think is the most logical and most lucrative choice, rather than one they feel passionate about serving. For the sake of your own success, read through this section, even if you don't think you need to. Trust me. If your target market isn't specific enough or the right one for you, the rest of the book won't be as effective. And besides, you just might be surprised at what you discover.

There are three primary reasons to choose a target market:

1. It helps you determine where to find potential clients who are looking for what you have to offer. If you have a target market, you know where to concentrate your marketing efforts and what to offer that is compelling and well received. You know what associations to speak to, magazines and journals to write for, and influential people with whom to network—you know where your potential clients gather. Voila! You now know where to show up.

2. Virtually every target market already has some kind of network of communication established. For your marketing to work, your clients need to spread your messages for you. If they already have a network of communication set up, they can talk to each other about you and your marketing messages can travel that much faster. What are networks of communication? Environments that are set up to help a group communicate—as I mentioned earlier: associations, social networking sites, clubs, various publications, events, and more.

3. And, finally, choosing a target market lets the people in that target market, know that you've dedicated your life's work to them.

Marketing and sales isn't about trying to persuade, coerce, or manipulate people into buying your services. It's about putting yourself out in front of, and offering your services to, those whom you are meant to serve—people who already need and are looking for your services.

In order to reach the people you're meant to serve, you've got to know where to find them. That's why an essential step is for you to identify a very specific target market to serve.

No matter how much you might like to be everything to everyone, it's just not possible. Even if you could be, you would be doing a disservice to yourself and your clients in the attempt. You can serve your clients much better, offer them much more of your time, energy, and expertise, if you narrow your market so that you're serving only those who most need your services and who can derive the greatest benefits from what you have to offer.

If you're just starting out in your business, or if you've been working in your business for a while but are not yet booked solid, you may be tempted to market to anyone and everyone with the assumption that the more people you market to, the more clients you'll get. While narrowing your market to gain more clients may seem counterintuitive, that's exactly what you need to do to successfully book yourself solid.

Think of narrowing your market this way: Which would you rather be—a small fish in a big pond or a big fish in a small pond? It's much easier to carve out a very lucrative domain for yourself once you've identified a specific target market. And once you're a big fish in a small pond, you'll get more invitations than you can handle to swim in other ponds.

There are two primary ways to grow a service business. You can choose a target market and, over time, continue to add new products and services to this same target market. For example, if your target market is fitness professionals, and you're currently offering them web design services, as you grow, you might start offering them search engine optimization services and then pay-per-click advertising services. Alternatively, once you get booked solid in one target market, you can begin to market and sell the same services in additional vertical target markets. So, if you currently serve wood floor manufacturers, you might offer the same services to manufacturers of tile flooring. Once you get a foothold in that market, you might then begin to focus on carpet manufacturers.

One of my first clients, Dr. Mike Berkley, L.Ac., a doctor of acupuncture, specializes in the treatment of male and female infertility using acupuncture and herbal medicine. He's renowned for his work and he's booked solid. In fact, he's overbooked. You'd be lucky to get an appointment with him. Why? Well, he's great at what he does, but he has also chosen a target market that allows him to do his best work, the work that he is most interested in, and which allows potential clients to see him as the answer to their problems.

You might be thinking: "If I specialize and only work with a specific group of people, or specific types of companies within a specific industry, won't that limit my opportunities? And what if I get bored?" Let me answer the second question first. If you're someone who gets bored easily, you may have that problem no matter what you do. You may want to spend some time reflecting on why you're not able to stay focused on what you've chosen to do. Or it may be that you've chosen a target market that doesn't excite you, that you aren't passionate about or interested in.

Over time, you can move into other areas. Dr. Berkley now offers other services to the same target audience to solve their fertility issues including, but not limited to, nutrition, yoga, and psychotherapy. Once he became renowned for his work using acupuncture to treat infertility, he was able to offer his patients additional services.

When I started my business, I helped fitness and wellness professionals get booked solid. Once I was fortunate enough to create demand for my services, I leveraged the reputation I built servicing the fitness industry as a springboard into other vertical target markets, like financial services, and others. As you establish your expertise and reputation, if you choose, you can broaden your target market. (I now serve virtually every type of service professional.) So if you want to increase your speed to getting booked solid, choose a very specific target market and stay with that target market until you are booked solid. Then you can move into other markets if you like or stay with your original focus and grow your product and service line.

Your Passions, Natural Talents, and Knowledge Are Key

If you haven't yet chosen a target market, then this is your chance, and I am going to help you. I'm going to ask you to consider what you're most passionate about, what excites you, and what you enjoy doing so much that it feels more like play than work and that will allow you to make the most of your natural talents and your knowledge.

Why start by thinking of your own needs, desires, and passions rather than those of your clients? For one very simple reason: If you are not passionate about what you're doing, if your heart isn't in it, if it doesn't have meaning to you, you are not going to devote the time and energy required to be successful, then you'll never, in a million years, be able to convince people in your target market that you're the best person to help them.

I often discover when I'm working with clients that they've chosen a target market based on what they think makes sense or will earn them the most money. The end result is that they're bored, frustrated, and struggling to book themselves solid. Don't make that mistake. It is imperative that you work with a target market that excites you, that you can feel passionate about serving. If you don't, growing your business will quickly feel like drudgery, and you'll be miserable. When you choose a target market you're passionate about, growing your business will feel like play and will bring you joy.

Identifying a target market you feel passionate about may sound like a daunting task. Maybe you have the habit of making business decisions based on left-brained, logical thinking. Maybe you're not in the habit of tuning in to your intuition. If this sounds like you, I'm going to ask you to once again set aside any preconceived ideas you may have about how this *should* be done and be open to the possibility that there is another way to make this particular business decision.

Tuning in to your intuition, allowing yourself to open up to new ways of thinking and to the infinite possibilities available to you, may seem illogical, but if you can approach the process we are engaged in with an open mind, you may find that it makes perfect sense.

That's not to say that you shouldn't also consider your clients. If you've been in business for a while, even if you may not have as many clients as you'd like, the clients you do have can help with this process. Look at the clients you're currently serving. Look for common elements among them—for example, a particular industry, geographic location, age, gender, or profession. If you find that most of your clients share one or more common elements, it may be that you are naturally drawn to those elements or they are drawn to you. Perhaps your target market has already chosen you and you just haven't stopped to think about it long enough to realize it and then focus your marketing there.

1.2.1 Written Exercise: Take a few moments to think about the following questions and to jot down whatever comes to you. Doing so will provide you with clues to the target market you're best suited to serve. Your passion, your natural talents, and what you already know and want to learn more about are key.

- Who are all the different groups of people who use the kind of services you provide?
- Which of these groups do you most relate to or feel the most interest or excitement about working with?
- Which group(s) do you know people in or already have clients in?
- Which group(s) do you have the most knowledge about, or, on the flip side, would you find fascinating to learn more about?
- What are you most passionate about as it relates to your work?
- What natural talents and strengths do you bring to your work?
- What aspects of your field do you know the most about?

1.2.2 Written Exercise: Consider your life experience and interests. You'll be able to more sincerely identify and empathize with your target market if you share common life situations or interests.

- What life situations or roles do you identify with that might connect you to a particular target market?
- Do you have any interests or hobbies that might connect you with your target market?

Now that you've given some thought to these questions, are some new possibilities beginning to emerge? Let's take a look at a few examples that might help you to see how you can incorporate some of your answers into serving a target market.

- If you're a graphic designer whose whole family is in the construction industry, maybe you'd choose the construction industry as your target market because you know the sensibilities of the people in that industry, and you know a lot about its inner workings.
- Or perhaps you're a fitness professional and one of your parents suffered from a chronic illness all your life. You know a lot about what it's like to go through that kind of situation and you empathize with and want to help people with chronic illnesses.
- Maybe you're a chiropractor who used to be a semipro athlete and you'd really enjoy working with athletes.
- If you're an accountant and you grew up in a family business that went bankrupt when you were a teen, you might like to work with family businesses to help them avoid what happened to your family.
- If you're a hairstylist who used to be a stay-at-home mom, stay-at-home moms might be a target market you'd relate well to and enjoy working with.
- Perhaps you're a Web designer who is fascinated by—and would like to learn more about—fashion, so you choose the fashion industry as your target market.
- If you're a yoga teacher who loves and naturally connects with children, and you're very creative, imaginative, and patient, you might want to choose children as your target market.

Let's take this last example and examine it more closely. Say this yoga teacher is booked solid. Chances are her full roster isn't just because she's an expert on the specific techniques of yoga for children, but because she has a natural affinity with children. This differentiator is what helped her to book herself solid much more quickly than she would have if she focused on serving the general population.

Are you beginning to see the ways in which your passions, natural talents, knowledge, life experience, and even interests and hobbies might help you to choose a more specific target market? Play, explore, and have fun with this process.

1.2.3 Written Exercise: For now I just want you to answer this question: Who is your target market? If you're not ready to make this choice, list the possibilities that appeal to you. Sit with them for a while (but not for too long) and then choose one. Even if you're not sure at this point, it will become clearer to you as you work through the next few chapters.

Remember to tune into your intuition. I can't tell you how many times I've worked with clients who *knew* on some level the target market they most wanted to serve, and for one reason or another discounted it. Turn off your inner censor when doing this exercise and allow yourself to at least explore every possibility, no matter how wild, silly, or unrealistic it may seem on the surface.

If You Feel Stuck

For some, choosing a target market doesn't come easily. It can feel very challenging, and when you've been told how important it is to identify a target market and it doesn't come quickly and easily, the pressure to choose can feel overwhelming and uncomfortable.

Part of what keeps us stuck is that we take ourselves, and the process, too seriously. We turn it into a big deal and wind up getting increasingly frustrated with the whole thing, and with ourselves. Suddenly the process has become another thing to beat ourselves up about. Needless to say, the frustration and self-flagellation just further block our creativity and intuition, and the next thing we know, we're in this awful cycle, like a hamster on an exercise wheel, spinning around and around and getting nowhere.

Take a few deep breaths. Let yourself off the hook. See if you can approach the process with an attitude of play. Think of it as a jigsaw puzzle—challenging but fun. The point isn't to finish as quickly as possible; the point is to enjoy the journey and to find the target market that is right for you.

As with any jigsaw puzzle, first you sort through all the pieces to find the edges, the pieces easiest to identify and put together. Then you take your time sorting through the rest. You pick one piece up, you compare it to the bigger picture on the box, and you try to figure out where it might go. One piece at a time, the picture comes together. When you get tired or bored or frustrated, or you just feel drawn to do something else, get up and walk away, and as you go about the rest of your day, don't stress out about whether you'll ever get the puzzle finished.

Some days you might spend an hour or two with it, other times only minutes. Maybe every once in a while you stop for mere seconds, pick up a piece or two, and pop them right in where they fit as you pass by. Maybe a friend or family member stops by for a visit, picks up that piece that's been making you crazy for days, and pops it right into place for you.

Choosing a target market you can feel passionate about serving can be enjoyable and immensely rewarding if you approach the process with an open mind and an attitude of play, reaching out for help from family, friends, or a professional business coach to guide you.

Revisit the written exercises in Step 1 and approach them with a spirit of play. Don't analyze; just jot down whatever answers come to you. Make it a game, listing as many ideas and possibilities as you can think of. If you're still having difficulty, ask someone to play with you. Someone outside your process can offer ideas and suggestions that occur to them, which you may not have the objectivity to consider. Remember to turn your inner censor off for this process. If you need to, let go of the process altogether for a while and move on. Releasing the pressure of having to choose sometimes allows ideas that were blocked to come racing through.

Step 2: Identify the Urgent Needs and Compelling Desires of Your Target Market

Your target market's urgent needs and compelling desires prompt them to go in search of you and your services, so it's critical to be able to identify and address them when they come looking or you'll miss your window of opportunity.

> *You must offer what your potential clients want to buy, not what you want to sell or think they should want to buy. You must be able to look at your services from your client's perspective—their urgent needs and compelling desires.*

Your clients' urgent needs are the things that they must have right away, usually pressing problems, and often the things they would like to move away from. Their compelling desires are the things that they want in the future. Sure, they'd like to have them right now but they may be part of a bigger picture dream, and see themselves moving toward these desires.

1.2.4 Written Exercise: What are five of your clients' *urgent needs*? (What problems must they solve right away?)

Example: The urgent need that may have prompted you to buy this book might be a feeling of stress because you know you need more clients (and more money) but don't know where or how to begin marketing your business. Maybe the bills are really starting to pile up and you're afraid. Or maybe you know what to do to market your services but just aren't doing it. You're procrastinating and your business is suffering as a result.

1.2.5 Written Exercise: What are five of your clients' *compelling desires*? (What would they like to move toward?)

Example: Let's use you as an example again. Your compelling desire might be to feel confident and in control as you get as many clients as you would like. Maybe you want financial freedom. Maybe you just want to be able to take a real vacation every year. Or maybe it's all about having a thriving business that includes doing what you love and making oodles of money.

Step 3: Determine the Biggest Result Your Clients Get

This simple step might be the most important step in understanding why people buy what you're selling. What is the Number One result you help your clients achieve or get? And, when I say Number One result, I mean one big one. Of course, I know there are lots of things that you help your clients achieve, experience, or get. But, generally, when a client comes looking for you, they're looking to solve one big problem or achieve one big result. I mean, why did you buy this book? To get more clients. Period. End of story. Are there lots of other things you'll get from reading this book? No doubt—from more confidence to more accountability, and even more friends (we'll get to that later). But, bottom line, you want more clients and the Book Yourself Solid system delivers on that promise. In fact, every product or service you offer must have one big promise. Your job is to fulfill that promise in the delivery of your service.

1.2.6 Written Exercise: Describe the biggest result you provide?

Step 4: Uncover and Demonstrate the Benefits of Your Investable Opportunities

Do potential clients within your target market see your services and products as opportunities that will give them a significant return on their investment?

They must; if your potential clients are going to purchase your services and products, they *must* see them as investable opportunities; they must feel that the return they receive is greater than the investment they made.

My rule of thumb is that your clients should be getting a return of at least 20 times their investment in your services. This return will come in different forms, depending on what you offer, but the return falls into four related categories: financial, emotional, physical, and spiritual, which I'll refer to by the acronym FEPS. Not only should the return on investment be high, this potential reward must be evident before your clients purchase services from you.

Let's look at the financial component as an example. If I sell a product for $49, the buyer can expect a financial return of, at least, $1,000. If one of my coaching programs, at BookedSolidUniversity.com, requires a financial investment of $1,500, the average participant can expect a return of at least $30,000 in new client business (and don't forget about the other FEPS like increased confidence, focus, clarity, and more). If someone hires me to give a speech at $30,000, the financial return for the audience, as a whole, can be, at a minimum, $600,000. I'm afraid that sometimes, as service professionals, we forget how important our clients' return on investment is.

What kind of return on investment will your client get from working with you? Will it be greater than their financial, emotional, physical, or spiritual investment in your services? If so, how much higher? Twenty times?

Again, I'll use Dr. Mike Berkley of the Berkley Center for Reproductive Wellness as an example. When I started working with him, while his target market was well-defined, he was not positioning his services as investable opportunities. He was selling the features of his services—the science of acupuncture, how it works, how it balances the hormone levels—but he was not making the important *return on investment* connection. He didn't see that he needed to articulate the return on investment of his services from a financial, emotional, physical, and spiritual perspective. Do you think his potential clients would be more willing to invest in his services if they believed that doing so would substantially increase their chances of conceiving? Of course they would. The truth is that he already had a proven success record. A significant number of his clients conceive after an average of three months of acupuncture treatment combined with in vitro fertilization (IVF) treatment. Now that's an opportunity that most couples dealing with infertility would be willing to invest in. You can imagine the emotional, physical, and spiritual return on investment that provides.

The secret to having a successful business is to know what your clients want and deliver it. Rather than talking about what you do, focus instead on clear, specific, and detailed solutions that solve your clients' problems. People aren't buying what you do. *The science, technique, or technical name that you use won't get clients to hire you!* Clients who understand the return on investment you offer will jump at the chance to work with you.

To make it obvious that your solutions are investable opportunities for your potential clients, you need to uncover and demonstrate their benefits. The opportunities you offer—acupuncture, financial planning, web site design, career counseling, executive coaching, interior design—are just things that you do. They are the actual services you offer; they are *technically* what your clients buy but not what they *actually* buy.

For example, some of my offerings are *technically* these:

- A book that you can read on how to book yourself solid
- A coaching program that teaches you how to book yourself solid
- Live seminars that teach you how to book yourself solid
- A license to become a Certified Book Yourself Solid Coach

However, these are still only the features and technical offerings. The core benefits of these offerings are much deeper. Benefits are sometimes tangible results, but more often they're intangible; they're the effects your services have on your clients' quality of life. They are what make your offer an investable opportunity—the FEPS that clients can experience because of your services. They are what people buy. Don't ever forget that.

To get a stronger sense of how this works, think about this. If I asked you what you wanted to accomplish in the next 90 days, you might say you'd like to get more clients or earn more money, but what is getting more clients really going to give you? Will it give you more than money in the bank or a wallet fat with twenties, fifties, and hundred-dollar bills?

The truth is that you don't actually want clients or cash. The true bottom line is that you may want financial freedom, peace of mind, time with your family, or reduced concerns about how you're going to make ends meet. Am I right?

To accentuate this point, here are some more examples of the deeper benefits you'll get from reading this book and participating in my Book Yourself Solid live events and coaching programs:

- A paradigm shift in the way you look at marketing and sales so that you can forever create demand for your services in a way that feels authentic and comfortable to you.
- Increased confidence in yourself and your capacity to handle any business challenge that you are faced with.
- A feeling of pride and a sense of accomplishment as you take the actions you know you need to take and see positive results.
- Freedom from the physical and emotional stress and anxiety of not being able to cover the mortgage for the home you and your children live in.
- A deep spiritual connection to your purpose and the opportunity to be fully self-expressed.
- And so much more . . .

Do you see how identifying core benefits allows you to speak to and touch your target market on a much deeper and more personally and emotionally connected level? The more financial, emotional, physical, and spiritual benefits you uncover, the quicker you will start to attract new clients. People buy results and the benefits of those results. So think about the solutions you offer and the subsequent results and benefits they provide.

1.2.7 Written Exercise: What are the deep-rooted benefits your clients will experience as a result of your services?

Now do you see what clients are actually buying when they decide to work with you? Every time you communicate in person, by writing, on the Internet, in an advertisement, in business meetings, or on the phone, articulate and rearticulate these benefits. Use words that you hear your clients use and express very specific solutions to their very prominent problems.

Even if it seems simple, it's worth repeating. If I have a client who wants to establish her own personal brand and start earning money doing something she loves, then every time we meet, I will remind her that her personal brand will offer her freedom so she won't ever have to *settle* again when it comes to the clients she works with. I know that this is a compelling desire for her, and I remind her how inspired she is going to feel once she works only with her ideal clients. Keeping the benefits on the top of her mind, she clearly sees the fully realized vision of her business and stays focused on accomplishing her goals.

Relax, Be Playful, and Have Fun!

If some of these business concepts are getting heavy for you, remember to look for the lightness and humor in everything you do and think of ways you can have more fun and help your clients at the same time. I mean, we're just talking about getting clients, an important subject, no doubt, but not a heavy one. Start thinking about how you can incorporate more play into your life and work. Don't be afraid to:

- Be playful and quirky—be yourself.
- Be full of energy—enthusiasm is contagious.
- Help others laugh a lot—it's the best sales technique in the world.

It's been said that children laugh an average of 450 times per day, while adults laugh an average of only 15 times a day. If that's true, and based on my experience with my beloved son Jake, it is, how did we end up 435 laughs short of a good time? Embrace a childlike sense of play and you'll be one step closer to booking yourself solid.

Clients Want You to Help Them

Begin to view your role with your clients as that of a highly important and trusted advisor. You have a moral obligation to offer your services to those who need them. To do anything other than counsel, advise, guide, and coach your clients would be a huge disservice. Start to view yourself as a leader in their life.

We all want someone to believe in. Be that person and you can write your own ticket. If you view yourself as a trusted advisor, clients will never forget you. They will come back to you months or even years later. Trust is built over time, so a connection you make today may not develop until much later. Continue to share your vision, mission, and obligation to help people. Give clients benefit after benefit and show them exactly how they can fulfill the promise of your offerings.

There is an acronym that is often used in sales—A, B, C—*always be closing*. Yuck! Sounds like cheesy sales talk to me. Instead, I say—A, B, C—*always be communicating*. Let everybody and anybody know how you help people. But first:

1. Select a target market.
2. Identify your clients' urgent needs and compelling desires.
3. Determine the Number One biggest result you help them get.
4. Uncover the deep-rooted core benefits of that big result (financial, emotional, physical, and spiritual).

Got it? Good.

3

Develop a Personal Brand

Every time you suppress some part of yourself or allow others to play you small, you are in essence ignoring the owner's manual your creator gave you and destroying your design.

—Oprah Winfrey

Branding

Having established your target market and identified their urgent needs and compelling desires, the big result you help them get, as well as the benefits of the investable opportunities you offer, you are ready to develop a plan for deciding how you want to be known in your market—in an irresistible and unforgettable way.

You will do this by developing a personal brand. Brands are not just for big corporations. In fact, a personal brand will serve as an important key to your success. A personal brand will help clearly and consistently define, express, and communicate who you are, who you serve, and why you have chosen to dedicate your life and work to serving your target market so that you can attract your most ideal clients and not those who are less than ideal. Personal branding is far more than just what you do or what your web site and business cards look like. It *is* you—uniquely you. It allows you to distinguish yourself from everyone else: what is unique about who you are, what you stand for, and what you do.

Your brand is about making yourself known for your skills and talents. More than that—your brand is about what you stand for. Successful people find their style, build a brand based on it, and boldly express themselves through that brand. To let the world see your true, authentic worth is powerful and it makes you memorable.

Think about some of the most successful people you know. The entertainment industry is a great example. On the television show *In Living Color*, Jim Carrey established himself as a physical comedian using exaggerated body and facial expressions to make us laugh, while Jerry Seinfeld became well known for his intellectual comedic style of observing the obvious. Whoopi Goldberg took an entirely different approach, baring her soul in her standup routines talking about career, motherhood, and the perils of trying to have it all. She used stories and emotions to strike an emotional chord in us to make us laugh. Each of these very different comedic styles is attractive to different types of people. Some people love Jim Carrey's work, while others don't particularly care for it. The same is true for Jerry and Whoopi. The more bold, authentic, and concise your personal brand is, the more easily you'll attract those you're meant to work with.

That's how a personal brand works—it defines you, but first you must define it. Your personal brand will give you the ability to attract fun and exciting clients who understand and *get* you. And you *get* them. You can see that each of the comedians I described expanded their repertoire after they became well known. Well, all of them except Jerry Seinfeld, who carried on with the same style that had always been successful for him. I doubt you'll ever see Jerry do a thriller playing a deranged sociopath.

Develop a personal brand that looks like you, thinks like you, sounds and feels like you—one that is instantly recognizable as your essence. It should be:

- Clear
- Consistent

- Authentic
- Memorable
- Meaningful
- Soulful
- Personal

There are three components to your personal brand.

- The first is your *who and do what* statement, which is based on who you serve and what you help them do or get.
- The second is your *why you do it* statement, which is based on why you get up every day to do your work—what you stand for. Sure, you stand for lots of things but you're going to choose one big one to stake your name on.
- And, the third is your *tagline.* More on these three components in a minute. But, first . . .

Releasing Blocks

Before we begin to craft your personal brand, it's important to address any blocks you are inadvertently creating that may hold you back from achieving success. I know it can seem unusual to discuss personal blocks as it relates to personal branding, but this is your life we're talking about. You want to play the biggest game possible, don't you? Of course, you do. The following questions can help you gain clarity about how you want to be known in the world. Consider them seriously.

The greatest strategy for personal and business development on the planet is bold self-expression.

Are you fully self-expressed? Again, I know this may seem like an unusual question. But I ask it because to create a gutsy, passionate, ardent, provocative, courageous, valiant, vibrant, dynamic, luminous, and respected personal brand, you must be fully self-expressed. You can't hide behind the shingle that you've hung over your door and you can't water yourself down in any way, shape, or form. If you do, you won't be of interest to the people you're meant to serve.

As a business owner, you probably already work *on* your business—creating the framework that supports the business itself, such as setting up an automatic marketing system—and work *in* your business, serving your clients. How you brand yourself is equally critical and is a reflection of how you work *on yourself*.

Have you compromised yourself or watered yourself down in any area of your business? For example, have you been in a business situation where you walked away feeling like you settled for less or compromised your integrity? You may be thinking, "I don't sell out. I've never compromised or sold out." If you haven't, you are unique. It's completely normal to compromise yourself or to be out of integrity from time to time. We all are.

It will serve you well to know exactly where you have run into trouble in the past. Since working independently and starting and running your own business is challenging, you can eliminate a lot of pain and surprise right now by acknowledging the issues you may have buried or have had a difficult time confronting in the past.

1.3.1 Written Exercise: List the ways in which you've sold out, settled for less, or compromised your integrity in your business, either now or in the past.

1.3.2 Written Exercise: What about the flip side? Tap into instances in your business life where you've felt alive and vibrant—fully self-expressed. Everything you did just flowed. Draw on all of your senses. What was happening at that time that made you feel so alive?

1.3.3 Written Exercise: Now compare the two areas, the ones where you sold out and the situations in which you felt most fully self-expressed. How can you change your behavior to speak boldly and from a place of free expression so that you're working in situations that make you feel fully self-expressed? How will you communicate to make sure you stop compromising or watering yourself down in the future?

1.3.4 Written Exercise: Start with a few situations (fairly comfortable ones) in which you could practice speaking from a bolder and more self-expressed place.

1.3.5 Written Exercise: Write down a few more situations (that seem a little more difficult) that you'd like to work up to speaking more boldly about.

There are two reasons for the exercises you're doing. The first is so you can help clients understand how you can help them. The second is so you can make sure that your personal and professional intentions are clear.

Clear intentions allow you to gracefully and confidently move toward your goals. Conflicting intentions will undermine your success without your even knowing it. They will hold you back from your dreams. They are the mother of energy drain and confusion. From a perspective of a personal brand identity, conflicting intentions will eventually lead to a bland message and a less successful you.

Here's a story to illustrate this concept. My father is an accomplished psychiatrist. I have always had great respect for him and his work. And, above all, I've always wanted him to be proud of me and my accomplishments. That's natural, right?

When I first launched my service business, I spent lots of time getting clear on my offerings and how I would communicate them to the world.

And then I did just that—or so I thought. I let everybody know what I was up to. However, not too much was happening. I got a few clients, but as I mentioned earlier, I couldn't really pay the bills, and I certainly wasn't happy with the response I was getting. So a few months later, when I was at my wits' end, I did a formal evaluation of my brand. I started with my web site. I locked myself away and read every word on my web site from start to finish. I sat back in my chair, staring at the screen in amazement and shock. The entire feeling of the site was not really me—it was almost as if my father were talking. In fact, I was communicating what I thought he would approve of.

I am not my father. I'm certainly not a medical doctor. Not having his credentials, I shied away from being bold and brave and instead played it safe, secretly hoping that he would approve of what I was doing. The reason this is relevant is that when I started my business, I was focusing more on personal development issues as they relate to business development. I wanted to help people become happier and more successful in their work. So I had two very conflicting intentions. One intention was to build a wildly successful business and the second (my conflicting intention) was to make my father proud. The underlying dynamic was not to do anything that he wouldn't approve of. And, here's the rub, if you think about it, many business problems are simply personal problems in disguise.

Even now, as a business coach, author, and speaker, much of the work I do helps people move through personal problems, as they relate to their business problems. I'm not practicing psychotherapy by any stretch of the imagination. However, I often relate to people on a very deep level. By remaining within conventional boundaries—the ones I *thought* my father would approve of—I limited myself dramatically. I didn't give myself the freedom to be truly me. I was inhibited and unable to offer the full extent of my experiences, point of view, and passion. The result was a rather confusing and bland identity. And the truth is, I had no proof or real reason to believe that my father wouldn't approve of my being authentically me. In fact, just the opposite is true; he wouldn't want me to be anyone but me. It was just a good story for me to hide behind.

In order to set clear intentions for yourself, you must remove the conflicting intentions that you currently have. Your reality is created by your present intentions. If you want to change your reality, you must change your intentions. My vision for you is that, through this book, the intentions for your business, as well as your life, will become clear to you and to your clients.

1.3.6 Written Exercise: Identify one of your most important intentions as it relates to your business.

Example: I intend to book myself solid.

1.3.7 Written Exercise: Take a good hard look within to see if you can identify any potentially conflicting intentions for the intention you identified. These are likely to be subconscious and more difficult to identify, and they are nearly always based on fear.

Example: If I book myself solid, I won't have time for myself. Or, in order to book myself solid, I'll have to promote myself, and self-promotion will make me feel pathetic and vulnerable. Or maybe you want to book yourself solid but you *think* self-promotion is unappealing.

1.3.8 Booked Solid Action Step: Identifying and acknowledging your conflicting intentions is the first big step in releasing them. Awareness is key, but not always enough to prevent conflicting intentions from affecting and blocking our positive intentions. The next step in the process is to identify the underlying fears. Once you've identified them, you can begin to take steps to relieve them.

For this step, it's critical that you very carefully choose one or two sincerely and highly supportive friends to share your new insights with. They must be truly supportive and willing to help you change. Often as we begin to make changes in our lives, whether business or personal, some of our most dearly loved friends and family can feel threatened by the process of change. While they may consciously want you to be successful, they may have their own subconscious conflicting intentions and be highly invested in wanting to maintain their own comfort zone by keeping you in yours. These are not the folks you want to ask for help from to do this exercise.

Share the intentions and their conflicting counterparts with one or two others and ask your friends to help you in recognizing whether these are genuine concerns or unfounded fears. Then brainstorm ways to address the problems.

While you can take this step on your own, we're often too close to our own fears to see them clearly. Having a supportive friend, mentor, or professional coach who has a bit more objectivity than we do can help put them into perspective.

You Are Uniquely You

It's often those qualities that make you uniquely you—the ones that come so naturally to you that you don't even think about them—that become the best personal brands. Susan's story illustrates the point.

A pleasant woman in her early forties, Susan, came to me and asked me to help her discover "what she was born to do" so she could launch her own business. It was a particularly tough time for her. She had recently been divorced and needed to support herself. As you might imagine, she was concerned about what she would do. Years earlier, she had been a successful trader on Wall Street. Yet it had now been over 20 years since her glory days. I asked her, "What are your quirks?" "Quirks?" she replied. "I don't have any quirks." She sounded moderately offended. "Okay," I said, "Then tell me about your friendships; what are they based on?" Without a moment's hesitation she said, "My female friends are always asking me for advice on sex and intimacy." "Interesting. Now we're getting somewhere," I thought.

She told me about her unusual habit of giving scarlet-colored thongs (not the ones of the flip-flop variety) as gifts. Remember, this is the same woman who told me she didn't have any quirks. After more prodding and investigating this unique, special, and entertaining quirk, it became clear that she was fully self-expressed when she was thinking and focusing on how women 40 and over can be, should be, and are, remarkable sexual beings (and more). She decided, even though she would have to resolve many conflicting intentions about doing so, that she was going to exploit her quirk and create *The Scarlet Thong Society*, an invitation-only social club for women over 40 who want to acknowledge their sexual prowess.

You may not have scarlet thongs to hand out, but chances are you do have something unique, maybe even quirky, that you really want to express and that others will notice and respond to.

1.3.9 Written Exercise: To know which secret quirk or natural talent is waiting in the wings to bring you wealth, happiness, and unbridled success in your business, answer the following questions:

- How are you unique?
- What are three things that make you memorable?
- What are the special talents that you are genetically coded to do? What have you been good at since you were a kid?
- What do people always compliment you on?
- What do you love or never grow tired of talking about in your personal life?
- What do you want to say that you would never grow tired of talking about when you are asked about your work?

Many times we are too close to see the qualities or quirks that stand out to others. Send a few of these questions to different people in your life to get their responses about you and your personality. Not only will you start to see some of the same truths about who you are, but you'll get back the most touching and warm e-mails—I promise. Try it.

1.3.10 Booked Solid Action Step: Send an e-mail to five or more people (include friends, family, clients, neighbors, and acquaintances from all the different aspects of your life).

- Ask them to provide you with your top five personality traits or quirks.
- Ask for fun or unique experiences they've had with you.
- Tell them to be brave and not to be shy.

Remember that your work is doomed to fail if you don't love it and share it with the world. And here's the biggie: *When you're fully self-expressed, you will love marketing.* You won't have conflicting intentions about promoting yourself. You won't feel that the world is coming to an end when you get a rejection. You'll smile and move on to the next opportunity because your ability to express yourself is directly proportional to your level of confidence and vice versa.

With all of this new and insightful information about yourself, you should be thrilled that you've already made it through the challenge of choosing your path and being an independent business owner. That's no easy task. Keep all of these insights in mind as you begin to craft your own personal brand.

The Three Components of Your Personal Brand

As I mentioned at the beginning of this chapter, there are three components to your personal brand:

1. Your *who and do what* statement.
2. Your *why you do it* statement.
3. Your *tagline*.

I want you to laser-beam your focus on these three aspects of your personal brand until you feel totally and utterly fully expressed when you put words to your *who and do what* statement, your *why you do it* statement, and your tagline. The process may take a week or it may take a few months. It took me six months, but I didn't have this book to help me do it faster. The important thing is to give yourself the time to really give thought to it all.

Your *Who and Do What* Statement

Your *who and do what* statement lets others know exactly who you help and what you can help them do. It is the first filter that people will put you through when considering your services for hire. Your potential clients will look at it to see if you help people like them in their specific situation.

Your *Why You Do It* Statement

After potential clients identify with your *who and do what* statement, they will want to know if they connect with you on an emotional, philosophical, or even spiritual level. They'll want to know if they connect with your *why you do it* statement—the reason you do what you do, what you stand for. The reason you get up every day to do the work that you do. Those who resonate with your *why you do it* statement will feel it on a deep level and be strongly, almost magnetically, attracted to you. Many others in your industry will share your *who and do what* statement. Similarly, your *why you do it* statement and even your tagline don't necessarily need to be wildly unique. Just deeply meaningful to you—and to the people you're *meant to serve*.

Your Tagline

I have become known as "The guy to call when you're tired of thinking small.®" This is no accident; I've been saying this over and over since the day I realized that being "The guy to call when you're tired of thinking small" was a perfect tagline to represent and demonstrate my *why I do it* statement, that I want to help people think bigger about who they are and what they offer the world.

Your tagline, based on your *why you do it* statement, is something you'll never get tired of hearing. And the first time you hear someone refer to you by it, you'll want to cry tears of joy. You'll formulate one simple sentence that allows people to define you in a manner of your own choosing. You'll never get tired of saying it or hearing it because it's based on what you stand for, what's important to you. And, most importantly, not only will it very deeply and truly mean something to you, it will resonate with the people you're meant to serve. Reading or hearing your tagline will be the defining moment people need to decide whether to purchase your services, products, or programs.

Your *tagline* lets others know what it's like to be around you. It says something about who you are at your core, and it's the essence of what you want to achieve or experience in the world. Think of it as the bigger vision that is the inspiration for what you do in your business, Your *why you do it statement* and associated *tagline* is the way in which you want to touch others' lives in a positive and meaningful way.

You may have noticed that my tagline is not necessarily specific to my target market. It may resonate with many people; professional service providers aren't the only ones who want to think bigger about who they are and what they offer the world. But I've chosen to offer my services to this inspired group of people, not to every single soul on the planet. Your tagline is not necessarily about your target market; it's about the emotional connection you make with people in general *and* with your ideal clients in your target market. Many people serve the same target market you serve, but your *tagline* is what will resonate with some people and not with others: It will resonate with those you're meant to serve.

Why have you dedicated your life to serving others? How do you want to make a difference?

If you don't want to make a difference, consider making your living as something other than a service professional. The operative word is service.

Wrap up review:

1. *Who and do what* statement (for example, I help service professionals get booked solid.)
2. *Why you do it* statement (for example, I want to help people think bigger about who they are and what they offer the world.)
3. *Tagline*: (for example, The guy to call when you're tired of thinking small.®)

1.3.11 Written Exercise: Start with the basics. Keep it simple and straightforward. What is your *who and do what* statement? Who do you help and what do you help them do? Refer to your target market from Chapter 2. The first time around, just come up with something accurate and clear for now—make sure a five-year-old can understand it. List as many possibilities as come to mind. Finish this statement, "I help. . . ."

   Example: I help . . . service professionals get booked solid. (Or, for the five-year-old, "I help the store sell more stuff.")

1.3.12 Written Exercise: It's time to step out of your comfort zone again. Set aside that inner critic and give yourself permission to think big—I mean really *big*, bigger than you've ever dared to think or dream before. Be your most idealistic, inspired, creative, powerful you. What is your purpose? What is your vision of what you hope to achieve through your work? Remember, your work is an expression of who you are. List whatever comes to mind.

1.3.13 Written Exercise: Keeping the preceding in mind, craft a minimum of three possible *why you do it* statements.

1.3.14 Booked Solid Action Step: If your *why you do it* statement is not immediately and easily identifiable, get together with a group of supportive friends or associates who know you well and ask them to brainstorm it with you. It's often the things about you that are most natural and that you don't even recognize that become key elements of your *why you do it* statement. Having some outside input and a few more objective perspectives can make all the difference.

1.3.15 Written Exercise: Craft three to five possible taglines that represent and demonstrate your current favorite *why you do it* statement.

Roma Non è Stata Construita un Giorno (Rome Wasn't Built in a Day)

Neither was my personal brand. I went through many, many versions, even one a month, before I got to a *why I do it* statement and tagline that worked for me. I didn't get caught up in trying to find the perfect brand message or positioning statement. I didn't worry about it because I knew I could change it. I knew that creating a tagline that represented what I stood for was a process and that I'd just keep changing it until I got there. If I didn't start with something, though, what would I have had? I'd have had nothing.

First I got clear on my *who and do what* statement, that "I help professional service providers get more clients."

Then I got clear on my *why I do it* statement, that "I want to help people think bigger about who they are and what they offer the world."

What took longer was nailing down my tagline. I worked really hard on trying to find it. It took about six months. I thought about it every day, but the amazing thing was that it came to me by accident. I was with a bunch of people and we were masterminding and brainstorming about our businesses and everyone was talking about what they did. I was giving the others a hard time, teasing and questioning, asking, "Why would I hire you for that?" I was playing devil's advocate until finally, one of the women gave it right back to me and said, "Yeah, well why would I hire you?" I blurted out, "Because I'm the guy to call when you're tired of thinking small.®'" Suddenly the whole room went silent, as if everyone was holding their breath. After a few moments the same woman shouted out "Yes! That is *so you!*" Everyone in the room was cheering and the air was charged with excitement.

Even so, I didn't really think much about it until a couple of weeks later as I was talking to a colleague about an idea I had for the Think Big Revolution, a free online social network where people could come together to think bigger about who they are and what they offer the world. I was excited about it, but I questioned it: "I'm not sure about this *big* stuff. I came up with this tagline that I'm 'the guy to call when you're tired of thinking small,' but I'm not sure about it. Do you think anyone will actually care about that? " She laughed and said, "Michael, are you dense?" I said, "Yes, but you're going to have to be more specific." She explained to me that she likes being around me because I help her think so much bigger about who she is and what she offers the world. And, I'm happy to report that it became a reality at ThinkBigRevolution.com, based on my *New York Times* best-selling book, *The Think Big Manifesto* and, yes, it's still free; it will always be. No one owns big thinking. I hope you join me in the Revolution.

I realized then that because it was so natural to me to want to help people think bigger about who they are and what they offer the world, it didn't seem like such a big deal. It took discussing it with others who weren't as close to it as I was to get the perspective I needed. The exact thing that came most naturally to me was the thing that was drawing people to me, instilling in them the desire to purchase my products and enroll in my programs and seminars.

As I began using my *why I do it* statement and tagline to let others know why I do what I do, I found that the people for whom it resonated would immediately comment on how much they connected with it. Those who didn't *get* it, wouldn't. That's okay. It's all about attracting those people who are meant to work with you. The rest will be attracted to someone with whom they will resonate, and you won't end up with less-than-ideal clients.

Recall the story about the old man, the boy, and the donkey. The process of booking yourself solid isn't about how to please as many people as possible. It's about how to convey your own unique message to those who are waiting to hear it. That can't be achieved with personal branding that's been watered down in an attempt to appeal to everyone. It can be achieved only through bold, no-holds-barred self-expression. It's about being uniquely you and standing for something—in a big way.

4

How to Talk About What You Do

A conversation is a dialogue, not a monologue. That's why there are so few good conversations: due to scarcity, two intelligent talkers seldom meet.

—Truman Capote

A primary reason that many service professionals fail to build thriving businesses is that they struggle to articulate in a clear and compelling way exactly what solutions and benefits they offer. They don't know how to talk about what they do without sounding confusing or bland or like everyone else—and without using an elevator speech. Yes, you heard me, *without* using an elevator speech.

The elevator speech (aka: the elevator pitch or 30-second commercial) reflects the idea that it should be possible to wow someone with what you do in the time it takes an elevator to go from the first to the fifth floor.

I've been polling audiences of thousands for years on this issue. During each speech I ask, "How many of you love, love, love *listening* to someone else's elevator speech?" No hands go up. I then ask, "How many of you love, love, love *giving* your elevator speech?" Same thing. No hands. So what gives? If we don't like listening to or giving the speech, why is it still being taught? Because, of course, we need to be able to talk about what we do—I get the concept. However, in this case, the elevator speech has been inappropriately appropriated by the service professional. Not only does it not work well, it makes us look foolish, or, worse yet, obnoxious.

The elevator pitch was born so that the *entrepreneur* could pitch an idea to a venture capitalist or angel investor in the hopes of receiving funding, not for the service professional to try to build a relationship of trust with a potential client. Venture capitalists often judge the quality of an idea on the basis of the quality of its elevator pitch. Makes perfect sense, in that situation. But this is not how a relationship develops between a client and a *service professional*. You're trying to earn the status of a trusted advisor not trying to raise money to create some new product like metal-detecting sandals. Totally different context. Totally different dynamic.

To support my beautiful community of service professionals, I'm on a mission to kill the elevator speech, to remove it from the business vernacular—for the service professional. I hope you'll join me on this mission and learn how to talk about what you do without ever resorting to an elevator speech. So, what do you do instead?

By using this crazy concept that I call a *conversation*. Weird, I know. Over the course of this chapter, I'm going to teach you a Book Yourself Solid Dialogue, a creative—but not scripted!—conversation that will spark curiosity and interest about you and your services, products, and programs. The Book Yourself Solid Dialogue will allow you to have a meaningful conversation (*conversation* being the operative word) with a potential client or referral source. The dialogue is a dynamic, lively description of the people you help, what challenges they face, how you help them, and the results and benefits they get from your services. It is intended to replace the static, boring, and usual response to the question, "What do you do?" "I'm a business consultant," "I'm a massage therapist," or "I'm a graphic designer"; answers that often elicit nothing more than a polite nod, comment, or awkward silence and a blank stare. Once you get that response, anything more you say about yourself or your services will sound pushy. Worse yet, you could supplement the rote answer with an overblown, high-highfalutin, hyperbole-laden elevator speech that's supposed to make you look like a rock star in 30 seconds. Unfortunately, I doubt the one-two punch of boring answer, followed by excessively exuberant elevator pitch is going to compel the listener to whip out his credit card right then and there.

Instead you'll learn the Book Yourself Solid way to create a meaningful, connected *dialogue* with a potential client or referral source. Think of it as a conversation between two people each of whom actually cares about what the other has to say. The beautiful thing is that the interchange is based on successfully understanding why people buy what you're selling. And because of the work we did together in Chapter 2, you already know why people buy what you're selling.

You previously created your *who and do what* statement. That's a fantastic first step and an excellent tool for starting a conversation about what you do. Now you must be sure that you can captivate and actively engage the person you're talking to in a conversation that elicits questions rather than just polite acknowledgment. You must talk *with* people, not *at* them, which means listening to them, too, and really hearing what they're interested in, and what their needs are. After all, their needs may be exactly what you serve. Never give anyone a prepared script. Doing so is a train wreck waiting to happen. The long, medium, and short version of your Book Yourself Solid Dialogue will allow you to have conversations with different people in different situations, so you're always prepared. You tell them about the people you work with and then you listen to their response. You build on their response, and before you know it, you are having a conversation that is informative and inspiring—and that's the key to talking about what you do without being bland or confusing or, worse yet, obnoxious, albeit, unintended.

> *We hear the question "What do you do for a living?" all the time. Your professional category alone is the wrong answer.*

You are so much more than your profession. Let's toss out the generic labels for now. Teacher, doctor, designer, accountant, acupuncturist, personal fitness trainer, yoga teacher, consultant, coach, or other dictionary description defines you as one of the masses.

Think about it for a second. Let's say you're a yoga teacher and you meet someone who really needs your help who would also be an ideal client. The only problem is that she has a preconceived notion of what yoga is all about and what a yoga teacher is like, and it's not a preconceived notion that sets you up for success.

Imagine this scenario: The potential client asks you what you do. You say, "I'm a yoga teacher." Before you know what's happened, you see the potential client's face contort, her left eyebrow lifts along with the left side of her upper lip, and her nostrils begin to flare. The potential client says, "Oh, yeah . . . I had a yoga teacher as a neighbor once. She was really weird and made my life miserable. In fact, I had to move out of that apartment because of her and I loved that apartment! She had scores of people coming in and out at all hours of the day, blasting strange music and chanting like the world was about to end—I think they must have been members of a cult. Oh, and you wouldn't believe the awful smell that I was subjected to from the perpetual cloud of incense that invaded my home."

Uh-oh.

Would you like to get that kind of response when you tell someone what you do? And this can happen to any service professional, not just to a yoga teacher. Say a stockbroker meets someone whose only introduction to stockbrokers has been the movie *Boiler Room* (a movie that came out in 2000 about stockbrokers who try to swindle innocent people out of their life's savings). Not a pretty picture.

How much more are you than your professional title? Your Book Yourself Solid Dialogue will allow you to set yourself apart from everyone else whose professional title is the same as yours. It provides you with the opportunity to highlight the ways in which you and your services, products, and programs are unique—and do so with passion.

If your Book Yourself Solid Dialogue reads like your resume, you'll bore people to tears, and although they may not say it, they'll be thinking, "Who cares? So what? What has any of that got to do with me?" Your potential client wants to know: "What's in it for me?"

Developing Your Book Yourself Solid Dialogue

We're going to break this down into its smallest components and gather all the information we've worked hard to compile in the previous pages. You've chosen your target market and you've begun to develop your personal brand by crafting your *who and do what* statement, your *why I do it* statement, and your tagline. Now we're going to go back through all the exercises you've done and clean up your core message. If you've kept up on the exercises, crafting your Book Yourself Solid Dialogue will be a relatively simple process, and yet this powerful piece will make all the difference in your business and your message.

Five-Part Book Yourself Solid Dialogue Formula

Let's put it all together and create a few different versions of your Dialogue: short, medium, and long. Please, please, bear in mind, we are not crafting a speech. I am just giving you some structure so that you can begin to imagine the possible content of the Book Yourself Solid Dialogue that is a *conversation*.

1.4.1 Written Exercise: Each of the following five parts has already been answered in previous exercises. All you need to do is pull the pieces into the formula below.

Part I: Summarize your target market in one sentence.
Part II: Identify and summarize the three biggest and most critical problems that your target market faces.
Part III: List how you solve these problems and present clients with investable opportunities.
Part IV: Demonstrate the Number One most relevant result you help your clients achieve.
Part V: Reveal the deeper core benefits your client's experience.

You now have an outline that will help you clearly articulate what you do without sounding confusing and bland. In fact, you'll sound like a superstar because you can use this outline or framework to have a meaningful conversation with another human being. I know I'm being redundant here, but it's so important that I'm willing to. This is not a speech. Don't stay married to the format. Be sure to improvise. Using the structure can be helpful but you may not need to go through every element of this framework in every conversation. The person you're engaged with might end up doing all the talking and even supply your side of the dialogue accurately. Then you can just sit back and relax. The point is, if you're prepared with these five elements, you have the required ingredients for talking about what you do so you can cook up a sweet and tasty business, booked solid with high-paying, high-value clients. (Make note of how each part of the exercises you've just done fits into the conversations that follow, and note also how each part flows as the result of a natural conversation.)

Short and Sweet

Start by trying the short version, which is essentially an expanded *who and do what* statement.

- I help [Part I] . . . [insert Part V].

Example: Checkout line at the supermarket.

BOBBY: Nice to meet you, Michael. What do you do?
MP: I'm a small business advisor—I help [Part I] small business owners [Part II] get more clients.
BOBBY: Oh, that's very interesting. My wife has a home-based business. Can you help her?

MP: Tell me a bit about what she does and what kind of support you think she needs.

Now, we're talking . . .

The Mid-Length Version

You can easily adapt the Book Yourself Solid Dialogue as needed. Try a mid-length version and just tighten it up a bit.

- I help [Part I]
- You know how [insert Parts I and II]?
- Well, what I do is [insert Parts III and V].

Example: Industry conference.

LISA: Nice to meet you, Michael. What do you do for a living?

MP: I'm a small business advisor—I help [Part I] small business owners [Part II] get more clients.

LISA: That's so important . . . getting more clients.

MP: Ain't that the truth. Business owners are always looking to find more clients but often complain that they hate marketing and selling [Parts I and more of II].

LISA: Can I confess something to you, Michael? I'm one of those business owners, and I always need new clients, but I really hate marketing and selling!

MP: I hear that! But it so doesn't have to be that way. In fact, I teach people just like you how to *love* marketing and selling, and at the same time, get as many clients as their heart desires (More of Part II, Part III and V).

LISA: Tell me more! Please tell me more!

And now we're really talking!

The Long Version

Easy-peasy-lemon-squeezey. All I you need to do is insert Parts I through V into the following formula:

- You know how [drop in Part I] do, are, or feel [include some of Part II]?
- Well, what I do is [articulate Part III].
- The result is [reveal Part IV].
- The benefits are [insert lots of Part V].

Example: Casual conversation at a cocktail party.

JOE: Hey, Michael, what is it that you do?

MP: Thanks for asking, Joe. You know how many self-employed professionals (Part I) go out on their own looking for the freedom that working independently promises but they wind up isolated, frustrated, and often struggling financially? (Part II) Do you know people like that?

JOE: Oh, yeah, I definitely do. Actually, that sounds exactly like my sister, Jane.

MP: Oh, no kidding . . . is she working more hours than she should or wants to, never seems to be able to relax, and is constantly stressed about money? Or worse . . . has she become disillusioned about working for herself (more of Part II)?

JOE: Yeah, that's exactly right! I've been trying to encourage her, but frankly I'm all out of ideas as to how to help her.

MP: I hear you. Please tell her that she's not alone. Her situation is remarkably common. So common, in fact, that I teach a system for people like her to book themselves solid in my seminars and coaching programs (Part III). Fortunately, over 90 percent of the people who have gone through my programs increase the number of clients they serve by over 30 percent and improve their revenues by over 40 percent within a year of taking the program (Part IV). So, there's hope!

JOE: Oh, wow! That's pretty cool. I just wish Jane could have the clients she wants.

MP: Well, yeah, it's very cool, but it's about more than just getting clients and making money. Jane would begin to think a heck of a lot bigger about who she is and what she offers the world so she won't have to worry so much anymore. She'll be able to passionately share her work with the people she's meant to serve (Part V).

Joe sighs, takes a meaningful pause, then says . . .

JOE: I'm so glad I asked you what you did. How can I get my sister in touch with you? She could really use your help.

MP: Would you like to give me your card and I'll follow up with you on Monday so you can introduce me to your sister?

JOE: That would be great, Michael. This way, I don't have to put it on my already overly long to-do list.

MP: You know . . . I wrote a book based on my system called *Book Yourself Solid*. Why don't I send a signed copy to your sister as a gift from you?

JOE: That would be great. Wow, thank you. When you e-mail me, I'll give you her address so you can mail it to her.

That's a pretty good way to have a real conversation with someone about what you do. Of course, I've written this scene so it works perfectly. In real life, it won't always be this smooth or successful. But, if you listen well, are flexible, and can adapt to the dynamic and specifics at hand, more often than not, you'll knock it out of the park.

Or I could start by saying I'm a *New York Times* best selling author of four books, appear regularly on network and cable TV shows, am one of the most sought-after speakers in the business, and run one of the most respected coaching programs in the world. But then I'd sound like an arrogant jerk. These kinds of credentials should come out over time, when appropriate, not three seconds after someone says, "What do you do?"

Of course, you can go back to the way you've always done things and say, "Hi, I'm [your name here]. I'm a [add professional title]." Or, you could try to use an elevator speech, but I think you see that you're not going to have quite the same impact and more than likely than not, you'll end the conversation rather than start a relationship.

Once you've clearly identified your target market, understand their needs and desires, and can articulate how you help them by identifying the core benefits associated with the results of your services, you'll never be caught off guard again. I suggest you continue to hone and refine your message and then practice over and over. I do.

Getting into a Book Yourself Solid Dialogue with Ease

Start in the comfortable confines of your home; it may take some time for your Book Yourself Solid Dialogue to feel natural. While you don't want your dialogue to sound stiff and rehearsed, you do want to practice it. The more you practice it, the more comfortable you'll get with it, the less rehearsed it will sound, and the more improvisational you will be. You only get one chance to make a first impression. Present yourself and your business in a powerful and compelling way.

Practicing in this way will help you to become comfortable with the multitude of ways in which your Book Yourself Dialogue will unfold when you're speaking with a variety of people. It is truly a dialogue, not a speech or script, so every time you have a dialogue with someone about what you do, it will be unique. Since the people you'll be speaking with won't be reading a script, they may or may not respond in similar ways to what I outlined earlier, but you'll soon discover that when you know your Book Yourself Solid Dialogue well, it won't matter. You'll easily and effortlessly respond in the most appropriate way.

1.4.2 Booked Solid Action Step: Practice with a colleague or two. Call one another spontaneously to ask, "What is it that you do?" The most important principle of the Book Yourself Solid system is actually using what

I teach you. Learning it is only a means to an end. Taking action will get you booked solid.

After you've practiced with your colleague, answer these questions for one another:

- Did I sound relaxed and comfortable?
- Could you sense my passion and excitement for what I do?
- What really grabbed your attention?
- What did you like best or least about my Book Yourself Solid Dialogue?

Use this exercise as the great opportunity it is to get honest, open feedback so that you can fine-tune your Book Yourself Solid Dialogue and make it the best it can be.

Speak from the Heart

Be sure to speak with lots of expression. Get excited and show the passion you have for the problems you solve and what you do in the world. If you're not very interested in what you do, no one else will be, either.

When you're passionate and excited about what you do and you let it show, it's incredibly attractive. Real passion can't be faked and there's nothing more appealing and convincing than knowing someone is speaking from the heart.

And don't forget to:

- *Smile.* I mean really smile—a big, bold, friendly smile.
- *Make eye contact.* You can't connect with others on a deep level if you aren't making eye contact.

- *Be confident.* Use confident, open body language. Stand up straight, yet be relaxed.
- *Listen!* Stop and listen intently to the needs and desires of the person you're speaking to so that you can address whatever is most important and relevant to her.

A well-crafted Book Yourself Solid Dialogue that is delivered with ease and sincerity and infused with your own unique brilliance and passion is incredibly powerful. Claim your passion, claim your voice, and share it with the world one person at a time.

Building Trust and Credibility

To be booked solid requires that you are considered credible within your marketplace, that you be perceived as likeable, and that you earn the trust of the people you'd like to serve. Now that you've got a solid foundation, it's time to look at how to develop a strategy for creating trust and credibility so that you stand out from the crowd and begin to build relationships with your potential clients. Your strategy will be based on:

- Becoming and establishing yourself as a likeable expert in your field
- Building relationships of trust over time through your sales cycle
- Developing brand-building products and programs

In the first module, you spent time contemplating the people you want to serve, how best to serve them, how to express yourself uniquely through the services you offer, and how to talk to people you hope to serve about how you can help them. Now it's time to step things up a notch and look at what you have to do to earn the trust of the people you're meant to serve.

As before, I walk you step by step through the process and you'll begin to see that marketing and sales doesn't have to be so hard after all. In fact, I think you'll find that it can even be exciting and fun.

CHAPTER 5

Who Knows What You Know and Do They Like You?

All credibility, all good conscience, all evidence of truth come only from the senses.

—Friedrich Nietzsche

Have you heard the expression, "It's not what you know that's important but who you know"? There's some truth to it but, if you're a professional service provider, consider the importance of "Who knows *what* you know and do they *like* you?" If you want to establish yourself as an expert in your field, a "category authority," potential clients as well as marketing and referral partners need to know that you know what you know . . . and they need to like you.

Even before we discuss how to position yourself as an expert within your field, let's get down to the nitty-gritty—the standard credibility builders. The standard credibility builders are the things that you need to do and have in place to appear credible and professional. Once you have all your basics covered, then and only then can we discuss how to establish your reputation as an authority in your field and look at how your like-ability influences your ability to get booked solid.

The Standard Credibility Builders

The standard credibility builders may seem obvious, but without them you won't be taken seriously, so they're worth reviewing:

- *You must have a professional e-mail address*, preferably one that includes your domain name. juicytushy@aol.com doesn't qualify. Neither does 175bb3c@yahoo.com. If you don't yet have a web site, then at least use your name: johndoe@gmail.com.
- *Invest in quality business cards.* Business cards with perforated edges that you've printed at home, or the free cards with the printing company's name on the back, will undermine your credibility. On the flip side, over-produced cards with hyped-up text or a highly stylized headshot may undermine your authority. Only do something unusual with things like business cards if you're an expert at that kind of differentiation. If you're a designer and brand specialist, it might make sense to have a very unusual business card because it's likely so well done that it'll come off as remarkable. Otherwise, keep it simple.
- *If you don't have a web site, have one built now!* Actually, wait until you read Chapter 16, the Book Yourself Solid Web Strategy. If you do have a web site and it's out of date or created using a lower-end, old-school free template, build a new one. Please don't design your site yourself unless you're a professional or an exceptionally skilled amateur. Have a professional design your site. Nothing will detract from your credibility more than having a web site that is gathering flies on the Net.
- *Have professionally produced photographs taken.* Display them on your web site and in promotional materials. A photo of you in your

pajamas with your cat is not going to inspire a lot of confidence (unless, of course, you own a pet store that also sells pajamas). Find any way you can to use pictures or video to demonstrate your professionalism on all promotional materials both online and off. When you're at seminars, have your picture taken with other well-known professionals within your industry and use them in your promotional materials. And certainly display photographs of yourself speaking to groups of people or engaged with your customers and clients. Not having a photograph readily available on your web site or marketing materials leaves your potential clients wondering what you have to hide and doesn't give them the opportunity to connect with you.

- *Obtain and showcase specific testimonials rather than general testimonials.* A comment from a client named H. G. that says, "Pam was great. She really helped" is not going to hold a lot of weight and it's certainly not going to get you booked solid. However, a very specific testimonial from a person with a name, a company, and maybe even a web site address, if applicable, that says, "In two months, Pam helped me lose 15 pounds. I could not have done it without her!" will carry weight (no pun intended). The testimonial is results oriented. If Pam is a nutritionist, the client's satisfaction will represent the results that many of her clients want to achieve. Even better would be a highly recognized testimonial. For example, if Cindy Crawford was a client of Pam's and she offered the same testimonial, wouldn't you want to work with Pam? You'd figure, if she's good enough for Cindy, she's good enough for me. I would. This is important because testimonials can come off as mundane and may not serve as true differentiators unless they are from highly recognized individuals. So, ask everybody you work with to offer their specific, positive praise of you and your work and reach out to people you respect. Connect with them, and when the time is right, ask them to supply you with a testimonial of your work.

- Bonus: *Establish an advisory board.* If well-known individuals will lend you their names, it will help you establish credibility within your target market. Just your association with other recognized experts will do wonders for establishing your credibility.

Standards of Service

These are the basic standards of service that are essential for any decent service professional to adhere to and that your clients will expect. They help establish your credibility. The mistake that many service professionals make is thinking that these standards of service are all that are necessary to help them stand out from the crowd.

- *Quality of service.* Of course you should have a high quality of service. A potential client expects that you offer a high quality of service.
- *Methods and tools.* It's expected that you have the best methods and tools.
- *Responsiveness.* Your clients and customers expect you to be responsive. If you own an ambulance service, maybe responsiveness is paramount, but if you're a photographer, I expect you to respond to my calls and e-mails, but I don't expect you to come to my house on a whim at 3 A.M. on a Sunday to take a family portrait.
- *Credentials.* For most service professionals, clients don't care as much about credentials as you might think, unless, of course, you're in the medical, legal, or financial field; then credentials are expected and assumed. But you don't get a lot of brownie points for having a degree in acupuncture. If I'm going to come to you for acupuncture, I'll expect that you're credentialed, and if there is a plaque on the wall that displays your credentials, I'm satisfied. However, if you won the Nobel Peace Prize for your work as an acupuncturist, that might be impressive.
- *Client importance.* Your clients and customers expect to be considered important. It's essential to always make your clients feel

important—more than important, in fact. You want to make your clients feel like the sun rises and shines just for them, because it does, if you want to book yourself solid. Making clients feel as important as they truly are builds your credibility, and it should be a given.

- *Appropriate price.* People don't generally buy on price (even though they say they do) and certainly not when it comes to their personal satisfaction, family, or their business, which I guess, is almost everything. Offering the lowest price is not necessarily going to help you establish credibility. In fact, many potential clients may be leery if your prices are significantly below market value. More on pricing later.

Please do not assume that these standards of service will set you apart. They won't. They're what every savvy consumer will expect. However, there is something very special that will make you stand out from the crowd every day of the week.

Becoming and Establishing Yourself as a Category Authority

Although being a category authority and establishing yourself as one may, at first glance, appear to be the same thing, they're not. This isn't about faking it until you make it. Before you can establish yourself as a category authority you must *be* one. How do you do that? You truly become a category authority by learning everything you possibly can about the one thing you've decided you want to become known for.

For many of us, the leap into learning all we can about our field can be immediately overwhelming, as the first thing we often learn is just how much we don't know. But this is a good thing. You can't seek knowledge that you don't know you need, so it is much better to first study what you didn't realize earlier that you didn't know, even if it deflates your ego.

If the thought of becoming and establishing yourself as a category authority immediately induces a sense of panic at the thought of all you'd have to learn and do, you're not alone. Or maybe you feel you already know enough to be an expert, but the thought of having to put yourself so boldly—and publicly—front and center of your target market makes you want to run home for Mom's homemade chicken soup.

For some, the idea of putting yourself out in front of the people you'd like to serve in a big, bold, public way, where you'll be subject to public scrutiny, can trigger a multitude of insecurities. You'll know your dark side has taken over when thoughts start racing round and round inside your head like, "Who am I to call myself an expert? What do I know? I'm such a fraud. I don't know enough yet. Maybe I'll never learn enough to be an expert. I don't even know where to begin." Or worse yet, "What if I put myself out there and fall flat on my face? What if I look silly and embarrass myself? What if everyone hates me? What if I get made fun of or criticized?" Does this sound familiar? I'll bet it does. Again, you're not alone! It doesn't have to be that way. If your dark side is running rampant, lock it in a soundproof closet and give control back to the bold and brilliant you that you know you really are, and keep reading.

Do I Have To?

If, now that you've avoided the dark side, some other side of you has taken over and is whining, "Do I have to?" the answer is a firm and resounding, "Yes, you do!" Like it or not, becoming a category authority, an expert in your field, isn't optional if you want your business to be as successful as it can be. It's a must. Becoming and establishing yourself as a category authority will have such a powerful effect on the success of your business, and will be so incredibly rewarding, that it's well worth the effort and *perceived* risk (which means no real risk at all).

Becoming a category authority will:

- Create the credibility and trust necessary for potential clients to feel comfortable and confident about purchasing your services, products, and programs.

- Gain you the visibility you'll need to reach all of your target market.
- Allow you to get your message out to the world in a big way as it raises awareness of yourself and your business *within* your target market. The idea is to be the first to come to mind when someone needs the kind of services, products, and programs that you offer.
- Help you gain clients and increase sales more easily and effortlessly while also allowing you to earn higher fees. It will give you the edge you need to stand out from the crowd of others who offer similar services, products, and programs. Suddenly, you'll no longer be just one of the masses.
- Make it much easier to move and expand into new markets of your choosing.
- Increase your own confidence in your ability to provide the best possible services, products, and programs to those who most need and want them.

Where to Begin

You first have to identify what you'd like to become known for within your target market. If what you want to be known for is too broad or you try to become a category authority on too many topics, you'll overwhelm yourself and confuse your target market.

By identifying and focusing on the one thing you most want to become known for, you simplify and speed up the process, leaving no question in the minds of those in your target market about your area of expertise. This will allow you to create a synergy, not only among your services, products, and programs but among all the techniques you'll use to establish yourself as a category authority.

To powerfully establish yourself as a category authority, you need to saturate your target market using a variety of techniques that demonstrate your expertise on a single subject. To do that, you must focus, focus, focus!

2.5.1 Written Exercise: Please answer the following questions:

1. In what areas are you currently an expert?
2. In what areas do you need to develop your expertise?
3. What promises can you make and deliver to your target market that will position you as an expert?
4. What promises would you like to make and deliver to your target market but don't yet feel comfortable with?
5. What do you need to do to become comfortable at making and delivering these promises?

2.5.2 Written Exercise: Keeping the answers from the previous written exercise in mind, if there was *one thing* you could be known for within your target market, what would it be?

2.5.3 Written Exercise: What do you need to *learn* to become a category authority in the area you'd like to be known for?

2.5.4 Written Exercise: List the ways in which you could learn the things you identified in the preceding written exercise.
   Example: Books, Internet research, training programs, apprenticing with a mentor who is already a category authority.

Even if you're already very knowledgeable about whatever it is you want to become known for, continuing to learn and staying up to date with the latest information in your field is not only a good idea but is required to remain booked solid. I recommend that you read at least one book a month, if not more, on your chosen subject, which will increase your knowledge, challenge you to see a different perspective, or spark new ideas and thoughts, all of which will enhance the value you provide to your clients.

2.5.5 Written Exercise: Research and list five books that meet the preceding criteria.

2.5.6 Booked Solid Action Step: Buy these five books.

Making the Mental Shift

We've discussed what you need to have and do to be credible, and by now you understand the importance of becoming and establishing yourself as a category authority. I hope it's clear that you must actually *be* an expert. You might think the logical next step would be to implement a plan to establish yourself as a category authority within your target market, but it's not. There's a critical mental shift that must take place first.

All of the Book Yourself Solid marketing strategies that you're going to learn in Module Four will put you out in front of your target market in such a big way that you will establish yourself as a category authority. First consider what you need to learn and what you need to do to establish your expertise so that when the time comes to implement the Book Yourself Solid 7 Core Self-Promotion Strategies, you will *be* an expert. You will make the crucial mental shift of thinking of yourself as an expert. If *you* don't believe it, you'll have a hard time persuading anyone else to believe it.

Begin to think of and refer to yourself as a category authority—an expert in your field.

When the time comes to establish yourself as a category authority within your target market, you'll be comfortable with, and confident of, your expertise. If you already consider yourself an expert, then by all means begin including that in your current marketing materials.

Just remember—when communicating with your potential clients, be clear about what you know and clear about what you don't. People who are credible don't actually know everything, and they are just as comfortable saying that they don't know something as they are saying that they do.

There is one other very powerful mental and emotional factor that has a profound impact on your efforts to establish yourself as a category authority, one that may surprise you. I urge you not to discount or underestimate it.

The Power of Likeability

Now that you know what you need to do to become and establish yourself as a category authority, we're going to look at an even more important factor to consider: Do your potential clients like you? Do they perceive you as likeable? And I mean *really* likeable.

The fact is that if they don't, none of the rest of your efforts to establish yourself as a category authority will matter. That's a pretty bold statement, and it may come as a surprise to you, but bear with me as I shine some light on the subject, with the help of Tim Sanders and a few concepts from his book, *The Likeability Factor: How to Boost Your L-Factor and Achieve Your Life's Dreams*.

When you get right down to it, Sanders points out, "Life is a series of popularity contests." We don't want to admit it, we don't want to believe it, we've been told it ain't necessarily so, but ultimately, if you're well liked, if your likeability factor is high, you're more likely to be chosen and to get booked solid.

Mark McCormack, the founder of International Management Group (IMG), the most powerful sports management and marketing company, agrees: "All things being equal, people will do business with a friend; all things being unequal, people will still do business with a friend." If a potential client perceives you as the most credible and likeable, you're probably the one she'll hire. And even if all things are *not* equal, even if you aren't the candidate with the most experience or expertise, if your potential client likes you, it's your likeability that will win the day and the client.

To make choices, we go through a three-step process. First, we *listen* to something out of a field of opportunities. Then we either do or do not *believe* what we've heard. Finally, we put a *value* on what we've heard. Then, we make our choice.

With so many demands on our attention these days, we have to filter and carefully select what we give our attention to. This is why becoming and establishing yourself as a category authority is so important. Your target market and your potential clients need a reason to deem your message important enough to sit up and pay attention, to *listen* to it. If you're likeable, they're much more likely to do so and to remember what they've heard.

Once you've got their attention, they're listening, but will they *believe* what they're hearing? This is where your credibility comes into play. With so many advertising messages coming at us from every direction each day—through spam e-mail, radio and TV commercials, and infomercials, to name a few—we've become highly skeptical of much of what we hear. If you're credible, you're much more likely to be believed.

But wait, that's not the only factor that comes into play when someone is determining whether to believe you. Again, your likeability is a critical factor in establishing trust. Think about it for a moment. You're much more likely to trust, and to *believe*, someone you like. Sanders says, "When people like the source of a message, they tend to trust the message or, at least, try to find a way to believe it."

Let's suppose that you've made it through the first two steps of this process. Your potential client has listened to you and believes you. Now she must determine the value of you and your message. Consider this example:

Susan owns a spa and is interviewing two massage therapists. The first candidate has been a professional for 12 years, is certified in Shiatsu, deep tissue, sports, Swedish, and relaxation massage. The second candidate has only recently completed a basic massage-certification training program and has minimal experience but comes with good references. They both expect to earn approximately the same amount per session.

The first massage therapist walks into the interview 10 minutes late, frowning and obviously agitated. She then launches into a litany of complaints about her day to explain her delayed arrival. This candidate leaves Susan feeling on edge and irritated. Susan realizes very quickly that her clients and staff are likely to have a similar negative reaction to this massage therapist's demeanor.

The second massage therapist is waiting patiently for her interview when Susan finishes with the first. She beams a radiant smile at Susan as she enters the office. Her upbeat temperament has a profound and immediate effect on Susan, and she feels herself relax as she smiles back. She already knows that her clients and staff will love her.

Who do you think is hired? You darn tootin' right it's the less experienced but highly likeable message therapist who gets the nod.

Your likeability factor has an enormous impact on your perceived value. Develop your credibility, establish yourself as an expert, strive to be your best, most likeable self, and you'll quickly become the best and most obvious choice for your potential clients.

6

The Book Yourself Solid Sales Cycle Process

It is a mistake to look too far ahead. Only one link in the chain of destiny can be handled at a time.

—Sir Winston Churchill

Building Relationships of Trust

All sales start with a simple conversation. It may be a conversation between you and a potential client or customer, between one of your clients and a potential referral, between one of your colleagues and a potential referral, or between your web site and a potential client. An effective sales cycle is based on turning these simple conversations into relationships of trust with your potential clients over time. We know that people buy from those they like and trust. This is never truer than for the professional service provider.

If you don't have trust, then it doesn't matter how well you've planned, what you're offering, or whether you've created a wide variety of buying options to meet varying budgets. If a potential client doesn't trust you, nothing else matters. They aren't going to buy from you—period. If you think about it, this may be one of the main reasons you say you hate marketing and selling. You may be trying to sell to people with whom you have not yet built enough trust. All sales offers must be proportionate to the amount of trust that you've earned.

What are your potential clients thinking?

- Do they really believe you can deliver what you say you can?
- Do they trust you to hold their personal information confidential?
- Do they like the people who work for you?
- Do they feel safe with you?
- Do they believe hiring you will give them a significant return on their investment?

If you want a perpetual stream of inspiring and life-fulfilling ideal clients clamoring for your services and products, then just remember—all sales start with a simple conversation and are executed when a need is met and the appropriate amount of trust is assured.

Turn Strangers into Friends and Friends into Clients

Seth Godin, author of *Permission Marketing*, implores us to stop interrupting people with our marketing messages and instead turn strangers into friends by adding value and friends into customers by getting permission from them to offer our products and services. In its most effective form, the Book Yourself Solid Sales Cycle not only turns strangers into friends and friends into potential clients but potential clients into current clients and past clients into current clients.

In order to design a sales cycle for your business, you must first understand how you're going to lead people into your sales cycle. Then we can actually build out a sales cycle process that will attract more clients than you can handle and do so with the utmost integrity.

The Book Yourself Solid Six Keys to Creating Connection: Who, What, Where, When, Why, and How

The Book Yourself Solid Sales Cycle works when you know:

1. *Who* your target clients are.
2. *What* they are looking for.
3. *Where* they look for you.
4. *When* they look for you.
5. *Why* they should choose you.
6. *How* you want them to engage with you.

Know your responses to these six keys and you will ensure that the offers you are making in your sales cycle process are right on target.

Key Number One: Who Is Your Target Client or Customer?

We've covered in depth how to choose a target market, but I'm going to reiterate it here because of its importance. You need to choose whom you'd like to bring into your cycle. The more specific you are the better; choose one person (or organization) within your target market to focus on.

Identifying and gearing your marketing to a specific individual (or organization) allows you to make the important emotional connection that is the first step in developing a relationship with your potential client. When you have made the effort to speak and write directly to your ideal client, he'll feel it. He will feel as though you truly know and understand his needs and desires—because you will. That task alone will go a long way toward building the trust you desire with the clients you seek.

If you're not super clear on whom specifically you're targeting, whom you want to reach out to and attract, it's going to be hard to develop a sales cycle that works because you'll be chasing after every potential opportunity and you won't be making a strong connection with anyone.

2.6.1 Written Exercise: *Who* is your target client or customer? Describe what she is like. Get really creative with this one. List as many specific details as you can.

Example: My friend Lorrie Morgan Ferrero, an excellent copywriter, describes her target customer like this: "Nikki Stanton, a 37-year-old divorced entrepreneur with a web conferencing business. She's Internet and business savvy. Invests most of her profit back into the business. Lives in San Diego in a gated community with her 10-year-old daughter, Madison. She's involved in her daughter's school and drives her to dance classes. Has a home office and makes approximately $117,000 a year. Jogs three times a week in the neighborhood. She loves to find bargains on designer clothes and dreams of visiting Italy with her daughter someday."

Your turn. Describe whom you'd like to attract into your sales cycle.

Key Number Two: What Are They Looking For?

You've got to understand what your ideal clients or customers are looking for—the kinds of products or services they think will solve their problems or help them reach their goals. It's very important to be clear on your answers because if you don't know what your potential clients are looking for, you won't know what kind of product and service offers to make in your sales cycle. We usually make offers that *we think* are relevant. It's time to put your target market first and work to truly understand what *they know* is relevant. Then you can decide on what you're going to offer them that will meet their needs, according to the amount of trust that you've earned, at various stages in your sales cycle.

2.6.2 Written Exercise: *What* are your potential clients looking for?

Examples: In my case, they want a book that can help them get clients. They want to read an article or report on how to use social media. They want private coaching. They want to attend a marketing seminar. And so on.

Key Number Three: Where Do They Look for You?

Do you know where your target market looks for you? Do they search online? Do they read magazines? Do they call their friends for referrals for the kind of service that you're providing? What other types of business professionals do they trust to get their referrals from? If you don't know, survey your current clients. This should always be one of the first questions you ask a new client: "How did you come to find me?" If you don't have any clients of your own yet, ask a colleague how her clients find her.

2.6.3 Written Exercise: *Where* do your ideal clients look for you?

Key Number Four: When Do They Look for You?

When do the people (or organizations) in your target market look for the services you offer? What needs to happen in their personal life or work life for them to purchase the kind of service you have to offer? How high do the stakes need to be before they decide to purchase the service you're offering? They may be interested in what you do, and your offerings may resonate with them, but they might not need you at the moment they find you.

This is why the Book Yourself Solid Sales Cycle is so important. You'll want to make it easy for them to step into your environment and move closer to your core offerings over time. When their stakes rise, they'll reach out to you and ask for you. But you've got to keep the conversation going.

2.6.4 Written Exercise: Describe the situations that are likely to drive potential clients to seek your services, products, and programs. *When* do they look for you?

Examples: They've lost their job. They're starting their own business. They're so disorganized that they're losing business. They are experiencing extreme discord in their relationship. They've just had a baby and can't seem to lose their baby weight.

Key Number Five: Why Should They Choose You?

That's a big question. Why are they going to choose you? Are you a credible authority in your field? What makes you the best choice for them? What is unique about you or the solutions you offer?

For this exercise, it's crucial that you set your modesty aside and express yourself clearly and with confidence—no wishy-washy answers to these questions. Think back to the last time you went in search of expert help. When you first spoke to the service provider to inquire about his services, his expertise, and whether he could help you, the *last* thing you wanted to hear was, "Well, I kinda know what I'm doing. I might be able to help you. I'll give it a shot."

> *While it may feel uncomfortable at first, you've got to get comfortable saying, "The best thing for you is me!"*

Granted, saying you are the best may be a bit too bold for you, but at the least you've got to be able to say, "You've come to the right person. Yes, absolutely, I *can* help you. I'm an expert at what I do and this is how I can help."

Bragging is about comparing yourself to others and proclaiming your superiority. Declaring your strengths, your skills, your expertise, and your ability to help is not bragging but expressing confidence in what your potential clients expect, want, and need to hear from you.

2.6.5 Written Exercise: *Why* should your potential clients choose you? (Don't you dare skip this one! Be bold! Express yourself fully. Remember, this is not the time for modesty.)

Key Number Six: How Do You Want Them to Engage with You?

Once potential clients have learned about your services, how would you like them to interact or engage with you? Do you want them to call your office? Do you want them to sign up for your newsletter on your web site? What is it that you want potential clients to *do?*

Naturally, we'd love for them to immediately purchase our highest-priced product, program, or service, but this is rare. Most of your potential clients need to get to know you and trust you over time. They need to be eased gradually toward what they may perceive to be your high-risk offerings. It's often said that, on average, you will need to connect with a potential client seven times before they'll purchase from you. Not always, but if you understand this principle, you will be on the road to booking yourself solid a lot faster than if you try to engage in one-step selling. "Hi, I'm a consultant. Wanna hire me today?" isn't going to be effective. That's definitely not the Book Yourself Solid way. Maybe we should call one-step selling one-*stop* selling because that's what it'll do—stop your sales process dead in its tracks.

2.6.6 Written Exercise: *How* do you want your potential clients to interact or engage with you? (Note: Establishing a line of communication is the first step in developing a relationship of trust.)

Clearly defining these six keys will help you to determine what you want to offer your potential clients in each stage of your sales cycle and will help you craft the most effective sales cycle possible. Moreover, defining these six keys will also help you tremendously when implementing the Book Yourself Solid 7 Core Self-Promotion Strategies.

The Book Yourself Solid Sales Cycle Process

Your services have a high barrier to entry. To potential new clients, your services are intangible and expensive—whether you think they are or not—especially to those who have not used the kind of services that you offer or who have not had good results with their previous service providers.

The Book Yourself Solid Sales Cycle is a sequence of phases that a client moves through when deciding whether to buy your services or products. You begin your sales cycle by making no-barrier-to-entry offers to potential clients. A no-barrier-to-entry offer is one that has no risk whatsoever for a potential client so that she can *sample* your services. I'm not talking just about offering free services, which is a common practice for many professional service providers. I take this concept much further with much more success.

In Module Four, you'll learn how to use the Book Yourself Solid 7 Core Self-Promotion Strategies, including networking, direct outreach, referral, keeping in touch, speaking, writing, and using the Web to create awareness for the solutions you offer. However, rather than attempting to *sell* to a client, you will simply offer her an invitation that has no barrier to entry.

You already know that "who knows what you know" is important when working toward booking yourself solid. Do you realize how many more clients you could be serving if they just knew what you had to offer? The best way to inform them is to have at least one, if not a few, compelling offers that have no barrier to entry. As opposed to the typical sales cycle, which has the same start and end points for all prospective clients, the Book Yourself Solid Sales Cycle works in a way that allows buyers to enter at any point in the process, depending on their situation. A client hires you when the circumstances in his life or work match the offers that you make. If you're a mortgage specialist, I may not need your services right now. But perhaps, six months from now, I stumble upon a "FOR SALE" sign in the front yard of my dream home. You can bet that I'll not only want your services, I'll need them immediately. Do you see how the stakes have changed? Chances are that if you haven't built trust with me over the last six months by offering great value along the way (without expecting anything in return, mind you), it's unlikely you'll cross my mind when I look to secure a mortgage for my dream house.

The following example will give you a framework for the process. Your sales cycle may include 3, 10, or even 15 stages, depending on your particular business and the different services and products you offer. I'm going to teach you the principles that govern an effective sales cycle so that you can craft one that serves your particular business and meets the individual needs and tastes of your clients and customers.

I will explain each stage and give you a real example from my business to help you visualize exactly how each stage works. I'm going to also ask you to write out your objective for each stage and how you're going to achieve your objective. This way, by the end of the chapter, you'll have completed your very own Book Yourself Solid Sales Cycle. I'll do my best to make it as easy as possible to absorb and implement the information. If you do get a bit overwhelmed, please stay with it. This is an important part of the Book Yourself Solid system, and understanding the principles behind these techniques will ensure that you're well on your way to being booked solid.

As you work through this process, remember all that you are doing is having a simple conversation with someone. You are making a connection that will build trust so that you will then be able to share your services with another person. How cool is that?

Book Yourself Solid Sales Cycle—Stage One

To book yourself solid, perform daily tasks that will keep your name in front of potential clients. In Stage One, your objective is to get a potential client to do something—go to your web site, call a number, fill out a form, or another action that begins to affiliate them to you. To best do this, you need to create awareness for the services, products, and programs you offer using one or all of the Book Yourself Solid 7 Core Self-Promotion Strategies. You will have your choice of:

1. The Book Yourself Solid Networking Strategy
2. The Book Yourself Solid Direct Outreach Strategy
3. The Book Yourself Solid Referral Strategy
4. The Book Yourself Solid Keep in Touch Strategy
5. The Book Yourself Solid Speaking Strategy
6. The Book Yourself Solid Writing Strategy
7. The Book Yourself Solid Web Strategy

Your objective for Stage One of the Book Yourself Solid Sales Cycle should be simple and measurable, like driving prospective clients to your web site. Or maybe you want them to call your office directly. It's up to you. But once you've chosen an objective, you'll choose the strategies you would like to use to achieve it.

The Book Yourself Solid Sales Cycle is most effective when used in conjunction with a keep-in-touch plan. The size of your network, and especially the number of potential clients in your network, is directly proportional to how booked solid you are. I strongly suggest working diligently on growing your network, which includes potential clients and marketing and referral partners alike. Sometimes this network is referred to as your database or followers or subscribers or, simply, your list. Your list is made up of people who have given you permission to communicate with them on an ongoing basis. Building a large list and having permission to communicate with them will make it easy to secure new clients whenever you need to. All you have to do is send out a newsletter or e-newsletter, publish a blog post, or tweet a compelling offer, and *voilà!*—you'll have new ideal clients. I am not being glib, you'll see for yourself just how easy it is once you build trust with a large group of raving fans who have given you permission to add value to their lives and make offers to them at the same time.

Please note, you can never, ever, no way, no how, just add people to your list because you think they'll like what you have to offer. That, my dear friend, is spam, any way you slice it—even if you know them personally. All your marketing, follow-up, keeping in touch, and publishing must be permission-based, which means, the recipient of your message has consented to receive a broadcast from you, regardless of whether it contains marketing messages. You can send a personal e-mail to connect and build your relationship, but you cannot add just anyone to any sort of broadcast list.

Michael's Stage One Example My Stage One objective is to drive potential clients to my web site. (This is the answer to the sixth key to creating connection, "How do you want your potential clients to engage with you?") To do so, I use the Book Yourself Solid Speaking, Writing, and Web Strategies.

2.6.7 Written Exercise: Book Yourself Solid Sales Cycle Stage One:

- What is your objective in Stage One of the sales cycle?
- How are you going to achieve it?

Book Yourself Solid Sales Cycle—Stage Two

In this stage you will demonstrate your knowledge, solutions, and sincere desire to provide value to your target market free of charge, with no barrier to entry and at no risk to them. The benefits include increased trust—they will feel as though they know you somewhat better.

To familiarize your prospective clients with your services, you need to offer them solutions, opportunities, and relevant information in exchange for their contact information and permission to continue communicating with them over time. What does that communication look like? You may provide a tip sheet, special report, or white paper that addresses their urgent needs and compelling desires. You might give a discount coupon for an initial session. It could be your always-have-something-to-invite-people-to offer, which I discuss in detail at the end of this chapter. No matter what you select, it should be something that speaks not only to their needs but also what you want them to know about how you can serve them.

Michael's Stage Two Example My Stage Two objective is to encourage my web site visitors to subscribe to my newsletter by entering their name, e-mail address, and location. If they do, they will also get a free chapter from each of my books, *Book Yourself Solid*, *Beyond Booked Solid*, *The Contrarian Effect*, and *The Think Big Manifesto*, along with a high quality 60-minute audio recording in which I expand on certain concepts, principles, and strategies.

2.6.8 Written Exercise: Book Yourself Solid Sales Cycle Stage Two:

- What is your objective in Stage Two of the cycle?
- How are you going to achieve it?

Book Yourself Solid Sales Cycle—Stage Three

Now that you've started building trust between you and your potential clients, you're going to work on developing and enhancing that trust and cultivating the relationship.

In Stage Three of the sales cycle your objective is twofold: to continue to add value by helping your potential clients incorporate the information that you gave them in Stage Two of the cycle and to make a sale. If you gave them a free report, you should follow up with automated e-mails that help them use the content in the report to create value. Or if you invited them to your always-have-something-to-invite-people-to event, you'll tell them more about it, make sure they know how to take advantage of it, and of course, what the benefits of participating in it will be. You should also offer them something that will surprise them. It could be a complimentary pass to a workshop you're doing or a personal note on your stationery or branded postcard with a list of books on your area of expertise that you know will speak to their urgent needs. Remember, the value you add doesn't have to be all about you. If you recommend a resource to your potential clients, they will very likely associate the value they received from that resource with you.

As I mentioned, this is the first time in the sales cycle where you might also offer your potential clients a service or product that will cost them money: an in-person seminar or intake session. It might be one of your information products: e-book, published book, CD, DVD, work-book, manual, guidebook, or teleseminar, all of which we'll get to in the book. When you send your follow-up e-mails, you will let your potential clients know of the opportunities you have for them that speak directly to their urgent needs and compelling desires, and you'll continue to add value without expecting anything in return.

What's important to understand is that the monetized offer you are making does not have a very high barrier to entry. You're not going to rush out of the gate and surprise potential clients with your highest-priced offer, just as you wouldn't propose marriage on a first date, no matter how smitten you are. You want to offer them something they are ready for, and if they're ready for more at that moment, they'll ask for it. Of course, you'll always let potential clients know how to view the page on your web site that lists your various services, just in case they are ready to walk down the aisle.

Michael's Stage Three Example My Stage Three objective is to give those who previously opted in for my newsletter, four free chapters, and 60-minute audio the incentive to purchase one of my books from Amazon .com. (You don't have to have a published book to do this. You can offer an intake session, needs assessment, e-book, CD, class, or any other low-barrier-to-entry offer.)

2.6.9 Written Exercise: Book Yourself Solid Sales Cycle Stage Three:

- What is your objective in Stage Three of the cycle?
- How are you going to achieve it?

Book Yourself Solid Sales Cycle—Stage Four

Your focus now is to help your potential clients move to the next level of your sales cycle. Let's say a potential client bought your low-barrier-to-entry product or service or has even become a client, thanks to your efforts in Stage Three of the sales cycle. Now is the time to overdeliver on the product or service he purchased. What does that mean? Here's an example: Your client has recently purchased your e-book, and you notice that you have a workshop or presentation scheduled on the very same topic. To overdeliver, you could call the customer, send the customer an e-mail or card inviting him to the workshop or, if he can't attend, send him a copy of the notes after the event. What a great way to give more than the potential client expected to receive.

When he has received great value from that service or product, you then offer your next level of product or service, something that requires more of an investment than the previous product or service he purchased. Notice how this client is moving closer and closer to your core offerings and your higher-priced offerings. This is usually the case but only after you've increased the client's trust factor and proven that your solutions work and that you deliver on the promises that you make.

If the potential client does not engage in one of your Stage Three offerings right away, don't despair. Just remember that you are building relationships of trust that will grow and, you hope, last a lifetime. When the time is right, a potential client will become a current client.

Michael's Stage Four Example   My Stage Four objective is to enroll ideal clients in my online and on-the-telephone courses on marketing, business growth, and even information product creation, the same people who have already visited my web site, opted in for free chapters and the audio recording, and purchased my book.

I believe that when people have read one of my books, thoughtfully done the exercises, and taken the action steps necessary, they will be well on their way to achieving their goals. They will also be confident that what I have to offer them is valid and valuable and that I can serve their most relevant, personal, and immediate needs and desires. However, they may also want the opportunity to work through the concepts, principles, and strategies in the book with me, my team, and other inspired service professionals for a number of reasons: opportunity for more personal coaching and attention, higher levels of accountability, networking opportunities, or maybe they want to bathe in the Book Yourself Solid fountain of inspiration.

The point is, I don't want to try to sell them these online and phone-based coaching courses until they've had the opportunity to read one of my books. I want them to be excited about meeting me and my team and know that we can serve them before they sign up for a coaching course. That one factor, knowing that we can serve them, will give our participants better results, and that's our goal—to help our clients get the results they want. Isn't that your goal? I know, too, from past experience that it will also increase attendance at the events. Will there be people enrolled in the courses who have not yet read one of my books? Sure, but more people will enroll in the courses after they have read one of my books. Your goal throughout the sales cycle is to help people move closer and closer to your core offerings by ensuring that they are getting the results they need at each stage of the cycle.

Each stage of this cycle applies to you regardless of whether you're holding live events for 400 people or you have a small graphic design firm. To do the following exercise, you are going to simply replace my offerings with the appropriate offerings for you and your clients. Remember, your sales cycle will have as many stages as is appropriate for you and your business right now. You might only have three stages in your sales cycle at present. It will evolve and grow as your business evolves and grows.

2.6.10 Written Exercise: Book Yourself Solid Sales Cycle Stage Four:

- What is your objective in Stage Four of the cycle?
- How are you going to achieve it?

Book Yourself Solid Sales Cycle—Stage Five

Your objective in Stage Five is similar to the previous one: to help potential clients move to the next level of your sales cycle by offering them a higher-level product or service. What's important to understand about this process is that not every person or organization who enters into your sales cycle will move all the way through it, and the time that each potential client takes to do so will be different as well.

Michael's Stage Five Example   My Stage Five objective is to enroll ideal clients into my in-person small group coaching and mentoring programs and or larger live events. Again, there are many people who join one of these programs, or attend a event, without participating in an online coaching course, or right after they read my book, or even before they do, simply because they were referred to me by a person they trust. But you can't count on that. You'll have better success if you lay out a plan for how you introduce people to your offerings.

The in-person small-group coaching programs require more of a financial investment than do the online and over-the-phone coaching courses. That's why it's very important to me that those who join these programs know that it is the right place for them to continue their business development and trust that my team and I will overdeliver on our promises. I imagine you would want the same thing. After clients participate in an online and over-the-phone coaching program, which is my Stage Four offering, they will believe this deeply. This is why the Book Yourself Solid Sales Cycle is so effective. You're building trust with people over time, trust that is proportionate to the size of the offer you're making to them.

> *All of your sales offers should be proportionate to the amount of trust that you've earned.*

As a professional service provider you don't want to try to convince people that what you're offering is right for them. You want to provide value upon value until they believe that your services are right for them. They will get better results that way and be more satisfied with your services, a factor that is way too important to forget about.

2.6.11 Written Exercise: Book Yourself Solid Sales Cycle Stage Five:

- What is your objective in Stage Five of the cycle?
- How are you going to achieve it?

The Book Yourself Solid Always-Have-Something-to-Invite-People-to Offer

This strategy might just be the most effective marketing and trust building strategy on the planet for the professional service provider. You'll want to consider your own always-have-something-to-invite-people-to offer as you design the first few stages of your Book Yourself Solid Sales Cycle. It might be what you choose to direct potential clients to when you use the Book Yourself Solid 7 Core Self-Promotion Strategies.

People generally hate to be sold, but they love to be invited—as long as the invitations are relevant and anticipated. Meaning, they've given you permission to make an invitation. What if I could help you eliminate your need to sell with this one solution? Would that be exciting to you? I bet it would. By my second year in business, this one strategy actually doubled my income.

When I started my business, I offered a complimentary teleseminar (very large conference call) that I called the "Think Big Revolution." I offered it on a weekly basis, and it was designed to help people think bigger about who they are and what they offer the world. Sometimes I would discuss a topic that was specifically related to getting more clients, and other times I discussed different principles and strategies that would help the callers be more successful in business and in life.

Note that the membership was free. If I met someone I thought would benefit from membership, I'd invite her to join. With the release of my fourth book, *The Think Big Manifesto*, I turned the weekly call into a 24/7 online social networking community, a place where big thinkers can connect with other big thinkers to actually make their dreams come true. Membership is free and it will always be because no one owns big thinking. I'd like to invite you to join. I bet you'll love it. You get an opportunity to participate in something that should add great value to your life and test me out at the same time. And for me it's fantastic because I don't have to *sell* anything. I can offer really great value to the lives of potential clients and customers at no risk to them. And then they have the opportunity to ask me for more business help if they are so inclined.

There are many ways you can set up this kind of always-have-something-to-invite-people-to self-promotion strategy. You are limited only by the scope of your imagination. If ideas for your own always-have-something-to-invite-people-to offer are just not springing to life for you right now, don't fret. I'm going to give you plenty of specific ideas and ways of brainstorming your own.

To accept my invitation to join the Think Big Revolution, go to ThinkBigRevolution.com and sign up there. See how easy that was? No selling; just an invitation.

> *This strategy works! Of the 93 percent of my clients who successfully book themselves solid, all of them use it in one form or another.*

There is another added benefit of this kind of always-have-something-to-invite-people-to offer. It can serve as one of the most effective ways of establishing your personal brand. Notice how the Think Big Revolution is an extension of my *why I do it* statement. Once you join the Revolution, you'll immediately see that I want to help you. And if you're someone who wants to think bigger about who you are and what you offer the world, then you'll know you're in the right place, not just intellectually, but in your soul as well. Your always-have-something-to-invite-people-to offer is the perfect way to integrate and align your *who and do what* statement (whom you help and what you help them do) and your *why you do it* statement (the philosophical explanation for why you do what you do).

Consider another example: I worked with a man who is a personal trainer and a healthy-eating chef. When he came to me, he was facing two challenges that he needed my help with. He was not living up to his full income potential because of working with clients on just a one-on-one basis, and he hadn't created a relentless demand for his services. Both of these concerns caused him to be anxious over what his future held.

I first asked him to look at how we could adapt his services from just offering one-on-one training, to group programs. Then we created his always-have-something-to-invite-people-to offer: the *Fitness Fiesta for Foodies*. One Sunday evening a month, he would host a party at which he would teach his guests how to prepare healthful meals that help them stay fit. There were two requirements for attendance, however. He would put that month's menu on his web site and each guest was required to bring one item off the menu. Each guest was also asked to bring someone new to the event, thus creating a new audience for his work. He barely had to market himself. It was magical. People loved it and they loved him for doing it. And they joined his programs because of it.

A financial planner could do something similar either on the phone or in person. Even a simple Q&A about building wealth would do the trick. Are you beginning to get your own ideas on how this could work for you?

The value you add in your offer meets the needs and desires of the people you serve. This no-barrier-to-entry offer is an essential component of the Book Yourself Solid Sales Cycle. Then as you continue to build trust over time by offering additional value and creating awareness for the services you provide, you'll attract potential clients deeper into the sales cycle, moving them closer to your core offerings.

You'll notice that the two always-have-something-to-invite-people-to examples I offered are done in a group format. There are three important reasons for this:

1. You'll leverage your time so you're connecting with as many potential clients as possible in the shortest amount of time.
2. You'll leverage the power of communities. When you bring people together, they create far more energy and excitement than

you can on your own. Your guests will also see other people interested in what you have to offer, and that's the best way to build
credibility.

3. You'll be viewed as a really cool person. Seriously, if you're known
   in your marketplace as someone who brings people together, that
   will help you build your reputation and increase your likeability.

Please give away so much value that you think you've given too
much, and then give more. I had a friend in college who, when he
ordered his hero sandwiches, would say, "Put so much mayonnaise on
it that you think you've ruined it, and then put more." Gross, I know
(I believe that he has since stopped eating his sandwiches that way and
his arteries are thanking him), but adding value is not a dissimilar experience. Remember, your potential clients must know *what* you know. They
must really like you and believe that you have the solutions to their very
personal, specific, and urgent problems. The single best way to do that
is to invite them to experience what it's like to be around you and the
people you serve.

Use the Book Yourself Solid Sales Cycle to Unconditionally Serve Your Clients

You can have as many stages in your sales cycle as you need to build trust
with potential clients for the kinds of offers you make. Just thinking about
your sales cycle will help you clarify and expand your offerings. Gone
are the days when you can simply have one offering and be guaranteed
to book yourself solid. The marketplace is too competitive and diverse.
Every day another inspired professional stakes a claim and joins the ranks
of free agents around the world. More and more people are feeling the
call to stand in the service of others.

Expanding your offerings to create a Book Yourself Solid Sales Cycle
may just enhance your business model—the mechanism by which you

generate revenue—from only one offering with one stream of revenue to multiple offerings with multiple streams of revenue.

The Book Yourself Solid Sales Cycle is not just about getting new clients to hire you. It is designed to unconditionally serve your current clients as well. It is much harder to sell your services, products, and programs to a new client than to those who have already received value from you as a client or customer. The most successful businesses, both large and small, know this. It's one of the reasons Amazon.com is so successful. Once you've become a customer, they know you, they know what you need, what you read, and they work to continue to serve you. The typical client-snagging mentality suggests that you make a sale and move on. The Book Yourself Solid way requires that you make a sale and ask, "How can I overdeliver and continue to serve this person or organization?" This is not a small thing.

Now it's your turn to develop your own unique sales cycle. Don't limit yourself to just the few examples I've already touched on. There are a multitude of ways to build trust with your potential clients and to ease them toward purchasing your higher price point offerings. Use your imagination and creativity to tailor your sales cycle to what works best, feels most natural, and resonates most with you.

7

The Power of Information Products

Know where to find the information and how to use it—that's the secret of success.

—Albert Einstein

Brand-Building Products and Easy-to-Follow Programs

Nothing helps to build your credibility like products and programs designed to serve your target market's very specific urgent needs and compelling desires. People love to buy packaged learning and experiences. They're easy to understand, and therefore easy to buy. Perhaps you think that your service may not be as easily defined as a packaged product or program, and necessarily has a high barrier for entry. I think you underestimate what you have to offer. As you continue to develop and enhance your Book Yourself Solid Sales Cycle, you will want to produce products and programs that will fully round out the many possible stages of your sales cycle, including the early stages, where barriers to entry must be low.

I'm sure your bookshelves are lined with products and programs that you've purchased from other service professionals over the years. In fact, you're reading one right now. How would you like to create your own self-expression product or program? I use the phrase *self-expression* because the kind of programs and products that I'm referring to gives you an opportunity to express yourself to the world and serve your target market at the same time. That's the beauty of being a service professional.

> *You are in the business of serving other people as you stand in the service of your destiny and express yourself through your work.*

I just love the opportunity offered through information product creation because you can follow a simple step-by-step system that leads you to the production of the kind of revenue and satisfaction that comes from bold self-expression. Let's take a quick look at the other red-hot benefits that you get from producing information products:

- Products create opportunities for multiple streams of passive or leveraged income. They can be in retail stores or online, at your web site and the web sites of your affiliates, 24/7/365, with world-wide availability. You can consistently get orders for your products from people all over the world.
- Having a product enhances your credibility with your prospects, your peers, meeting planners, and the media because it establishes you as a category expert and sets you apart from your competitors.
- Products can help you land more clients because they speed up the sales cycle. Since your services have a high barrier to entry, your potential clients may need to jump a few high hurdles to persuade themselves they need to hire you. Having a product to offer based on your services gives potential clients the opportunity to test you out without having to take a big risk. Then if they connect with

you and are well served by your product, they will upgrade from the lower-priced product to the higher-priced service.

- If you use public speaking as one of your marketing strategies, having a product at the back of the room when you speak gives you credibility, and you also have a relatively low-cost way to introduce prospects into your business and generate ancillary revenue at the same time.

- Products leverage your time. One of the biggest problems service professionals face is the paradigm of trading time for money. If all you ever do is trade your time for money, your revenues are limited by how much you charge per hour. For example, if you speak in front of 100 of your prospects and you're able to sell a couple dozen of your information products at $50 each, then you've just increased your hourly rate from $100 to more than $1,000 an hour. Again, remember, many more people are willing and able to buy an information product than they are willing and able to hire you for your higher-priced service.

Start with the End in Mind

You may be in the beginning phase of building your business and just be setting out on the course to book yourself solid, but as Dr. Stephen Covey *(The 7 Habits of Highly Effective People)* says, "Start with the end in mind." If you want to seriously build a long-lasting career as a service professional, you'll want to start thinking just as seriously about creating information products.

Don't let the idea of creating products intimidate you; you can start where you are and then the sky's the limit. For example, you can:

- Publish a free-tips book.
- Write an e-book.
- Produce an audio CD.

- Write an article.
- Write a workbook.
- Compile and publish a glossary of inspirational quotes.

Here are a few thoughts on your first information product:

- Keep it simple.
- Don't overwork it or feel that it needs to be perfect.
- Don't worry about being wildly original.
- Tips, guides, or resource manuals are great formats.
- Continually strive to add value to your clients' lives in any way you can.

When considering how to create an information product, start by examining the different possibilities and ask yourself, "How can I leverage my existing knowledge and experience to create a quality product that I can produce and launch in the shortest amount of time possible?"

Be sure you don't overlook any content you may already have created. If you've written an article, you have content that you can leverage into multiple formats. You can quickly and easily turn your article into an e-course, use it as the foundation for an e-book, print book, or program, or present it as an introductory presentation or teleclass. A single article can be leveraged into any or all of these formats, making it possible to create an entire sales cycle from a single source of content.

Define Your Product or Program

Choose the one product idea that you're most passionate or excited about right now—and most important, one that is in line with your current business needs. If you're starting out and need to build your database, you'll need to create a *lead-generating* product first, a product that you give away to create connection with a potential client. You will then leverage that free lead-generating information product into other monetized information products over time. If you already have a lead-generating product and you're ready to produce higher-priced information products like an audio program or a book, then go for it!

As you define your product, you will need to consider not only the type of product you will create but to whom you're selling it, the promises it makes, the benefits and solutions it offers, the look and feel you want your product to convey, and the ways in which you can leverage the content.

2.7.1 Written Exercise: For now, keep it simple. Just get your ideas out of your head and onto paper.

1. What type of product or program would you most like to create? What would you be most passionate about creating and offering to your target market?
2. To whom would you be offering this product? (Refer to target market.)
3. What benefits will your target market experience as a result of your product?
4. How do you want your product to look and feel? What image or emotion do you want it to convey?
5. How might you leverage the same content into a variety of different formats and price points for your sales cycle?

Assess the Need

It's important to be clear about your intentions for your product or program, and it's critical that your product or program meet the needs of your target market. No matter how much you might love to create something, if your target market doesn't need it you'll be defeating your purpose.

2.7.2 Written Exercise: Answer the following questions: Why does your target market need your particular product now?

- What does your product need to deliver for it to meet your customer's need?
- What about your product, if anything, will be different from similar products on the market?
- *Bonus:* How can you overdeliver on your promises by adding unexpected value to make your product remarkable? If you're unsure of your target market's need for a particular type of product or program, doing market research will help you ensure you're creating something your target market will find valuable. Survey friends, clients, and groups, such as online discussion groups or local organizations. And certainly search Google, using keywords that your target audience would use. It's the best research tool out there.

Five Steps to Developing Your Product

The five simple steps to developing your product are discussed in the following subsections.

Step 1: Choose the role you are playing
Step 2: Choose your product framework
Step 3: Choose a title that sells
Step 4: Build your table of contents
Step 5: Create your content

Step 1: Choose the Role You Are Playing

Whatever product you choose to create, as the author you will essentially be telling a story. To do so, you'll need to choose the role you wish to play when delivering your content. I'll use books to illustrate my point because books are simply bigger information products:

- *Expert.* Here's what I've done, and here's my theory on why it works. This is the role that I chose as the author of this book. Or maybe you're the Mad Professor, the Reluctant Hero, or the Reclusive Genius?

- *Interviewer.* Compile information from other experts. You can compile a product by interviewing others who are experts in their respective fields. A good example of that is Mitch Meyerson's book, *Success Secrets of the Online Marketing Superstars.* He interviewed more than 20 online marketing experts and compiled their interviews into a book.

- *Researcher.* Go out and gather information to serve the needs and desires of your target market. Compile the results to create a product that meets those needs and desires. Research can turn you into an expert at a future date. Jim Collins's book, *Good to Great,* is a perfect example. It's a research study, and it has made him an authority on creating great results in large corporations. You don't need to do a 10-year clinical study as Mr. Collins did, but the concept is the same.

- *Repurposer.* Use and modify existing content (with permission) for a different purpose. Many of the guerilla marketing books are excellent examples of this. Jay Conrad Levinson created the "Guerrilla Marketing" brand, and then many other authors co-opted that material and offered it for a different purpose—for example, *Guerrilla Marketing for Job Hunters* by David Perry.

2.7.3 Written Exercise: Which role most appeals to you or is most appropriate to your product or program, and why?

Step 2: Choose Your Product Framework

You'll need a framework in which to organize and present your content. A framework will make it easier not only for you to develop your content but also for your potential client to understand it and get the greatest possible value from it.

You may find that your content is ideally suited to a particular framework. If, for example, you're developing content for a product on pregnancy, the chronological framework may be the logical choice. Your content, however, may work well in more than one framework. An information product or program often uses a combination of frameworks. Here are six of the most common:

1. *Problem/Solution.* State a problem and then present solutions to the problem. *The Magic of Conflict: Turning Your Life of Work into a Work of Art* by Thomas F. Crum is written in this framework. He presents a number of problems that people face in their life and at work and presents solutions to those problems using the philosophical principles of the martial art of aikido.
2. *Numerical.* Create your product as a series of keys or lessons. A well-known example of this would be Stephen Covey's *The 7 Habits of Highly Effective People.*
3. *Chronological.* Some products need to be presented in a particular order because that is the only way it would make sense. Step A must come before Step B, as in *Your Pregnancy Week by Week* by Glade B. Curtis and Judith Schuler.
4. *Modular.* This book is a perfect example. The book consists of four modules: Your Foundation, Building Trust and Credibility, Perfect Pricing and Simple Selling, and the Book Yourself Solid 7 Core Self-Promotion Strategies. Within each module are additional tracks presented in a chronological framework. So you see that the book has both a main framework (modular) and a secondary framework (chronological).

5. *Compare/Contrast.* Showcase your creation in terms of presenting several scenarios or options and then compare and contrast them. Jim Collins, in his book *Good to Great*, compares and contrasts successful and not-so-successful companies.

6. *Reference.* Reference is just as it sounds. You may be creating a product that becomes a valuable resource to members of your target market. A compilation of information is best showcased in a reference format like that in *Words that Sell* by Richard Bayan. It's a reference guide of good words and phrases that help sell.

2.7.4 Written Exercise: Which framework will you choose and why?

Step 3: Choose a Title that Sells

The title of your product or program can make a big difference in whether your product sells. It's the title that initially catches consumers' attention and determines whether they look any further. Your title must be compelling enough for the prospect to want to know more. The consumer should be able to know exactly what you're offering by reading or hearing your title. Investing time to craft a captivating title can have a significant impact on your bottom line. Here are six types of titles that you can adapt to your needs:

1. Suspense: The Secret Life of Stay-at-Home Moms
2. Tell a story: The Path of the Successful Entrepreneur
3. Address a pain or a fear: The Top 10 Fears Every Leader Has and How to Overcome Them
4. Grab the reader's attention: Caught! The Six Deadliest Dating Mistakes!

5. Solutions to problems: Focus: The Seven Keys to Getting Things Done Even If You Have ADD
6. Emotional connection: What My Son's Tragedy Taught Me about Living Life to the Fullest

---

2.7.5 Written Exercise: Choose one of the title types that fits your product or that you find especially appealing, and brainstorm a number of different title ideas. Have fun with this. Just get your creative juices flowing.

Step 4: Build Your Table of Contents

Your table of contents is another key piece in organizing your content so that it's easy for you to present and easy for your potential clients to understand and follow. Regardless of which role you present your content in, the creation of a product gives the impression that you are an expert, and this is how your target market will view you.

The table of contents should be very well organized and professional. It should be easy to scan through to gain an understanding of the concept and the main points. Creating a table of contents also allows you to break your content into manageable pieces. The thought of writing even a simple article, e-book, special report, or book may at first glance seem overwhelming, but it doesn't have to be. Use your table of contents, or outline, to break the process down into smaller steps that will be much easier and less intimidating to work on.

2.7.6 Written Exercise: Create your table of contents. Keep the following questions in mind:

■ What are the steps in understanding your content?
■ Is the flow logical and easy to understand?

Step 5: Create Your Content

Using your table of contents, create a schedule for completing the first draft of each section. Don't let this become overwhelming—it doesn't have to be. If you write as little as a paragraph or two a day, you could have your content for your product or program completed in as little as a week for an e-course or a month or two for a more in-depth product or program.

I suggest that you adhere to the *Philosophy of the First Draft*. What? You've never heard of this ancient Greek philosophical movement? Okay, maybe not. But it might help you mitigate the feeling of being overwhelmed and get unstuck. The *Philosophy of the First Draft* suggests that you get it down quickly, just do a data dump, and then adhere to the next level of philosophical thinking: the *Philosophy of Tweaking*, which suggests that your product will be a work in progress. Do not expect an end result at this point. First follow the five-step plan for developing the structure of your product, as indicated earlier. Then, use this simple three-part formula for creating your first draft, the second draft, and so on until the final draft.

Three-Part Formula for Creating Your First Draft

Step 1: Based on your table of contents, choose two to five key points for each section

Step 2: Flesh out each of the key points per section with supportive content

Step 3: Repeat Step 2 until you've created the final product

Yes, it should be that straightforward. I'm even going to get down on my knees right now and beg you not to make it more complicated. Keep it simple and focus on getting it done so you can get down to the business of getting booked solid.

The Simple Three-Step Product Launch Sequence

Listing your product on your web site is a fabulous idea. It's a great start. However, if you don't, at present, have an overwhelming number of visitors browsing through your site, it's unlikely you'll get many orders—*even if you're giving it away for free.* On the other hand, if you want to make a big splash with the new product you've created, consider using the following simple three-step product launch sequence to get your product into the hands of eager and inspired potential clients.

> Step 1: Pre-Launch
> Step 2: Launch
> Step 3: Post-Launch

Step 1: Pre-Launch

Upon completion of your product, you may be tempted to immediately begin promoting it. Hold off for a bit. Instead, consider how you're going to warm up your audience with tidbits of content in the form of video, audio, PDF, and any other format that is easy for them to consume. (I'll show you how to begin to build your audience in a minute.) During the pre-launch stage, you should focus on giving so much value that you think you've gone too far and then give more. This teaser content should be designed to get your audience thinking about the specific problems that your upcoming product offer addresses and the results it promises—without mentioning the product itself—not yet. This early stage pre-launch period can last a few days or a few weeks and can give you the opportunity to evaluate how your audience is responding to your content and adjust your product accordingly.

Perhaps a strength and conditioning coach who created a breakthrough video product on how to increase performance doing three, 30-minute Kettlebell workouts a week might consider writing a series of articles, blog posts, and online press releases (we cover these in Chapter 16) that include links to two-minute video clips lifted from the product. This content, sent to her e-mail list, posted on her blog and in article and press release directories, is designed to stimulate discussion on the topic rather than to explicitly promote the product. Instead, she's encouraging her audience to consider particular issues and solutions to those issues before she releases the product itself.

Toward the end of this early stage pre-launch, make mention of an upcoming product in the same places that you seeded with valuable content. Now that momentum and interest in the topic you've been addressing has spiked, among your readers, it's time to enter the late stage pre-launch. This is when you announce the details of your upcoming product offer. An offer so packed with value that, again, you and they will think you've gone too far. But you'll go even further adding more value by piling on additional features, opportunities, and bonuses like:

- Follow-up implementation coaching calls.
- Additional videos, interviews, or e-books.
- Quick-start PDF guides.
- Related software.
- A live event.
- And, certainly, a no-hassle guarantee of some sort.

Your potential buyers should feel like they're getting a significant return on investment; value should overwhelm cost. You'll attempt to focus their attention on the incredible benefits of your product and the problems it solves. Hopefully, by the time you launch, your potential buyers will have very few objections to your product and believe that it is a high-powered vehicle that'll get them where they want to go.

Pre-Launch Checklist
- Software to database and manage buyer's information.
- Shopping cart and merchant account.

- Sales page.
- Launch blog.
- Completed product ready to ship or deliver digitally.

Remember to test every part of the process prior to launch. Guaranteed (well almost), you'll miss something—at least I usually do. Run sample orders to make sure that you clear up any glitches. View all of your pages and videos in all of the most popular browsers, including Internet Explorer, Firefox, Chrome, and Safari. Notify your web host, merchant account provider, and shopping cart solution of your upcoming launch date if you expect a lot more traffic to your site than is usual. Sometimes, hosting companies will freeze an account if they detect activity that is unusual or different than the norm. This happens more often than you might think and can seriously squash your product launch.

Step 2: Launch

The success of your launch is, in large part, due to the structure of your offer. How you make it, what comes with it, how long it lasts, and more. A word to the wise: be careful of what kind of tactics you use to encourage people to buy. I discuss pricing models at length in Chapter 8, so I won't discuss them here. I suggest that you carefully consider how you want to be perceived, however, when promoting your information products. Will you create a hyperkinetic, high-intensity product launch based on the principle of scarcity? Will you try to tap into the buyer's fear that they'll miss out if they don't act right away, or the perception that if they don't buy what you're offering they'll never move forward and will, basically, fail at whatever it is you're offering to help with? Or, will you create a reasoned, sensible, and appropriate product launch based on integrity? Look, I'm comfortable with special time- and space-limited offers as long as they are based on integrity and they're not too hyped up and aggressive. There is a well-known marketing expert who says, "If you're not annoying some of your prospects, then you're not pushing hard enough." I'm not hip to that concept. You are how you market. Consider what you stand for and how you want to be known. And, of course, how the people to whom you are trying to sell want to be treated.

Okay, so, now the big day is here! It's time to press "Send" on your "we're live" e-mail as well as announce the product launch on the social network sites to which you belong, your blog, or any other relevant platform. This is where all of your hard work pays off. Take a deep breath.

Don't stress the process. You know already the launch is unlikely to unfold as planned. Hey, it might go better than planned. The live period of the launch usually lasts from three to seven days, depending on your preference. The first day or two is a great time to introduce the urgency of acting as the time or available units are dwindling (but please see the earlier note). Feel free to share new and exciting testimonials as they come in or added bonuses.

Step 3: Post-Launch

Sales generally die down after the first few days of the launch. There are ways to reignite them, however. For example, you can announce an added bonus. This may encourage people sitting on the fence to go for it and hit the buy button. This bonus will also please all previous buyers, as they'll get extra value that they had not anticipated. Maybe you're holding a special live event to which the buyers of the product get free tickets? Or perhaps, you've added an entire product to the offer that is complimentary to the topic covered in the initial product? Sort of like the extended free trial that comes with this book, of the Book Yourself Solid® software that does your marketing for you using all the strategies and tactics you're learning in this book. Go to BookYourselfSolid.com/software to get your extended free trial. See?

When you close out the launch, what do you do with the product? Are you planning on continuing to sell it from your site but at a different price point or, maybe, you're taking it off the market for six months and will then do a second launch? If you do take the product off the market, make sure you put up a special web page thanking visitors for their interest in the product and suggest that they opt in to a web form so they can be the first notified when the product becomes available again. This way you'll have the opportunity to earn their trust before your next product launch.

Joint Venture Partners and Affiliates

When you don't yet have a substantial group of followers or subscribers, or even if you do, for that matter, one of the keys to increasing your reach is to team up with what are usually referred to as joint venture (aka JV) partners or affiliates. I discuss this concept in Chapter 16 as it relates to driving traffic to your web site, so for now, I'll just touch on a few important points of joint venture marketing relationships with respect to product launches.

Other professionals, who already have established relationships of trust with your target market, might be willing to partner with you and promote your product in exchange for a commission on each product sold or some other incentive. Note that I said *might*. As you'll learn when we discuss Direct Outreach in Chapter 11, before you make any kind of JV request of a successful professional, it's wise to have already established a relationship with them and to understand what incentivizes them. You might be surprised to learn that they are not, in fact, interested in what you think is a financial incentive. When a JV partner promotes your product for you, she expends a considerable amount of her social and professional capital. There is also an opportunity cost associated with every promotion made to a group of subscribers or followers. Be prepared to demonstrate the viability of your offer with sound metrics. You need to have a sound commission structure in place as well as a detailed analysis of your opt-in and conversion rates. When you ask someone to promote a product for you, you're asking a lot—more than you might realize at the moment. You're asking for access to what might be his most prized business asset—the trust he has built with his subscribers. Read the chapter on Direct Outreach before you attempt any kind of joint venture campaign.

If you want joint venture partners to enjoy working with you, you'll want to make promoting you easy and breezy. Once you have your joint venture partners in place, have the following materials available for them:

- E-mail copy ready to use during the pre-launch and launch periods.
- A contest with prizes to excite and rally the partners with a little friendly competition (just make sure you get their approval before you include them in any competition among JV partners).
- A separate, password protected, JV partner blog for updates on the contest and continued motivation for them to promote your product. It's sort of like doing a launch within a launch.
- Affiliate accounts for your JV partners in your shopping cart system that provide custom affiliate links.

Big, deep, authentic success is truly only realized when we share our gifts with others through mutually valuable, long-term partnerships. Some of your JV partners may even become your best friends and closest allies.

If you are new to the concept of launching a product on the Internet, some of this can seem daunting. It can be a big process with many more moving pieces than I included in this section. Nonetheless, you can do this. Keep your launch simple at first and take it one small step at a time. Look at it this way, once you create a successful launch, you can do it again and again. Just duplicate your initial success with some small changes for the new product. Most of the hard work is done the first time around. If you need more help on how to launch your product, David Jehlen, an expert in information product launches and a Certified Book Yourself Solid Coach, can help you. Visit his site at DavidJehlen.com.

A Necessary Step in Your Business Development

Creating a product or program is a powerful—and possibly necessary—step in your business development. When you do so, your business has the potential to skyrocket. One product will turn into another and another—the possibilities are endless.

Just imagine this: You open your e-mail first thing in the morning and you see 15 new orders—one from Switzerland, one from Australia, one from India, and a dozen from all over the United States—all for the product you recently made available on the Web. It's 7:00 A.M., you're still sipping your first cup of coffee and only half awake, and you've already earned $3,479.27.

While this scenario may seem more like a dream than reality to you right now, it's entirely possible to achieve, and it's much easier to do than you might imagine; just follow the steps I outlined earlier for creating an unlimited number of information products on virtually any topic you can think of! Before you know it you'll be hearing the beautiful, melodic *ka-ching, ka-ching* sound of your web-site-turned-cash-register as the orders come rolling in.

Simple Selling and Perfect Pricing

To be booked solid requires that you price your offerings at rates that are compelling to your ideal clients and that you're able to have sales conversations that are effortless and effective. It means that you must:

- Perfect your pricing strategies using the right models and incentives
- Master simple selling techniques so you can have sales conversations that feel as easy as a day at the beach

Module Three consists of two chapters. These two chapters are the culmination of the Book Yourself Solid system because you'll learn how to make offers that are proportional to the amount of trust that you've earned and how to have a sales conversation that books new business. This is the ultimate goal—to get new clients so you can earn new business.

Remember how the Book Yourself Solid system works.

1. You'll create awareness for the products and services you offer using the 7 Core Self-Promotion Strategies (you'll learn these in Module Four)

2. Once you create awareness for what you offer, potential new clients will check out your foundation for stability and security (you built this foundation in Module One)

3. If they like what they see, they'll give you the opportunity to earn their trust over time (you do this using the strategies you learned in Module Two)

4. When the circumstances are right, potential clients will either raise their hand and ask you to have a sales conversation or they'll accept one of your compelling offers and you'll book the business (this is the focus of Module Three)

All you have to do now is decide how to price your offers and learn how to be comfortable and confident during sales conversations. Let's get right to it then . . .

8

Perfect Pricing

Price is what you pay; value is what you get.

—Warren Buffett

What is the value, for example, of having the talent and skills to create a compelling web presence for someone or maybe a training manual for a corporation? Is it the length of time it takes for you to produce it, or the number of pages created, or, how about the number of images used? The answer is . . . D, none of the above. Unfortunately, that's how many service providers price their products and service offerings—as stuff.

I asked Certified Book Yourself Solid Coach Cara Lumen (caralumen .com) for her perspective on the matter because she deals, directly, in ideas and how to make them sell. In fact, as the idea optimizer, she's got it right when she says that "the only way to put a price on ideas is to put a value on what they will produce."

"But it only took me two hours to create it," you might say. How long it takes you to write something, or design something, or think up an idea, or even the amount of time you spend with a client, is irrelevant. What (should) matter to the client is the financial, emotional, physical, and spiritual return on investment your product or service provides—remember,

I introduced you to the all-important, life-changing FEPS benefits (financial, emotional, physical, and spiritual). Think about the value you provide.

- How much income will your service create?
- How long will what you create be a productive, useful resource for the client?
- How much pain will you relieve?
- How much pleasure will you create?
- How are you helping your client connect to their purpose or spirit?
- Will your work create substantial and long-lasting peace of mind?

No less important than the value you create, according to Cara, is "how you value yourself." And this might just be the difference between simply making ends meet and earning healthy heaps of money. Remember your ideal client. Remember doing your best work. Remember standing in the service of others as you stand in the service of your destiny. You want to work with people who value what you bring to your partnership. But if you don't value it, they won't either.

3.8.1 Written Exercise: Think of a client who gave you rave reviews. Make a list of all the FEPS benefits the client received from working with you. Don't be stingy here. Think big. Now, put specific dollar values on all of those benefits. Again, think big. No, bigger than that. Because . . . hold on to your hat. . . . you may just find that you have been undervaluing yourself and, as a result, underpricing your products and services. You are giving generously of your talents and skills and, it's likely, the value you provide is worth much, much more than what you've been charging.

Don't Buy Into a Poverty Mindset

Maybe you think . . . I don't want to price my services such that people can't afford them. Or, maybe it was something like . . . I have a new client that says they can't afford much so I'm thinking of lowering my price for them. These thoughts don't necessarily mean you have a "poverty mindset" but they most definitely play you small. Allow your expectations to be stretched. People rarely buy professional services based solely on price. In fact, people express their values through what they buy—so let them.

Only you can offer you. Whatever it is you offer—it is unique—to you. Only you can offer a particular combination of services, skills, talent, and personality. Only you can offer the exact combination of information, style of communication, and value that makes you so uniquely you. Know that. Know and accept, and revel in your value. Come from a place of service. Raise your intention to be well compensated for what you offer. Expect to be paid well. Then ask for it. Put out a price that makes you feel valuable and see others joyously flocking to take advantage of the great value you offer.

3.8.2 Booked Solid Action Step: Right now raise your prices until it makes you slightly uncomfortable. You'll know you've reached the right number when you experience a slight feeling of nausea. That's your new price. Over time you'll grow into it—not the nausea, the price—and, over time, you'll continue to raise your prices, sans nausea.

Ask for what you are worth and you will receive it. But first, truly know and believe you have great value. Then others will know and appreciate all you have to offer. You have to know that what you offer is valuable and you have to charge an amount that shows it is valuable. Only you can choose to think big about who you are and what you offer the world.

Pricing Models

I'm sure you've seen a number of different pricing models employed in various service industries. Some seem to benefit the provider and others are more favorable to the client. However, the picture of perfect pricing has each party thinking that they got the better end of the deal. If the client thinks he snagged a deal, he'll be tickled pink and if the service provider thinks she's scored, she'll feel like the cat who ate the canary. The key is to figure out how to create this win–win dynamic so that both parties feel fortunate. Here are a few of the often-used pricing models for selling professional services:

- *Time for money trade.* A rate is set for a predetermined, agreed-upon amount of time—hourly, daily, weekly, or some other combination thereof (for example, $100 per hour, $1,000 per day, $10,000 per week). A very common model and one with which clients are generally comfortable.

- *Open-ended time for money trade.* A rate is set that trades your time for money, usually hourly, but no constraint is put on the amount of time required to complete the job. Service providers (especially contractors) like this model for the same reason that it petrifies the client—runaway time piles on additional fees. You know that three-week kitchen remodel that's going on thirty-three weeks? No one likes surprises that cost them money. Imagine, instead of getting gifts on Christmas morning, you woke to find you had to pay for every box that had your name on it.

- *Fixed price for pre-set result.* A price is established for the entire project and fees are usually paid in percentages at predetermined dates or upon completion of project milestones (that is, 25 percent up front, another 50 percent halfway through, and the remaining 25 percent upon completion). This model often causes anxiety for the service provider for fear of "project creep" (aka: functionality creep, feature creep, scope creep, and mission creep). This is when the scope of the project gets bigger and bigger but the fee established stays the same. It's different from working on a *project with a creep*. That sucks, too. Which is worse, however, depends on how much creep or creepiness occurs on the project or with the client, respectively.

- *Recurring fee for an open-ended amount of time.* Commonly referred to as a *retainer*, for which a monthly or quarterly payment is offered for a certain amount of work. Sometimes a time period is associated with the retainer but the arrangement is typically not associated with a period of time and can be canceled at will or with some reasonable amount of notice.

- *Retainer plus back-end.* Includes a retainer that covers expenses and some modest payment might be offered but most of the service provider's revenue is earned on the back end. If the project makes money, the service provider makes money. This pricing model isn't typical but can be very lucrative. Personal injury attorneys use this model. If they win the case, they take a significant percentage of the settlement. Software programmers, especially hungry, entrepreneurial types, also employ this model.
- *Flexible pricing.* Offer the same service to clients at different prices. This is very common in the business–to–business market in which sales are often based on negotiated contracts. You may also offer flexible pricing based on need. Service providers often offer flexible pricing, also known as sliding scale pricing, based on the client's ability to pay or a provider's desire to work with the client.
- *Bundle pricing.* Offering a combination of products and services together in a single package to increase the size of the sale can offer savings to both the buyer and to the seller. The buyer gets more value for less money and the seller gets more profit for less marketing effort. However, if you bundle your services, "Don't wrap all the Christmas presents in one box," says economist Richard Thaler. The benefits of the product or service should be enumerated rather than lumped together. So, if you buy "this" we'll also throw in "that." And, if you buy "that" we'll also through in "this." Or, if you buy "this," you can also have "this" at a reduced price. You want to be sure the client values and appreciates each and every product, program, and service they're getting from you.
- *Penetration Pricing.* Offer very low prices to get into a market. Once you've created a name for yourself, begin to raise your prices.
- *Loss-leader pricing.* This is a more common approach to selling products than it is to selling services but can be exploited by service

providers, nonetheless. You can offer specific services at a very low price point to get clients in the door who will then, hopefully, buy additional products or other services at a higher price point. You may be willing to take a loss up front for a financial gain down the road.

- *Economy Pricing.* Offer the lowest prices in the market as a way of differentiating yourself. This is unlike loss-leader pricing in that all your prices are always low when you use economy pricing—it becomes part of your brand, like Walmart. Using the economy pricing model is different from undervaluing yourself. In this case, you're building a model that allows more people to take advantage of your services—which, over time, can actually add value to your brand. Certainly, low prices are often perceived as low value services, but that need not necessarily be the case.

- *Prestige pricing.* You may choose to price your services at a price point higher than is typical for your industry in order to create a sense of prestige around you and your company. You may serve fewer clients but end up making more money.

When considering which of the various preceding pricing models you are going to employ first consider your objective. You may be thinking, *Uh, Michael, are you dense? I want to make as much money as I can—that's my objective!* Well, yes, but you're reading this book to think more strategically about your business and how you grow it, so humor me for a moment. Consider the following five different pricing objectives:

1. *To maximize long-term profits.* This should be your default approach. You're building something to last a lifetime, something that will support your dreams, not to mention your family, so you always want to focus on long-term pricing. Any of the pricing models can be applied to achieve this objective.
2. *To maximize short-term profits.* Generally chosen when you need to make a bunch of money fast. Prestige pricing may be the way to

go but only if you've been in business for a while or are starting up with some sort of very unique selling proposition. Or, you
might consider bundle pricing to sell more of what you already
offer. Or, maybe, aggressive loss-leader pricing will help. Lots of
options here.

3. *To gain market share.* That's just a fancy way of saying you're starting up the business or introducing a new product or service line
and need to get clients—now. Loss leader or economy pricing or
flexible pricing models may be the way to go. They'll help you get
in the game and build up a large group of ideal clients that are out
in the world talking about your best work. Which, of course, will
bring you new ideal clients.

4. *To survive.* Hey, look. Sometimes things get rough. You might
face, oh . . . what was that little thing that happened in 2008? Oh,
yes, a complete global economic recession. Sometimes survival *is*
enough—and that's coming to you from *the guy to call when you're
tired of thinking small.* This is when you employ whatever strategy
you think is going to get you through to the next quarter: flexible
pricing, time for money pricing, retainer plus back-end pricing,
and so on. Do what you have to do to make it.

5. *To do good.* This is the strategy I use on many of my offerings. My
accountant, who is also my uncle, doesn't like this pricing model
because he thinks I leave a lot of money on the table. And, he's
right. But don't shed any tears for me. I do just fine. I intentionally
keep my prices low, compared to my colleagues, for my online
and teleseminar courses. This way, newer small business owners
(possibly like you) are able to enroll in the courses. Sure, it allows
more people to participate and you might think that I make bigger profits due to volume but it's not the case because my expenses
are also higher. My most profitable offerings are my small-group
in-person coaching workshops and big corporate speaking gigs.
And yes, they're at prestige prices. Worth every penny, I might add.
Even so, you'll often see me using the sliding scale pricing model

for these prestige-priced offerings as well. If I think I can help you, and I think you're going to make a positive difference in the world with the help I provide, I'll adjust my prices to fit your current economic situation. The relationship between money and happiness is a complicated one, for sure. The vast majority of research points to this, though: once you are living above the poverty line, most happiness is a result of meaningful interpersonal relationships and connection to those around you. So, go on, do some good in the world. As my mother says, "C'mon, it won't kill you."

When to Lower Prices, Discount, and Offer Specials

The answer is not always clear but the question remains the same: *When should I lower prices or offer discounts and specials?* Sometimes you want to offer price discounts or special packages to motivate potential clients to act. Other times, you'll feel the need (or desire) to lower prices because of factors beyond your control like economic conditions, supply and demand issues, competitor's prices, or other market conditions. Or maybe, you're in complete control and have found a cheaper, more economical way to produce your services that allows you to lower your prices while increasing your profit margins. Either way, leveraging a variety of discounting tactics and other incentive devices to get clients faster and increase sales can be, to put it mildly, a godsend.

Use discounting and incentives with care. There's a fine line between over-the-top infomercial-like promotional pricing and authentic, clean, believable, appreciated-by-the-customer, and respectful use of discounting tactics and special offers. You'll know when you step over the line. If you do, take a step back. However, don't be afraid to be fully self-expressed in your sales promotions. There's nothing wrong—in fact, there's something very right about giving your ideal clients an opportunity to take advantage of your services at reduced prices. Remember, what I said before, people buy to express their values. And, you're giving them an opportunity to express their values through the work you do together.

- *Quantity discounts.* You may be able to encourage clients to buy more of your services if they can get better prices the more they purchase. This model is very common for personal trainers and others like yoga teachers who sell sessions on an ongoing basis. For example, a yoga teacher may sell sessions in 5, 10, 15, and 20 packs. The price per session will decrease for each subsequently larger pack, making the 20-pack the best deal. She may even decide to offer a value-added bonus to the buyer of the 20 pack: a free, three-hour yoga retreat for the client and 20 of her closest friends, for example. Yes, you're right, what a great value add to the client as well as a remarkable marketing opportunity for the yoga teacher—20 brand new potential clients brought right to her door step, or in this case, yoga mat.

- *Cash discounts.* A business may offer cash discounts for the costs saved from not having to extend credit and bill the buyer on an open account. This mainly affects business-to-business rather than business-to-consumer sales. However, you'll also find many service professionals offer cash discounts as a way of keeping some, or all, of the work off the books, a practice I can't endorse.

- *Seasonal Discounts.* Encourage clients to buy at certain times of the year in anticipation of seasonal needs. Or offer off-season discounts. A landscaper can increase sales in the winter by closing the summer contracts at special off-season prices.

- *Markdowns and time sensitive discounts.* Mark down your prices for a particular period of time or until a certain number of sales are made. For example, "25 percent off until the end of March" or "the first three people to respond get 25 percent off." An interior designer who does one-day makeovers can make an offer in her newsletter at a 25 percent discount—but only for the first three people to respond. Will the designer come off as desperate, or pushy, or worse yet, like one of those over-the-top Internet marketers or late night infomercials? First, her clients love her and her potential clients are on the way to loving her, so they'll be thrilled at the opportunity to get a 25 percent discount for something that will express their values. Second, she can explain why she's offering only three spots. She has just a certain amount of time and, as much as she'd love to, she can't do an unlimited number of full-day makeovers.

- *Free Services.* Give away free sessions or services as a sales tactic to get clients. Does it work? Sometimes. Should you do it? Depends on who you ask. Some swear by it. Others have sworn off it. And yet, still others swear every time they do it because it's so frustrating. Generally, I don't recommend it. Think about it. How does it look to a potential client that you're offering free sessions to anybody who happens to stumble across your web site—in demand, successful, and valuable or sitting around with lots of time on your hands just trying to give your stuff away for free in the hope that someone will hire you? Much more likely the latter. Credibility is built in large part on perception. And, anyway, what happened to your Red Velvet Rope Policy? Sure, get on the phone with someone to see whether he'd get past your red velvet rope and give him an opportunity to fall in love with you at the same time. But don't set up a situation in which he perceives that he's supposed to get some big result from that one free session, because if he doesn't, he's disappointed and doesn't hire you, and consequently sees you as a low status service provider.

This doesn't mean that there is no way to use this strategy—there is. Here's how I used free sessions to "close" 65 percent of new business during my first year in business. I included an offer for a 20-minute laser coaching session into my sales cycle—but only after someone had demonstrated that she was serious about learning from me. If someone downloaded my seven-part e-mail mini-course (see why information products are important to the lead generation and conversion process?) I would send her the first two lessons during Week One. Each lesson included two paragraphs of education followed by a detailed written exercise. Then, instead of starting off Week Two with Lesson

Three, I would send a "congratulations and reward" e-mail, offering praise and appreciation for the work she put in to the first two lessons (all of this was automated). As a reward, I offered her a complimentary 20-minute telephone coaching session to address any questions she had about the material in the first two lessons. I called these phone sessions "laser coaching sessions." A number of criteria needed to be followed, however, to book the session, which I spelled out in the "congratulations and reward" e-mail:

- She had to schedule the session using my public calendar. I made only a few spots available on Friday afternoons so that a waiting list developed quickly. This way I didn't look like I was sitting around twiddling my thumbs, hoping someone would show up.
- If she missed the session or didn't reschedule with 24 hours notice, she missed the opportunity and could not reschedule (again, all of this was automated).
- If she were more than a few minutes late to the phone session, I wouldn't pick up.
- And, finally, one week before the scheduled session, she had to send me an e-mail with her responses to the exercises from the first two lessons. This helped because:
  - If she had not already done them, it got her to do the exercises. Getting clients to consume your work is as important as getting them to hire you.
  - By reviewing their written exercises, I knew what they needed before they dialed my number. It showed me what they were struggling with and how to help them. So, in just 20 minutes I could solve their problems and create an impressive result.

You might think that all these rules would put potential clients off. You're trying to get clients, not force them to jump through flaming hoops. But, you know what? Over 65 percent of the people who signed up for the free 20-minute session became clients. The other 35 percent, for the most part, truly couldn't afford it. But I'll tell you what, that other 35 percent generated even more business for me because they went out to their community and talked about me and the work I "gifted" them. Figure out a way to use this strategy in your sales cycle and you'll get the opportunity to do something valuable, and free of charge, for your potential clients. You'll enhance your reputation, build credibility, and book more business.

When to Raise Prices

Whenever you can, but there's no need to race to the top of the pricing ladder to be successful. Here are a few examples of why and how to do it.

- *Just for the heck of it*. Sometimes, raising prices may simply, and beautifully, lead to a much deserved increase in profit.
- *Economic conditions*. You may need to raise prices because of inflation (rising costs unequaled by productivity gains). Inflation usually gets carried over to the consumer—which is why it's such an economic problem.
- *You're in demand and overbooked*. If demand for your services has increased—I'll be doing the Book Yourself Solid happy dance for you—it may be a good time to raise prices.
- *Training and skill development*. If you've recently upgraded your certifications or completed a significant training that is highly relevant to your clients' needs, it may be a great time to raise prices.
- *Upgrading your packaging*. If you upgrade your web site with a complete redesign and in doing so seriously upgrade the look and feel of your brand, you can raise your prices. If you upgrade your offices, allowing you to become more efficient at what you do, you can up your prices. If you upgrade the packaging of your products, you can also improve your bottom line. Again, credibility is, in large part, based on perception.

Sometimes, when service providers get overbooked, they complain about it. Oh, how easily we forget what it was like when we were struggling our way up the ladder. Worse still, I've witnessed many a service provider resist raising prices, which would have allowed each of them to work with fewer clients, for fear of losing business. Here's a simple story that illustrates my point.

I see an acupuncturist from time to time. He might be the best-known acupuncturist in my town (I live in a small town). He's likely the most experienced, and has an overbooked practice because of it. Every time I see him he complains (in a nice way) that he's overworked and can't keep up with demand. He doesn't want to change the model of his business, in that he still wants to see patients himself and doesn't want to manage other acupuncturists, nor does he want to raise his prices. So, every time I see him, I complain to him (in a nice way) that his prices are too low and, in fact, should be doubled. His answer is always the same, "But, Michael, if I double my rates, I'll lose half my clients." I'll pause here to let that sink in just as I do with him. He never gets it. Maybe you will. First of all, he won't lose half his clients but even if he did lose half his clients, he'd still make the same money *and* have twice as much free time. More likely he'll lose just a few clients but make much more money overall, because of the price increase.

If you do raise prices it's a good idea to let clients know why. There's nothing wrong with saying that you're fortunate to be in high demand and are raising your prices so that you can give more attention to your clients. Or, that certain expenses related to serving your clients have increased and you're raising your prices accordingly. People like the truth. I'd prefer to be open and honest with my clients, running the risk of disappointing a few of them, than be manipulative or obtuse, running the risk of damaging my soul. Just be sure to let them know what the new rates will be and when they go into effect. Give them reasonable notice so they can adjust to the changes. And, most important, remind them of the continuing benefits they'll get from working with you.

On the flip side, you don't always have to carry over all costs or eke out every bit of profit on every sale. Sometimes you can earn long-term marketing juice by taking one on the chin for the sake of your clients. My son's favorite pizza place is an organic restaurant called Jules Thin Crust Pizza. At one point last summer, the price of cheese went down. Now, the average customer is not going to know this. I love cheese but I don't buy it in bulk. It would have been easy, and cheesy (sorry, couldn't resist), for Jules to just pocket the extra profit from the savings. But no, instead, they put up a big sign announcing the cheap cheese and that they were lowering prices because of it. All summer, their busy season, no less, prices were reduced. I asked the owner, John, whether the cheese experiment cultured nicely or stunk up the place (sorry, again, couldn't resist). He said it was a huge success—customers loved it, as you might imagine. Now, John's not the type to boast about sales but I'm pretty sure he saw more business because of his gastrointestinal-stimulus package.

Regulations on Pricing

Before you rush off and start pricing yourself, I should mention that there are various governmental regulations on pricing. If you sell outside of your own country, which you might do given that the Internet is a global marketplace, you'll need to familiarize yourself with laws in other countries. In the United States, price discrimination, offering different prices to different buyers, like our flexible-pricing model, has certain limitations. But the Robinson-Patman Act does allows for price differentials under certain circumstances, so if you choose to use that pricing model, just check with your attorney to determine what is legal with respect to your services in your particular industry.

Super Simple Selling

Art is making something out of nothing and selling it.

—Frank Zappa

As a service provider you may not want to think of yourself as a salesperson. You're in the business of helping others, and the sales process may feel contradictory to your core purpose. If you're uncomfortable with the sales process, it's likely that you view it as unethical, manipulative, and dishonest. Looking at it that way, who wouldn't be uncomfortable?

Many service professionals also feel uncomfortable charging for services that either come easily to them or that they love doing. There is often a sense that if it comes easily and is enjoyable, there's something wrong with charging others for doing it.

Add the fact that service professionals sell themselves as much as they sell a product, and the whole idea becomes even more uncomfortable. It may feel like you're bragging and being shamelessly immodest.

Becoming comfortable with the sales process requires that you let go of any limiting beliefs you may have about being worthy of the money you're earning. In fact, developing the right comfort level also requires a shift in your perspective of the sales process itself.

Letting Go of Limiting Beliefs

Most people who are successful get paid to do what they do well. You don't usually become successful doing something that you find difficult. You become successful when you exploit your natural talents. Imagine Tom Hanks saying he shouldn't get paid to do movies because he's really good at it and loves it. Or J. K. Rowling saying she should write the Harry Potter books for free because she enjoys it.

Tom Hanks, J. K. Rowling, and anyone else you can think of who is, or was, wildly successful at what they do, work to the bone at becoming even better at what they are naturally gifted at doing. They create extraordinary experiences for the people they serve, whether it's an audience, a fan, or a client. That's why they—and you—deserve to be paid top dollar.

If you've been feeling like you can't, or shouldn't, be paid to do what you love, you must let that limiting belief go if you're to be booked solid.

If you don't believe you are worth what you are charging, it is unlikely that a lot of people are going to hire you based on those fees. You need to resonate fully with the prices you are setting so that others will resonate with them as well. To do so, you may need to work on shifting your beliefs so that you feel more comfortable with charging higher fees, rather than lowering your fees to eliminate the discomfort.

There is an old joke about a guy who gets into a cab in New York City and asks the driver how to get to Carnegie Hall, and the driver responds, "Practice, practice, practice." You're going to increase your resonance with practice. It's just like practicing a martial art, or a sport, or singing. Singing is a great example because your voice becomes more resonant the more you practice. At first it's uncomfortable, but over time it becomes easier and more natural. The same thing will happen when you quote your fees. The more you feel comfortable setting your price, the more other people will feel that comfort and the energetic resonance that comes with that comfort, and they'll happily pay you what you're worth.

Shifting Your Perspective

The Book Yourself Solid paradigm of sales is all about building relationships with your potential clients on the basis of trust. It is, quite simply, about having a sincere conversation that allows you to let your potential clients know what you can do to help them. You aren't manipulating or coercing people into buying something they have no real need or desire to buy. You're making them aware of something you offer that they already need, want, or desire.

Thinking in terms of solutions and benefits is the *ah-ha* to the selling process. It's the key to shifting your perspective. It's so foolproof you'll never think of the selling process the same way again.

When you think in terms of solutions and problems solved, clients will beg to work with you. You are a consultant, a lifelong advisor. When you have fundamental solutions and a desire to help others, it becomes your moral imperative to show and tell as many people as possible. You are changing lives!

Successful Selling Needs the Right Amount of Trust at Just the Right Time

It's no accident that I introduce sales in Chapter 9—after I've taught you how to set your foundation and build trust and credibility. One of the reasons that so many sales conversations are *unsuccessful* is because they're had at the wrong time—usually too soon—before you've earned the proportionate amount of trust needed for the offer being made. Plus, your clients buy when it's right for them—when something occurs in their life or business that compels them to hire you. If these two factors, trust and timing, come together at just the right moment, you'll have a *successful* sales conversation and book the business. But this only works if you've built a solid foundation, demonstrating that you:

- Have a Red Velvet Rope Policy so you work only with ideal clients
- Understand why people buy what you're selling so you know exactly to whom you are selling and what they want to invest in
- Have developed a personal brand identity so you decide how you're known in the world
- Are able to talk about what you do without sounding confusing or bland, or like everybody else, and without ever using an elevator speech

If you've set this foundation, a potential client will give you the opportunity to earn his trust. But you'll only earn his trust if you:

- Use the standard credibility builders and have a high degree of likeability
- Have designed a sales cycle that starts with no-barrier-to-entry offers including your always-have-something-to-invite-people-to offer
- Have simple lead-generating information products that enhance your credibility and speed up your sales cycle

Then, and really only then, are you ready to have sales conversations that work.

The Secret to the Book Yourself Solid System

This simple four-step process is the secret to the Book Yourself Solid system.

1. You execute a few of the 7 Core Self-Promotion strategies, which create awareness for what you have to offer.

2. When a potential client becomes aware of your services she'll take a look at your foundation. If it looks secure, if she feels comfortable stepping onto it, she'll give you the opportunity to earn her trust— but only the opportunity. She's not necessarily going to hire you right then and there. She needs some time to consider the consequences before she will actually trust you.

3. That's when your plan to build trust and credibility comes into play. As a potential client moves through your sales cycle, she will come to like you, trust you, and find you credible.

4. When her circumstances dictate that she needs the kind of help you provide, she'll raise her hand and ask you to have a sales conversation. You have a sales conversation the Book Yourself Solid way and book the business.

The process is simple. The process is sound. It can turn your business life around. And, most important, the process is a complete, repetitive, and self-perpetuating system. While potential clients are going through this process, you're continuing to create awareness for what you have to offer using a few of the 7 Core Self-Promotion Strategies. This gets more new potential clients checking out your foundation for stability and security. They'll like what they see, stand on it, and give you the opportunity to earn their trust. You earn their trust (over time) and when the circumstances are right for *them*, they'll either raise their hand and ask you to have a sales conversation or they'll accept one of your compelling offers and you'll book the business. The process repeats itself over and over and over again. It's systematic. Once you've set up your own Book Yourself Solid marketing and sales system, it works like a charm. Just rinse and repeat.

The Super Simple Selling System

Now, let's talk about how to have the sales conversation. I've created the four-part sales formula for super simple selling—so simple the formula practically works on its own. Why? Because, once trust is assured and a need is met, using this four-part formula during your sales conversations *will* book the business. But, please, just like the Book Yourself Solid dialogue, this is meant to be an open and free-flowing conversation, not a sales script.

Book Yourself Solid Four-Part Sales Formula

When a potential client expresses interest in working with you, open with a simple question . . .

Part 1: *What are you working on? Or, what is your goal? Or, what are you trying to achieve?* Once you feel certain you know what he wants to accomplish and by when, simply ask . . .

Part 2: *How will you know when you have achieved it? What results will you see? What feedback will you hear? What feelings will you have?* Once you feel like the potential client has clearly articulated these benefits, make sure he is fully in the hiring frame of mind, and then ask . . .

Part 3: *Would you like someone to help you with that (achieve your goal, and so forth)?* If he says, "no," wish him the best of luck and keep in touch with him. If he says, "yes," then offer . . .

Part 4: *Would you like that person to be me? Because, you know, you are my ideal client.* (To which he'll say, "What do you mean?" because no one has ever said that to him before.) *Well, you are someone with whom I do my best work.* (He'll ask "why?" and you'll tell him . . .) *Because you are . . .* (Here is where you list the qualities that make him who he is and allow you to do your best work.) As you're listing these qualities you'll see his face brighten as he sits up straight and says, "Wow. That is so me! Thank you for noticing." You'll say, *"So shall we look at our calendars to plan a time to get started?"* And, the answer will be . . . drumroll, please . . . "Absolutely, yes!"

Don't use the preceding phrases verbatim. Instead, just use the Book Yourself Solid Four-Part Sales Formula as a framework for a super duper simple (successful) sales conversation.

> **3.9.1 Written Exercise:** Practice without pressure. Try this process with a good friend or colleague and see what happens. Ask her to call you at random a few times over the course of a week and say, "Hi, I've been getting your newsletter for a while and I think you may be able to help me, can we talk about your services?" And, instead of doing that thing that everyone does—talk about themselves and their business for 20 minutes—ask her what she's working on or what she's trying to achieve or what problem she's trying to overcome, and you'll be into Part 1 of the Book Yourself Solid Four-Part Sales Formula. Super simple.

If They're Uncertain

What if potential clients are not ready to start working with you? No problem. The good news is that someday the benefits you provide will be a priority. And, something in your potential client's life will change that compels him to hire you. However, if you haven't kept in touch and followed up, he'll look to someone else to help him reach his goals. But, since you're going to become a master at keeping in touch and following up, you'll be waiting in the wings, ready, willing, and able to help him accomplish his goals. (We dig deeper into exactly how to keep in touch in Chapter 13.)

These are the lovely, easy steps to simple selling and booking yourself solid. Start small, end big, and remember—successful selling is really nothing more than showing your potential clients how you can help them to live a happier, more successful life.

Cut the Crap Out of Selling

By now you probably can guess that I think traditional sales tactics have about as much validity as a three-dollar bill. I even wrote an entire book about it called *The Contrarian Effect: Why It Pays (BIG) to Take Typical Sales Advice and Do the Opposite.*

In fact, traditional, trite sales tactics, closing techniques, assuming the sale, overcoming objections, and so forth were originally developed in the late 1800s by John H. Patterson of the National Cash Register Company (who ironically enough was found guilty of violating antitrust laws). These contrived sales strategies, created by a convict, are still perpetuated by sales trainers. And for good reason. They give us something to do when we're lost. They provide a standard by which to measure. And the worst part is that they work . . . a little . . . sometimes. But clients detest them.

People don't buy because you want them to. And rarely do they buy because of a sales pitch or something clever you said to persuade them.

If you really want to be successful when selling, you've got to listen to your potential clients. If they don't like the old generic, overused, and clichéd tactics, why are you still holding on to them? (Maybe you're not, but you know, or work with, someone who is.)

Do what you must. Ditch the canned 1-2-3, sometimes pushy, usually insensitive, and almost always repetitive sales strategies glamorized from the past.

I've offered you the Book Yourself Solid Four-Part Sales Formula to use as a framework for your sales conversations but there is no perfectly packaged process, magic bullet, or foolproof method to crumble every gatekeeper in your path and book every piece of business. It doesn't exist. We must be willing to learn, adapt, and listen to our potential clients.

When you do this, you'll never have to use a canned close again. But you will connect brilliantly with the values your customers want to express. Remember . . .

- Trash the provocative questions, the level-setting statements, and the conversation helpers and just listen while customers tell you what they really want.
- Ditch the pitch of the day and only make relevant sales offers proportionate to the amount of trust you've earned.
- Use the Red Velvet Rope Policy and don't assume you are meant to work with everyone. Maximize your time and energy, and build credibility when you work with people you are meant to serve.

I'm certain you care about what you do: the people you serve, the services you sell, and the reputation you've earned. You wouldn't be reading this book if you didn't. Do not let your guard down for one second. Think bigger about who you are and how you will serve your clients.

When you keep your focus and maintain your integrity, you'll never, ever, be put in the same category as those stereotypical, shady, smooth-talking, handlebar-mustache-twirling, sleazeball "salesmen" ready to screw over the next poor sap just to take home the commission. Your service is important to the world. You are important to the world. Cut the crap out of selling and set yourself apart.

The Book Yourself Solid 7 Core Self-Promotion Strategies

You've diligently worked through Modules One, Two, and Three. You have a foundation for your business. You have a strategy for building trust and credibility. You know how to price and sell your services. Watch out, because you're not only on your way to liking marketing and selling, but you are now dangerously close to loving both.

By the time you complete Module Four, you'll be in a full-on, mad, passionate love affair not only with the idea of marketing and selling but also with the real-world application of the Book Yourself Solid 7 Core Self-Promotion Strategies.

Just like any new love affair, you want to give yourself time to absorb the newness of it all. Don't let the multitude of strategies, techniques, and exercises in Module Four overwhelm you. Pick the strategies that are most aligned with your strengths and run with them—you don't need to execute all of them. In fact, only four of the strategies are mandatory, whereas three of them are optional. Can you guess which are mandatory and which are optional?

The Book Yourself Solid 7 Core Self-Promotion Strategies

1. The Book Yourself Solid Networking Strategy
2. The Book Yourself Solid Direct Outreach Strategy
3. The Book Yourself Solid Referral Strategy
4. The Book Yourself Solid Keep-In-Touch Strategy
5. The Book Yourself Solid Speaking Strategy
6. The Book Yourself Solid Writing Strategy
7. The Book Yourself Solid Web Strategy

Give yourself an A+ if you guessed that the mandatory strategies are: Networking, Direct Outreach, Referrals, and Keep-in-Touch. You don't survive without using those basic strategies for creating awareness for what you offer.

You might have guessed that speaking and writing strategies are optional, but are you surprised to hear that the web strategy is also optional? Yes, having a professional web site that effectively starts conversations with potential clients is probably a good idea, but beyond that, you need not learn or use any of the additional web strategies. If you're not Web or tech savvy and have absolutely no desire to become so, then you shouldn't worry about all the various bells and whistles the Web offers. In fact, if you try to dive into the Web with no real interest or aptitude, you're sure to become overwhelmed, and fast.

Start with the strategies that speak to you first. The only possible mistake you can make is to try all of these strategies at once. You run the risk of watering down your efforts, becoming frustrated with the results, or worse, quitting before you see any results. I suggest that you use the four mandatory strategies, networking, direct outreach, referrals, and keep-in-touch, and pick one of the optional strategies, Web, speaking, or writing, to start.

The mandatory strategies will ensure that you're creating awareness for the products and services you offer and the one optional strategy will supercharge your promotional efforts. Then, over time, as you get more and more proficient with the mandatory strategies, feel free to add in more of the optional strategies. In the process, do your best to enjoy, embrace, and profit from the Book Yourself Solid 7 Core Self-Promotion Strategies.

Throughout this module, I will often refer to the Book Yourself Solid marketing software. This is an organization, planning, and marketing system to which, as a reader of this book, you get an extended free trial. What's the point of it: Well . . . we book your calendar with marketing so you can book it with clients. That's right. When you register, your marketing activities will already be scheduled into your day. You'll know exactly what to do and when to do it.

Knowing how to do something and actually doing it are two very different things. For years, I've seen many a talented service professional struggle to get clients because, even though they understood what they were supposed to do, they just didn't do it. Watching others struggle so much literally hurt my heart, and solving this problem, for the people I serve, became an obsession, which hurt my head. Thankfully, for me, and fortunately, for you, I believe we've solved the problem.

The Book Yourself Solid software will help you execute some of the self-promotion strategies I teach you in this upcoming module.

I have a deep understanding of what you actually need to get your marketing done and created a tool that is one of a kind. As you read through the next several chapters you'll see for yourself how much easier this system can make doing your self-promotion.

Over the course of Module Four, as the 7 core self-promotion strategies are revealed to you, you'll also discover the power of the Book Yourself Solid software. Get ready at last to set and achieve your goals.

If you would like to try out the Book Yourself Solid software, and take advantage of the special extended free trial offer that comes only with this book, go to BookYourselfSolid.com/software right now and take two minutes to sign up.

Remember, the Book Yourself Solid system is supported by both practical and spiritual principles. From a spiritual perspective I believe that if you have something to say, if you have a message to deliver, and if there are people you want to serve, then there are people in this world whom you are meant to serve. Not kinda, sorta, because they're in your target market . . . but *meant to*—that's the way the universe is set up if you're in the business of helping others.

From a practical perspective there may be two simple reasons why you don't have as many clients as you'd like:

- Either you don't know what to do to attract and secure more clients; or
- You know what to do but you're not actually doing it.

The Book Yourself Solid system is designed to help you solve both of these problems. Module Four will show you what to do to attract and secure more clients. But these 7 core self-promotion strategies must be executed every day. Yes, *every working day*. You don't need me to tell you that your future rests on your ability to execute these strategies with daily discipline. However, you might need me to help you:

- Identify exactly what you need to do each day to book more business; and
- Definitely get it done, daily.

This Module will show you exactly what do to daily. And, the Book Yourself Solid software can help you help yourself do what you know you need to do.

Of course, please know that, even if you don't use the automatic marketing system that I've created for you, you will still be able to execute the Book Yourself Solid 7 Core Self-Promotion Strategies. Provided, of course, that you do use some kind of tool to manage your marketing and relationship development. Don't let opportunities slip through your fingers because of a lack of organization or inability to get things done.

Most important, the concepts and action steps laid out in the following pages will help you create relentless demand for the services and products you offer so that you can energetically build a cadre of high value, high-paying, inspiring clients.

10

The Book Yourself Solid Networking Strategy

Some cause happiness wherever they go; others, whenever they go.
—Oscar Wilde

Networking, Ugh!

It's possible that—like the thought of marketing and sales—the thought of networking may make you cringe. When most service professionals hear the word *networking*, they think of the old-school business mentality of promotional networking at meet-and-greet events where everyone is there to schmooze and manipulate one another in an attempt to gain some advantage for themselves or their business.

Who wouldn't cringe at the thought of spending an hour or two exchanging banalities and sales pitches with a phony smile plastered on your face to hide your discomfort? If it feels uncomfortable, self-serving, and deceptive, chances are all those business cards you collected will end up in a drawer of your desk never to be seen again because you'll so dread following up that you'll procrastinate until they're forgotten.

Take heart, because it doesn't have to be that way. The Book Yourself Solid Networking Strategy operates from an entirely different perspective—networking is all about connecting and sharing with others. All that's necessary is to shift your perspective from one of scarcity and fear to one of abundance and love. With the Book Yourself Solid Networking Strategy, the focus is on sincerely and freely giving and sharing, and by doing so, building and deepening mutually beneficial relationships with others. Networking is all about making lasting connections.

Making the Shift to the Book Yourself Solid Way

The first step is to change your perspective of what networking really is. Do you believe that networking has something to do with the old-school business mentality of scarcity and fear that asks:

- How can I push my agenda?
- How can I get or keep the attention on myself?
- What can I say to really impress or manipulate?
- How can I use each contact to get what I want or need?
- How can I crush the competition?
- How can I dominate the marketplace?

The Book Yourself Solid Networking Strategy (one of abundance and love) asks:

- What can I give and offer to others?
- How can I help others to be successful?
- How can I start and continue friendly conversations?
- How can I put others at ease?
- How can I best express my sincerity and generosity?

- How can I listen attentively so as to recognize the needs and desires of others?
- How can I provide true value to others?
- How can I fully express myself so I can make genuine connections with others?

When we use the word *networking* let's think of *connecting*, instead. Does that help you fall in love with the concept of networking? We don't get contacts, we don't find contacts, we don't have contacts; we make *connections* with real people.

A connection with another human being means that you're in sync with, and relevant to, each other. Let that be our definition of networking.

When people ask me what is the most important factor in networking success, I always have a two-word answer: other people. Your networking success is determined by other people—how they respond to you.

If you keep asking yourself the preceding value-added questions and follow the Book Yourself Solid Networking Strategy that I'm about to present to you, you'll create a large and powerful network built on compassion, trust, and integrity, a network that is priceless and will reap rewards for years to come.

The Book Yourself Solid 50/50 Networking Rule

The Book Yourself Solid Networking Strategy employs the 50/50 networking rule, which requires that we share our networking focus evenly between potential clients and other professionals. Most people think of networking as something you do primarily to try to reel in clients. That's not so.

While the Book Yourself Solid Networking Strategy adds value to the lives of people who could become your clients, you'll also want to spend 50 percent of your networking time connecting with other professionals. Networking with other professionals provides you with an opportunity to connect and share resources, knowledge, and information. Bear in mind that working solo does not mean working alone. You can create so much more value when other talented people are involved.

Have You Got Any Soul?

The absolute best education I have ever received on the concept of networking was from Tim Sanders in his book, *Love Is the Killer App: How to Win Business and Influence Friends*. That's why I asked Tim to write the foreword of this book.

Tim Sanders's message is that being a *love cat* is the key to business success, and it's at the heart of the Book Yourself Solid Networking Strategy. He quotes philosopher and writer Milton Mayeroff's definition of love from his book *On Caring:* "Love is the selfless promotion of the growth of the other." Tim then defines his idea of business love as "the act of intelligently and sensibly sharing your intangibles with your biz partners."

What are those intangibles? According to Tim, they are your knowledge, your network, and your compassion. They are the three essential keys to networking success.

Networking requires that you consciously integrate each of these intangibles until they become a natural part of your daily life, everywhere you go, and in everything you do. Yes, I said *daily life*. Networking isn't something you do only at networking events. It's an ongoing process that will bring terrific benefits.

Share *Who* You Know, *What* You Know, and *How* You Feel

- *Share who you know.* This is everyone you know. It's as simple as that. Whether family, friend, or business associate, everyone in your network is potentially a good connection with someone else, and you never know whom you might meet next who will be the other half of a great connection.

- *Share what you know.* This means everything you've learned—whether through life experience, observation, conversation, or study—and everything you continue to learn.

- *Share how you feel.* This is all of your compassion, the quality that makes us most human. It's our ability to empathize with others. Sharing your compassion in every aspect of your life will bring the greatest rewards, not only for your bottom line, but also in knowing that you're operating from your heart and your integrity in all your interactions.

Note: Give each of these three intangibles freely and with no expectation of return. After all, that's how love is meant to operate, too. While it may seem calculated to plan a strategy around them, the fact remains that when you're smart, friendly, and helpful, people will like you, will enjoy being around you, and will remember you when they or someone they know needs your services.

Share Who You Know

I will do anything I can to support the people I like and respect. I go out of my way to serve the people who serve me. Do you?

Think about it: Whom do you want to give your business to or recommend to other members of your network? It's the people who have served you in some way; the people who are friendly, nice, smart, and helpful; the people who will go the extra mile, give that little bit more than anyone expects, and who genuinely strive to provide the best service they can with integrity. It's the people who are upbeat, always have a ready smile, and from whom you walk away feeling supported and energized.

If you are that person in each and every interaction you have with others, whether business or personal, your network is going to grow exponentially, and those people are going to remember you and want to do business with you. They're going to link you with others in their network with whom you can make beneficial connections, and they're going to refer you to everyone they know who could possibly use your service or products.

I can think of scores, if not hundreds, of friends and colleagues I have who are like this. There is one who comes to mind as the ideal example of what it really means to share your network openly, without reservation, and without expecting anything in return.

Caroline Kohles, of NiaNewYork.com, is a fitness, health, and wellness expert. She is one of the most authentic and talented people I have the pleasure of knowing, and I will do anything for her any chance I get. Why? Because she constantly sends me clients, connects me with people that I can partner with, gives me opportunities to market my services, and constantly shares things she's learned or heard about that she thinks will help me personally or professionally. The most remarkable thing about Caroline is that she expects nothing in return.

There is one thing that is essential to consider with respect to sharing your network. You must do what you say you're going to do—always. And if you don't, apologize and make it right. If you make commitments and don't fulfill them, you'll damage your reputation and close doorways that were once open to you. If you don't make commitments to connect, no one will do it for you. These habits of commitment making and fulfilling are essential to developing yourself into a masterful connector who truly and meaningfully adds value to the lives of others.

Each business day, introduce two people within your network who do not yet know each other but you think might benefit from knowing each other. This is not a referral for a specific work opportunity but rather a way to connect two people who may find some benefit in knowing each other. Maybe they are both in the same field or share some business connection. Maybe they are both into martial arts or golf. Or, maybe they just live in the same town. Either way, all you're doing is creating an opportunity for connection. If they're the kind of people who value meeting others, then something special might happen. Hey, you never know . . . you might be introducing two people who are going to save the planet from climate calamity or fall in love and get married.

Your Book Yourself Solid® software helps with this. Each day, the system suggests possible connections based on your contacts' hobbies, locations, professions, and more. You pick one of the suggested connections along with an e-mail template. The e-mail template is automatically populated with their contact information, you then edit the note and voilà, you're done. The system then tracks all the connections you've made ensuring that you never reconnect the same people. It also spaces out the connections so you are never too helpful (which can overwhelm your contact). Furthermore, the system manages your follow-up with each person so you continue to develop and nurture the relationship. You can learn more about how it works, see a demo, and get your reader's bonus extended trial at BookYourselfSolid.com/software.

4.10.1 Written Exercise: List five people in your network who consistently support you by sending referrals, giving you advice, or doing anything else that's helpful. Then identify someone in your network for each of these five people whom you could connect them with. Whom do you know who will add value to their work or life? Is it a potential client, a potential business partner, a potential vendor?

4.10.2 Booked Solid Action Step: Try it now. Go through your address book and find two people who share something in common, something that each one of them will find relevant about the other and introduce them to each other.

The people you listed in the preceding written exercise and the people you connected in the Booked Solid Action Step are going to appreciate the opportunity to connect or the recommendation that you make, and when someone they know needs your service or product, they'll be more likely to remember you and to reciprocate.

Remember, too, that the six degrees of separation theory says that you are only six people away from the person or information you need. (In your field, your degrees of separation from anyone you need or want to connect with are even fewer.) Everyone you meet has the potential to connect you (through his network and his contacts' networks) to someone or some piece of information that you need. So step out of your comfort zone and make a sincere effort to connect with people you might not normally interact with. The more diverse your network of connections, the more powerful and effective your network becomes. It opens doors that might otherwise remain closed.

4.10.3 Written Exercise: Think of the types of people or professions that are *not* represented in your current network. List five that would expand and benefit your network, as well as ideas for where you might find them.

Every once in a while I get some push-back about sharing your network that goes something like this: "But, Michael, I don't know that many people, so this won't work for me." Not so fast, my big thinking friend. Criss Ittermann, a business owner who took one of my courses at BookedSolidUniversity.com, showed me how you can create 45 connections from a network of only 10 people. Bump it up to 20 people and you've got 190 connections. It seems like funny math but it's not. It's factorial math (whatever that is).

Here's how it works for just 10 people.

Introduce person 1 to persons 2 to 10.
That's 9 connections.
Person 2 has met person 1, but needs to meet persons 3 to 10.
That's 8 connections.

Person 3 has now met persons 1 and 2 and needs to meet persons 4 to 10. *That's 7 connections.*

Person 4 has now met persons 1 to 3 and needs to meet persons 5 to 10. *That's 6 connections.*

Person 5 has now met persons 1 to 4 and needs to meet persons 6 to 10. *That's 5 connections.*

Person 6 has now met persons 1 to 5 and needs to meet persons 7 to 10. *That's 4 connections.*

Person 7 has now met persons 1 to 6 and needs to meet persons 8 to 10. *That's 3 connections.*

Person 8 has now met persons 1 to 7 and needs to meet persons 9 to 10. *That's 2 connections.*

Person 9 has now met persons 1 to 8 and needs to meet person 10. *That's 1 connection.*

That's a total of 45 connections created out of only 10 people.

If you start with 20 people, you end up with 190 connections because $19 + 18 + 17 + 16 + 15 + 14 + 13 + 12 + 11 + 10 + 9 + 8 + 7 + 6 + 5 + 4 + 3 + 2 + 1 = 190$.

Your world is much bigger than you might think. It's a good thing you have your Book Yourself Solid® software to do this funny factorial math for you.

Share What You Know

I recommend books all the time, and I'm often asked, "How do you read so much?" which always makes me smile because, when I was a kid, my father was worried that I wasn't going to amount to much because he couldn't get me to read beyond the Hardy Boys. But now I read about two books per month. What changed? I realized that the answers to most of my questions are offered in books. Even better, I get to choose what I learn and from whom. Then armed with this information, I am in a great place to share it with others.

You may be thinking, "But if I'm always referring to other people's work, won't they just forget about me and get everything they need from the book or resource I referenced?" Good question. First of all, if they love the book or information that you referred them to, it's highly likely they'll associate much of that value with you. They will feel connected to you because you helped them achieve a goal or change their life or simply learn something new, the value of which is not to be underestimated. The more knowledgeable you are, and are perceived to be, the more trust and credibility you'll build in your network. Reading books is, by far, the best and most efficient way to increase your knowledge.

Reading a book on a topic that is related to the services you provide offers an easy way to start a conversation with potential clients or contacts. In fact, they may start the conversation with you instead with one simple question, "What are you reading?" I realized this gem of a networking technique by accident. I was born and raised in New York City, where almost every New Yorker rides the subway. It's simply the best way to get around. It's also one of the best places to make new friends. Think about it; you're constantly bumped, pushed, and shoved by people you don't know. So instead of fighting all the time, most New Yorkers decide the path of least resistance is simply to strike up a conversation. If you have a book in your hand, what do you think this conversation is going to be about? You guessed it—the book. And what better way to get into your Book Yourself Solid dialogue than to explain why you're reading the particular book you're holding in your hand.

Of course, this doesn't just apply to New York subway cars. Everywhere you go you're running into, meeting, and connecting with other people. What if you always had a book in your hand that allowed you to share what you know about your particular area of expertise, for the betterment of the person you're talking with? I know that not every person you meet or run into is a member of your target market, or at first thought, can send you clients, but it doesn't matter. You're just finding opportunities to add value to those you meet by sharing what you know—as long as it's relevant to them.

4.10.4 Booked Solid Action Step: Try it with this book. Carry it wherever you go and explain to people why you're reading it. You'll have the opportunity to talk about the Book Yourself Solid philosophy of giving so much value that you think you've gone too far and then giving more, and how it's in sync with your values and what you do as a service provider. You'll then be able to get into your Book Yourself Solid Dialogue with ease.

Ask yourself what knowledge, once acquired, would add the greatest value and make you more attractive to potential clients and business partners, and then go after learning it. Your investment in books—buying them and reading them—will pay dividends you can't even imagine.

4.10.5 Written Exercise: List five books you've read that you know are must-reads for your target market. Think about and jot down the names of any specific people who come to mind for each book.

4.10.6 Written Exercise: List five books that have been recommended to you as must-reads or that you know contain information that would add value to your target market. Then go out and make the investment in at least one this week.

4.10.7 Written Exercise: Books aren't our only source of knowledge. As I mentioned earlier, our life experience, observations, and conversations are all sources of knowledge as well. Think about the many areas in which you're knowledgeable and list a minimum of five. Have fun with this and just let it flow. If you know a lot about skydiving, or *ikebana* (the Japanese art of flower arranging), include it! You never know what subject might help make a connection.

Let's take it up a notch. Once per week, send a book to someone with whom you'd like to develop a meaningful business relationship. Include a nice card with a note about why you're sending them the book—what it's meant to you and why you think it'll be valuable to them. Follow up three weeks later by phone to see how they're enjoying the book. This strategy is especially beneficial for those who are not particularly comfortable with small talk because now you've got something to talk about.

Now, let's take up one more notch. Sharing magazine, journal, and newspaper articles can work even better than books because the recipient of the information can consume it so quickly. Each day, send personally or professionally relevant articles to three people in your network. I know what you're thinking, *Michael, c'mon, how much time is that going to take? What do you think, I'm just sitting around with nothing to do?* No, of course not. I know how busy you are. That's why the Book Yourself Solid® marketing software is so valuable.

For example, if you've tagged Bob as someone who owns a small engineering business and focuses on high technology, and Monday morning the *New York Times* publishes an article about the state of the high-tech engineering industry, you'll be able to send the article to Bob before he even turns on his computer. Your e-mail will include a link to the article and a little note that says, "Good Morning Bob, I saw this article and immediately thought of you. Wonder if you've seen it? Pretty interesting when the author says that. . . ." You might just make Bob's day by sharing some very relevant and timely information that he might have otherwise missed. Not to mention, that Bob is going to feel so fortunate you're out in the world thinking about him and his needs. Of course, you can do this the old-fashioned way and just read the relevant publications on your list each day and then decide to whom you are going to send various articles and then make note of it in your address book. Doing this with three different articles for three different people manually usually takes about an hour. Doing it with the BookYourselfSolid.com/software usually takes about 10 minutes.

4.10.8 Booked Solid Action Step: Try it now. Go to your favorite online publication, browse through today's articles and when you find one that is relevant to someone in your network, send it to them with a note as suggested earlier.

Share How You Feel

In a business like yours that is based on service, people will generally not hire you unless they feel you have compassion for what they're going through. Expressing that compassion is the first step to a successful working relationship. How do you do that? Listen attentively. Be fully present when making connections, smile as often as possible, make eye contact, and ask engaging, open-ended questions that express your curiosity and interest.

Take the time to add value to the person you're connecting with by offering information or resources that speak to her needs. If you don't have what she needs, think about who in your network would meet her needs and how to go about acting as the link for them. Remember, this is done with no expectation of any immediate return.

4.10.9 Written Exercise: Note a recent situation, business or personal, when someone else expressed compassion for you. Think about how you felt following the interaction. How do you feel about that person because of the compassion she showed for you?

Can sharing your compassion be a marketing tactic? Absolutely. Do you do it manipulatively or to try to gain some favor? No, that is not the

Book Yourself Solid way. You can be deliberate and developmental in the way that you share you compassion—that's not manipulative!

At least once per week, send a card or e-mail to someone in your network just to share your compassion. If you know he's going through a difficult time, send a note expressing sympathy. If he's just been honored with an award, shower him with praise. If he recently experienced a family triumph, like the marriage of a child, congratulate him. These simple, yet powerful, gestures make people thankful to know you. It keeps you top of their mind. And, most important, you're making other people feel better about who they are and what they do.

These Booked Solid Action Steps are your new daily and weekly networking activities and you don't even need to leave the house to get them done.

- You'll share your network by introducing two people each day who may benefit from meeting each together. You'll come across as a real connecter, someone who thinks about the needs of others, and that's an amazingly attractive quality.
- You'll share what you know by sending one book per week, and three articles per day, to important networking partners. It'll make you look like a smartypants, give you something to talk to them about and in the process build your relationship.
- You'll share your compassion with one person in your network each day, making her feel better about herself and in the process thankful that she knows you.

These simple, yet meaningful, networking strategies will get, and keep, you booked solid for many years to come. You just have to do it—each and every business day. I believe the Book Yourself Solid® marketing system will be the key to your success. Using the software will ensure you get it all done. And, as you know, that's where the rubber meets the road.

Networking Opportunities

The possibilities for meeting people are endless. Any time you're sharing your connections, knowledge, and compassion, you're networking. Any time you're learning more about what others do and know, you're networking. Anytime you link or connect two people you know, you're networking.

Informal Networking Opportunities

These are the ones that we might not think of as networking but that we can't afford to overlook. We have dozens of these every day:

- Casual chat in line at the grocery store.
- While checking out videos at your local video store.
- Speaking with your neighbor while walking your dog.

Let's take the neighbor you see while walking your dog as an example. Every day you walk the same path with your dog. Each time, you smile and chat with your neighbor as your dogs sniff each other. After a while you begin to greet one another by name, and you know enough about him to ask after his family. He mentions he was looking forward to a special evening out with his wife the following night for their anniversary but then sighs and says, "But our babysitter canceled at the last minute. I wish [one of the phrases to always be listening for] that I knew of a good backup to call." You recall that your friend Sally seems to know every sitter in town. You pull out your phone, look up her number, and give her a call. "Sally, meet Bob. He's looking for a great sitter for tomorrow night, and you know everyone, so of course I thought you might be able to help," you say as you hand your cell phone to Bob.

Now this exchange has absolutely nothing to do with business, or does it? On the surface it has nothing to do with business. However, who do you think Bob is going to call when he, or someone he knows, needs your services? Bob is thrilled with you because you've saved his special night out. And Sally is pleased too because you've given her high praise and allowed her to show off her knowledge of who's who in the world of local baby sitters. Both of them feel better following their interaction with you, and that makes you memorable. And most important, you've increased your connection factor with each of them. Your connection factor is how much trust you've built with each person in your network. The more value you add to a person's life, the more she is going to trust you.

4.10.10 Written Exercise: Think for a moment: Have you recently missed any opportunities for making a deeper connection with someone? List five connections that would have been made if you had just shared your knowledge, your network, or your compassion.

Formal Networking Opportunities

These are the more formal, business meet-and-greet opportunities that can be fun and enjoyable and offer great rewards:

- Toastmasters International.
- Chamber of Commerce meetings.
- Networking or leads groups—for example, Business Network International.
- Trade association meetings.

4.10.11 Written Exercise: Do some research and come up with three additional business networking opportunities like the ones I've listed that you can attend with the intention of adding value to others as well as enhancing your network.

Networking Events—What to Do

- *Arrive on time.* This is not the time to stage a grand entrance by being fashionably late or to tell any stories about why you're late. Nobody cares. If you're late and it's noticed, apologize and leave it at that.

- *Relax and be yourself.* Contrary to conventional wisdom, you don't have to fit in. It may sound trite, but be yourself, unless when you're being yourself you end the evening with your tie wrapped around your head doing a nosedive into the shrimp salad. Seriously, people want to meet the person who is out in front, who is writing the rules and taking the lead, not the one who is following the pack. So don't be afraid to be fully self-expressed. If you are, you'll be more memorable.

- *Smile and be friendly.* Both men and women may worry that smiling too big will be construed as some sort of a come-on or that they're desperate for attention. This fear of being misunderstood will hold you back. Let it go! Better to err on the side of a big, friendly smile than to be considered unfriendly or standoffish.

- *Focus on giving.* If your focus is on giving of yourself, you're going to get returns in spades. If you focus on what you can get, you will be much less successful.

- *Prepare for the event.* Learn the names of the organizers and some of the key players. Identify what and how you can share with others at the function: who you know (without being a name dropper), what you know (without being a know-it-all), and what you can share from your heart (without making assumptions) with the people who will be at this particular event. You never know what might change someone's life.

- *Introduce yourself to the person hosting the event.* This person may be a very valuable addition to your network. Never forget to say, "Thank you."

- *Introduce yourself to the bigwig.* If there's someone you want to meet at a big seminar or event, someone famous in your industry, do you go up to her and say, "Here's what I do and here's my business card"? No! You start by offering praise. You say, "I just want to tell you your work had a great effect on me," or "Your work inspired me to do this or that." Then the next time you are at the same event, you could say, "I would just love to hold your coffee cup." Meaning, "I would love to assist you in some way that would add value to your life or work." She may say, "I don't think so," but what have you got to lose? Then again, she may respond by saying, "Yeah, you seem like a really genuine and considerate person. I've got some stuff you can do." Don't forget that successful and busy people always have more on their plate than they can reasonably handle. They're always looking for talented people to help make their life easier. If you can help reduce someone's stress level, you've made a friend for life.

- *Offer something when first meeting someone, whenever possible.* Offer praise (as in the earlier example), compassion, or a connection. When you can say, "I know someone you've got to meet," or "There's a great book I think may offer the solution to your problem," he is going to see you very differently from the person who shoved a business card in his face and said, "Let's stay in touch, dude." If you can leave him feeling even better, more uplifted, and energized after his interaction with you, he's going to remember you.

- *Start conversations by asking questions.* This is a great approach, especially if you're nervous. It takes the spotlight off you and allows the other person to shine. It allows you to learn something new at the same time.

- *Identify two or three things you'd like to learn from the people at the function.* People are drawn to others who are curious and interested.

- *Make eye contact.* It expresses respect and interest in the person you're speaking with. And stay focused on the person you're speaking with. If you're speaking with me, but your eyes are constantly scanning the room for someone more important or relevant to you, don't you think it might make me feel unappreciated?

- *Wear comfortable clothing.* If you're constantly fidgeting or worrying about how you look in clothes that aren't comfortable or don't fit properly, you'll be self-conscious and others will sense it.

- *Take the initiative.* Go up to people and make friends. People love to be asked about themselves, their hobbies, or their family. This is the time to get to know a few personal tidbits that will give you the opportunity to find a common interest that makes connecting easier and more natural.

- *Offer a firm handshake.* Hold your drink in your left hand. This eliminates the need to wipe your damp hand on your clothes before shaking hands. And, guys, don't think you need to shake hands differently with a woman from the way you do with a man. A firm handshake (not a death grip) is always appropriate.

- *Be inclusive.* Ask others to join your conversations; this is very important. Don't monopolize people, especially those who are in high demand, like the speaker from the event. It makes the speaker uncomfortable. Remember, she's there to meet lots of people too. It also annoys others who want to meet the person you're trying to keep to yourself. Tip: If you want to be helpful, ask the speaker if there is anybody you can introduce her to, or simply be sure to keep including people in your conversations with her. This way, you'll be seen as a very generous and open person by the others at the event, and the speaker will remember you as someone who helped her easily network and navigate the event.

- *Ask for a business card and then keep in touch.* It's your responsibility to ask for a card if you want one, and it's your responsibility to follow up. Quality, not quantity, counts when making genuine personal connections. If you race through an event passing out and collecting business cards from anyone and everyone as though there were a prize for the most cards gained at the end of the event, you'll do yourself a huge disservice. And remember, just because someone gives you his business card does *not* mean you have permission to add him to your mailing list or e-zine list. You do not. You can certainly send a personal e-mail as a follow-up, and you should, but you should not and cannot add him to your list. You don't have permission to do so.

- *Always have a pen with you.* When you receive a business card, write a little note about any commitment to follow up, what you talked about, any personal bits or unusual things that will help you to remember the person and to personalize future contact, and be sure to include the date and name of the function where you met.

Networking Events—What Not to Do

- *Don't try to be cool.* And don't overcompensate for your nervousness by bragging about your success; this is a major turn-off.
- *Don't let "What do you do?" be the first question you ask.* Let it come up naturally in conversation.
- *Don't sit with people you know for the majority of the event.* While it may be more comfortable to sit with the people you know, it becomes too easy to stay with them, and if you do, you'll defeat the purpose of being there. Step out of your comfort zone and get to know new people.
- *Don't juggle multiple items.* Travel light to eliminate the necessity of juggling your coat, purse, briefcase, drink, or buffet plate. Keep that right hand free for handshakes and for jotting down quick notes on business cards.
- *Don't complain about networking or the event you're attending.* Don't complain about anything. The cycle of complaining is easy to get drawn into, especially at events where almost everyone is a bit uncomfortable. While complaining is an icebreaker, it's not an attractive one. Change the subject—for example, "Have you tried the shrimp?"—or take the opportunity to recommend this great book, *Book Yourself Solid*, and how it's transformed the way you think about networking events. Wink.
- *Don't take yourself too seriously.* Remember to relax and have fun.

Online Networking—and Social Media Marketing

I'm sure you're familiar with social media—Internet-based tools for sharing and discussing information and sharing pictures, video, and more. You may already be using social media for both personal and professional purposes or it may be an entirely new frontier just waiting for you to stake your claim.

If you're wondering how significant social media will become, in an October 2009 *Wall Street Journal* article titled *Why E-Mail No Longer Rules*, the writer predicted that in the next 5 or 10 years, e-mail will become a thing of the past. It will become irrelevant in regard to sharing information and content with people:

> "E-mail has had a good run as king over communications, but its reign is over. In its place a new generation of services is starting to take hold. Services like Twitter and Facebook and countless others vying for a piece of the new world. Just as e-mail did more than a decade ago, this shift promises to profoundly rewrite the way we communicate in ways we can only begin to imagine."

There has been, and will continue to be, a migration from e-mail marketing to social media marketing and communications. Forrester Research suggests social media is the fastest-growing area of the Internet. In fact, at the writing of this second edition of *Book Yourself Solid*, Facebook is the fastest-growing online social network, boasting 500 million users.

On the one hand, the growth of social media is good for you and your ability to exploit it for networking and marketing purposes—it's mobile, it's easy, it's quick, and it's free. My friend, Chris Brogan, an author and blogger on the cutting edge of social media trends, believes that, "Not every demographic will engage in social media in the same way but every demographic will engage in social media in some way." On the other hand, the fact that it's easy, quick, and free is also a problem. It means more junk—more irrelevant noise clogging up the bandwidth. So use your social media wisely and well. If you do, it will speak volumes about who you are, what you stand for, and how you do business.

Social Media—for Marketing or Networking?

Social media can be used for marketing purposes through pay-per-click ad campaigns, promotions, and the like. However, when beginning to build a social media platform on Facebook, LinkedIn, and others, I suggest using it primarily as a tool for connecting, relationship building, and creating value by sharing your intangibles as we discussed before. When I introduce you to the Book Yourself Solid Web Strategy in Chapter 16, I'll teach you how to use Facebook, Twitter, and LinkedIn for both marketing and building relationships. It's too much to add to this chapter. Just remember the bottom line: *think relationships first, business second.*

You Are Always Networking

Your profits will come from connections with people who can send you business—whether that's by way of a satisfied client who refers others to you; or another professional who has the ability to book you for speaking engagements, write about you, or partner with you; or the manager at the video store who appreciates your big, friendly smile each weekend and the recommendation you made for a great babysitter when he desperately needed one.

With the Book Yourself Solid Networking Strategy, the prospect of creating a phenomenal network of connections doesn't have to be overwhelming or intimidating. We all connect constantly, with everyone, every day. Now we just need to do it consciously, with greater awareness, until doing so becomes a natural and comfortable part of our daily lives.

Then follow up. Keep in touch. It is imperative that you get every one of your connections into your database and act on each connection. If the contact isn't in your database or you don't take the action necessary to keep in touch, your networking is pointless.

So You've Got Spinach in Your Teeth

I've given you a lot of techniques in this chapter about what to do, what not to do, and how to interact with others when you're networking, but there's a big difference between techniques and principles, and it's the principles that are most important to remember and begin implementing. If you can incorporate the principles, you'll naturally do well.

For example, everyone says when you meet people at a networking event you're supposed to look that person in the eye, give them a firm handshake, smile, and nod your head, but if you do that and don't take the giver's stance, it won't matter how slick you are. However, if you always take the giver's stance and share who you know, what you know, and how you feel, even if you have spinach in your teeth and your palm is sweaty, you'll be fine, because people are going to respond to who you are as a human being. In fact, they'll share their compassion with you by gently letting you know about the large piece of spinach entrenched between your two front teeth.

So what do you think? Are you ready to network your way to more clients, more profit, and deeper connections with people? Sharing your knowledge, your network, and your compassion will bring you one step closer to being booked solid.

11

The Book Yourself Solid Direct Outreach Strategy

You miss 100 percent of the shots you don't take.

—Wayne Gretzky

As a business owner, you'll need to proactively reach out to potential clients to make offers and to marketing partners and other decision makers to create business opportunities. In fact, the most important direct outreach you do might well be to other service professionals, businesses, and professional associations to network, cross-promote, and build referral relationships.

Let's clearly define what direct outreach is *not* before detailing exactly what it is and how to do it authentically, easily, and successfully. It is *not* spam, which has typically been considered unsolicited mail or e-mail, sent, without permission, to mailing lists or newsgroups. However, I think the way people now see spam has grown in scope and definition. Today, there are many more ways you can be labeled a spammer—even when you think you're standing in the service of potential clients or business associates.

As you know, spam is not the Book Yourself Solid way. It never has been and never will be. Before the advent of the Internet, direct outreach was a very common marketing strategy. I suppose it's no less common today, but unfortunately, it is often perceived as spam. You must be very careful and discerning with respect to how you use the Book Yourself Solid Direct Outreach Strategy.

You can now be labeled a spammer by sending an unsolicited e-mail directly to a potential client that contains any kind of sales message or promotional or business offer. The same goes for cold calling. Many people just consider that another kind of spam, since it's unsolicited. Even direct outreach to an individual through Facebook, Twitter, LinkedIn, and other social media platforms can get you pegged as irrelevant or worse, a spammer. Posting comments on a blog or other social media site, yes, even your friends' Facebook pages, can get you called out for spamming if they smack of self-promotion.

Clients now find you. That doesn't relieve you of your marketing responsibilities. You need to create awareness for what you offer so that when potential clients go looking for the kind of services you offer they find you. If you don't like the fact that clients want to find you, rather than the other way around, then blame Google. It has changed the way customers and businesses interact. When people go searching online they're willing to wade through junk in search of what they want because they feel in control of the process. When they find what they want, and if it's you, they'll give you permission to market to them.

Just because it's easy to broadcast our messages through e-mail, blogs, and social media platforms doesn't give us permission to force people to pay attention. We have to earn their attention—more than ever. My colleague Seth Godin, the father of Permission Marketing, puts it this way, "Go ahead and make what you want, as long as you stand behind it and don't bother me. If you want to sell magnetic bracelets or put risqué pictures on your web site, it's your responsibility, your choice. Want to find a web site featuring donkeys, naked jugglers, and various illicit acts? It's junk, sure, but it's out there. You just have to go find it. Junk turns into spam when you show up at my doorstep, when your noise intercepts my quiet."

This is why, even though it's easier than ever to make noise and get noticed, direct outreach has become trickier than ever. When you reach out, unsolicited, to a potential client or business associate about a business opportunity, their default assumption is that you're a spammer interrupting their peace and quiet. Is it fair? Doesn't matter. Until there's a cure for selfishness, one that eliminates spammers and their spam, it's the reality that you and I have to deal with. Don't make noise that interrupts others' quiet.

You will find yourself using the Book Yourself Solid Direct Outreach Strategy time and time again when you want to reach out to:

- An ideal client or a referral partner within your target market
- The decision maker at an organization or association to cross-promote, secure speaking engagements, submit articles for publication, and more
- The press

Or a myriad of other business development opportunities.

Direct Outreach Gone Wrong

Sometimes the easiest way to understand a concept is to see real examples of what works and what doesn't. I don't want to scare you off from doing direct outreach. Just the opposite—I want to encourage you to do more of it, but in a way that will make sure you come across as a thoughtful, considerate, empathetic, relevant, and high integrity professional with value to add. To make sure you're always perceived this way, I'm going to show you a series of direct outreach messages sent to me that went terribly wrong. I've changed the names of all involved to protect the innocent but the following are actual messages from real people. In fact, I'm pretty sure they were sent by decent, hard-working professionals. Unfortunately, they haven't yet learned how to do direct outreach and, as a result, their messages landed like a ton of bricks.

Let's start with this brick, which landed in my LinkedIn inbox.

LinkedIn Recommendations

Maria Venter is requesting an endorsement for work.

> Dear Michael,
>
> I'm sending this to ask you for a brief recommendation of my work that I can include in my LinkedIn profile. If you have any questions, let me know.
>
> Thanks in advance for helping me out.
>
> —Maria Venter

Endorse Maria Venter. It only takes a minute. Your endorsement can help Maria Venter:

- Hire and get hired
- Win customers and partnerships
- Build a stronger professional reputation

This e-mail was sent to you by Maria Venter (email@website.com) through LinkedIn because Maria Venter entered your e-mail address. If you have any questions, please contact customer_service@linkedin.com.

This request from Maria is problematic for a number of reasons:

1. Let's start with the fact that I don't know her.
2. If I don't know Maria, why would I recommend she get hired, win customers and partnerships, and build a stronger professional reputation?
3. To send it, all she had to do was enter my e-mail address. Clearly no effort was demonstrated on her part.
4. My LinkedIn profile states that I don't check e-mail at LinkedIn. Rather, I request that people e-mail me at a public e-mail address, which I list.

What should have Maria done instead?

1. She could have started by giving me a recommendation first, if she thought I deserved one. Always better to offer something before asking for something.
2. If it was important to her that we connect, she could have attempted to meet me at an event, if it was convenient for her.
3. She could have commented on my blog posts or notes on my LinkedIn profile or Facebook Fan Page. This would have been noticed and appreciated.
4. She could have sent me an e-mail to my public e-mail address expressing some appreciation for my work or find some other way of making a personal connection through any number of other activities that don't ask for anything in return and don't make any assumptions.

My suggestions have nothing to do with professional status. I would approach anyone this way. Of course, if the person you're reaching out to is already familiar with your work or your name, the connecting process usually speeds up. And, if you're thinking that it's just novice business owners whose direct outreach goes wrong, think again.

This next e-mail is from a publicity and promotions manager at a marketing firm that represents best-selling authors and large publishing houses. I don't know the sender or the author and have no connection to the publisher of the book. Again, I've changed the names of all parties involved.

Dear Mr. Port,

I have not heard back from you on my e-mail below. This is a great opportunity to get your products out in front of a huge audience looking for this kind of material (our previous book campaign was seen by over 5 million people)! Not only will you be offering your subscribers an incredible package, you will also be directing more traffic to your web site and building your own mailing list. Remember, there is no cost involved.

Click on the link below to view a previous campaign we put together for

John Smith's New York Times bestselling book, XXXXXX:

http://www.longurltoasalespage.com

Please let me know right away if you would like to participate or if you have any questions.

Thank you,

Andrea Tiffonelli
Assistant Publicity and Promotions Manager
Progressive Marketing Firm, Inc.

What's so bad about a PR or marketing firm reaching out to an author to see if he'll help promote another author? Nothing. Nothing at all. In fact, one of the primary ways authors get noticed is through promotion from other authors. So, what's wrong with this one?

1. I don't know any of the parties involved and they're sending me what is clearly a form e-mail. It's not personalized in any way.
2. Andrea makes all sorts of assumptions about why I would want to promote this author. She has no idea what really makes me tick and didn't take the time to find out.
3. In the last line, Andrea tells me to let her know "right away" if I want to participate. She clearly demonstrated a lack of respect or appreciation for my time, schedule, life, and so forth. It's not wrong to try to encourage someone to act quickly when promoting a product or service, but this is not such a promotion (her mistake is that she thinks it is). Fundamentally, it's a request to a colleague to help out another colleague and at this point, after all the other offenses in this e-mail, telling me what to do and when to do it is off-putting.
4. This is actually the fourth e-mail Andrea sent to me about this "opportunity." If I didn't respond the first three times, might that be saying something? And, to add insult to injury, every

time Andrea sent me an e-mail I wrote back asking her to stop e-mailing me. Obviously, she ignored my requests. It just confirms my suspicion that I was added to a "list" of authors to whom they're trying to get to participate in their book promotions. That makes it real, honest-to-goodness, 100 percent spam.

What should Andrea have done instead? Well, since I didn't request any information on her promotions or the authors she represents, she could have sent me a short note to this effect:

Dear Michael,

My name is Andrea Tiffonelli. I'm the Assistant Publicity and Promotions Manager for Progressive Marketing Firm, Inc. We represent authors and help them promote their books.

I'm writing to you today to let you know that I'm a fan of your work and appreciate the way you teach marketing. It really helps people who don't typically like marketing and selling—like most of the authors I represent.

Again, just saying "hi" and thanks for your work. If there is anything I can do to be of service to you, please just say the word.

Sincerely,

Andrea Tiffonelli
Assistant Publicity and Promotions Manager
Progressive Marketing Firm, Inc.

What works so well about this alternative version of the e-mail?

1. She's not asking anything of me on her first contact.
2. She quickly tells me who she is and what she does right off the bat.
3. She praises me and demonstrates that, not only is she familiar with my work, she seems to know what I stand for.
4. She closes by offering her support with no expectation of anything in return.

This is how you start a relationship. Over time, a few more, relevant and personal interactions like this would earn her the proportionate amount of trust and credibility needed to see if I'd be interested in getting involved in one of her author promotions.

Here's another one. It's long. Very long. Which is just one of its many problems. There is, however, one simple fix that could have saved this effort. Can you tell what it is?

This is Jerry Faber and I'm working with Tom Rose, The ▆▆▆▆▆▆ Coach, looking for a few very special joint venture partners for his upcoming Quick-Start 3-Day ▆▆▆▆▆▆ Workshop.

▆▆▆▆▆▆ are Hot and getting Hotter! And anybody who wants to have a successful online business needs ▆▆▆▆▆▆ as part of their funnel. So we want to offer you the opportunity to host a preview call with Tom for his highly acclaimed ▆▆▆▆▆▆ Workshop.

Tom has been teaching this workshop for the past 5 years and has helped hundreds of frustrated writers become successful authors. (You can see his long list of testimonials at www.firstwebsite.com.)

I'm contacting you because Tom and I believe that you and Tom are speaking to the same target market, and that this offer will be very lucrative for you while providing great value for your list.

This opportunity pays from $200 to $1000 commission on every sale (depending on which level your subscribers register for).

For the complete details on this JV opportunity go to: www.secondweb site.com.

Basically, here's the way this JV works.

Once you agree to do a jv call with Tom (The call is on "The 7 Biggest Mistakes People Make When ▆▆▆▆▆▆ And How To Avoid Them" and it has converted from 11%–22%), we'll set up the pages for the call and send you a link to all of the materials you will need to promote it, including a promo e-mail series, blog posts and tweets to mail to your list.

(Continued)

(*Continued*)

Then, over the coming weeks, we'll "drip" great content on them (unless it's the week of the Workshop. We do a final Q and A call that week).

If they buy, on or after your call with Tom through your affiliate link, you will get the following commissions.

Platinum Plus Package pays $1000.

Platinum Package pays $500.

Gold Package pays $200.

You can see the sales page at: www.thirdwebsite.com.

If you're interested in doing a JV call with Tom, please let me know. You can e-mail me directly at: jerry@gmail.com.

If you have any questions, feel free to e-mail me at jerry@gmail.com.

Or, if you're ready to get started, e-mail me at jerry@gmail.com and I'll send you everything you need to get started as soon as we can get the web pages set up.

Thank you for your time. We truly appreciate it—and look forward to having the opportunity to joint venture with you. And we'd like to give you a gift for taking the time to read this e-mail:

www.fourthwebsite.com is a pdf with 28 ways to use Twitter. We hope it helps you prosper even more!

Best Wishes,

Jerry Faber
For Tom Rose
The [xxxx] Coach

P.S. If you want to know more about Tom, you can see his bio at: www. fifthwebsite.com.

You can see his videos at: www.sixthwebsite.com.

Holy cow. Where do I start?

1. It's insanely long.
2. Tom and Jerry are making all sorts of assumptions about why I would be interested in this joint venture.
3. It's filled with nonsensical hyperbole like ". . . are hot and getting Hotter! And anybody who wants to have a successful online business needs . . ."
4. Jerry mentions the marketing funnel, which demonstrates that he's not particularly familiar with my work because I write quite a bit about how I don't like the philosophy behind the marketing funnel.
5. He thinks he needs to tell me how a jv like this works.
6. He gives me his e-mail address three times within three sentences.
7. He wants me to look at six different web sites.
8. He offers me a "gift" of an ebook on how to use Twitter for taking the time to read his e-mail. Does he think I'm unfamiliar with Twitter and how to use it?
9. And, what might be the biggest offense of all, he tells me that I'll be blasting my e-mail newsletter subscribers, tweeting to my followers, and promoting Tom's product on my blog. If Tom and Jerry think that I would indiscriminately promote someone that I don't know to my subscribers, readers, and followers, for a few dollars in commissions, then it's obvious they don't know how I operate and don't have a lot of respect for their subscribers.

So, what should Jerry have done? Did you figure out the simple fix to this total disaster of a direct outreach attempt? If you're thinking that he should have simply sent me a short note asking if I even do these kinds of jv's, you're absolutely right. If he had, I would have told him that I don't and no love would have been lost. Instead, Tom and Jerry wasted my time (and theirs) asking me to read this unrequested e-mail about their jv opportunity. Here's what a better direct outreach attempt could have looked like.

Dear Michael,

My name is Jerry Faber and I work with Tom Rose, who teaches courses on ▬▬▬ creation. I enjoy your work and really like your style. I don't want to take up much of your time so, if I may ask one quick question . . .

I'm wondering if you ever promote products from other experts in exchange for commissions on sales? If so, would you consider learning more about Tom and a joint venture campaign we're putting together? If not, I completely understand and I thank you for your time, nonetheless. Both Tom and I appreciate your work and hope to have the opportunity to meet you at some point in the future.

If there is anything we can do for you, please don't hesitate to ask.

Sincerely,

Best Wishes,
Jerry Faber
For Tom Rose
www.onewebsitehere.com

Even if Tom and Jerry used the letter I suggested, they're still not guaranteed a response. But they would at least have come across as professional and respectful, two of the most important components of credibility.

Here's one more short one. Can you figure out what's wrong with this note? Besides the fact that I received it through my Facebook account—which clearly states, just like my LinkedIn Profile, *"Don't send e-mail here. Instead, please send to questions@michaelport.com."*

Michael, please accept my friend request. Tell me about what you do. I see you have written a book. What's it called? What's it about? I'm also working on a book and a project you might be interested in. I would like to discuss potential business opportunities with you.

Here, this woman, asked to friend me. Of course, my Facebook page explains what I do and lists all four of my books. So perhaps it's just my ego talking, but one would hope that she would make a little effort to, at least, scan the page—do a little homework on me. And, I think that's the rub. We all have some ego around something. To fast forward the process and ask for business without building some foundation is more than just ineffective, it's a turnoff.

You Will Connect More When You've Got the Skinny

It doesn't matter if you are prospecting, door knocking, outreaching, introducing, or just plain canvassing. If you do any or all of these without knowing the person or business you are contacting, you may as well be calling the president of the United States. At best, you'll find yourself winded, your time wasted, or your wares unwanted. Or, at worst . . . humiliated. No one wants to feel like a cheesy, shady, pushy, or unprepared salesperson.

So, you say at the end of the day you want to create a never-ending pool of heartwarming and bank account–filling clients? You want to capture more sales? You want to get booked solid? Make more money? Create a nest egg? Then, do me a favor. Show up front, center, and in the know with all the people you want to know. There's no minimizing your overall effectiveness and confidence when you're packin' preparation. So find out . . .

1. *What motivates the person?* What really gets the person's juices flowing? What makes his eyes sparkle? It might be business, family, or hobbies. Look at the photos, books, and other things sitting on or near his desk or on his web site or social media pages. What is he reading, referring to others, or genuinely interested in?
2. *What has the person accomplished?* Do an online search. Go to her site and do a Google Image search if you don't know what her smiling face looks like yet. Who is singing her praises? Has she won awards, received acknowledgments, public recognition, or publication announcements?
3. *What common interests might you have?* How have your paths crossed? Express your compassion, enthusiasm, and understanding for these

shared interests. Keep your focus coming back to the person. Use these common interests as a starting place to learn more about how they feel and think about the world.

4. *Who are the person's peers?* Do you have any mutual friends or social circle overlap? Do you have common Facebook friends or Twitter followers? And, are you involved in these circles? Be informed and stay connected.

5. *Who is his competition?* Know the opportunities and challenges he faces in his business. What challenges will you help him overcome? And what opportunities will you, ultimately, help him fulfill?

6. *What unique benefits do you offer?* What do others love about the way you do business? Be easy. Know your strengths. Show up as the kind of person people love being with and want to do business with.

7. *What excites you about knowing or working with this person?* We all want to feel appreciated, acknowledged, and respected. Share how the person's work and opinions have influenced or affected you. Stay positive, be yourself, and be complimentary.

8. *What do you believe is possible for the person?* No matter how confident or successful we appear, all of us have limiting beliefs. Can you see areas of business or life where the person has been holding back? Describe in detail (but keep it to yourself, for now) the true potential you see for the person based on what they want and need. As you get to know each other, you *may* decide to share what you see.

9. *What is your current status or role in the person's life?* Don't overrate or exaggerate who you are or why the person should work or connect with you. Be realistic about what you bring to the table and how you see the relationship unfolding. The best relationships grow slowly and with a foundation of trust.

10. *How can you become an indispensable asset to the person?* Do you truly know how and why the person should know or work with you? Do you believe that her life will be happier, easier, fuller, richer, or just plain better with the benefit of you and your services?

Sales aren't always sensible. Connecting isn't always cool. Even if your proposition seems picture perfect . . . life, decisions, and relationships are always wrapped up in underlying influences. Some of these foundational influences we can see quickly at first glance, while others take a bit more time.

But, when you show up knowledgeable and prepared, you address the human needs of the people you want to serve, and you are closer to meeting both the other person's needs and your own. You might have a shot at getting what you ask for. Plus, aren't conversations just easier and more fun when you know and share these commonalities. Doors stop slamming. People start playing and they start paying, too.

When initiating your direct outreach strategy, please make sure that your efforts are targeted, individualized, valuable, and legitimate so they are not perceived as spam and are instead appreciated and acted upon.

Using the Book Yourself Solid Direct Outreach Strategy is all about making personal connections. Whichever of the following direct outreach tools you employ, you should be reaching out to others from the heart, in a way that is genuine and authentic for you.

When I was an actor (that was my first career) I had a modicum of success. I appeared in *Sex and the City, Third Watch, Law & Order, All My Children, The Pelican Brief, Down to Earth*, and many other shows. I also did hundreds of television commercials and voiceovers, but hung up my hat for what I thought was the meaning and stability of a career in the corporate world. Boy was I wrong about the "meaning" thing. Anyhow . . . in my acting days, I recall blowing auditions because I was trying to knock it out of the park. Instead of focusing on getting the callback, I was focusing on getting the part. What I should have done was focus on getting the callback. Then, once I had the callback, work on getting the second callback. Then, once I had the second callback, work to get the producer's meeting. Once I had the producer's meeting, work to get the screen test, and so on. I want you to do the same thing with your direct outreach. Take it one step at a time and you'll do fine, and it will feel more authentic to you.

Only One Link in the Chain of Destiny
Can Be Handled at a Time

There are lots of different tools that you can use to reach out to other people. You can write e-mails, letters, or postcards. You can reach out to people through social media sites including, but not limited to, Facebook, Twitter, and LinkedIn. You can use the phone. And you can do what I call the whatever-it-takes direct outreach, as long as it doesn't get you arrested; like parachuting into the backyard of the CEO of Google because you think you have a great service to offer his company. It will get you noticed but not in a good way.

These tools can be instruments with which you can make beautiful music or they can be weapons of mass destruction. It just depends on how you use them. My mantra is Winston Churchill's quote: "It is a mistake to look too far ahead. Only one link of the chain of destiny can be handled at a time." Keep that on the top of your mind as you progress through the direct outreach process and you'll be able to avoid desperate direct outreach measures. You'll build trust over time instead and end up swimming in success.

When reaching out to others, you'll go through multiple stages of relationship development. At each stage of the process you'll, hopefully, build more trust and earn more credibility with your new friend, much like the Book Yourself Solid Sales Cycle Process that you learned in Chapter 6. And, just like the sales cycle, no relationship will develop in the exact same way. There isn't a secret formula that will guarantee everyone will love you and do exactly as you wish but there is a way to know whom to contact when, how to make contact, and whether to do it again—and the method requires a well-developed social intelligence.

Socially Successful Conduct

When I'm asked, "What are the best marketing and sales books ever written?" My answer is always the same, "Besides my books?" Kidding. In all seriousness, my answer is, just one: *Social Intelligence: The New Science of Human Relationships*, by Daniel Goleman, a popular science writer. Why a book that draws on social neuroscience research to help learn how to market and sell professional services? Because, social intelligence can be defined as a person's competence to comprehend his or her environment and react appropriately for socially successful conduct. And socially successful conduct is what ensures successful direct outreach.

Understanding the concepts people use to make sense of their social relations can help you understand things like, *What situation am I in and how do I talk to this kind of person?* You can also learn rules that help you draw references like, *What did he mean by that?* as well as plan your actions so you can decide, *What am I going to do about that?*

You may or may not like this concept, depending on your interpretation of self, but your ability to succeed in many entrepreneurial endeavors is, in large part, based on your self-awareness and social savvy. Being able to understand yourself and what's going on with others and then skillfully responding to them is a question of social intelligence, not how many different clever pitches you've memorized or methods you've got on hand to impress.

According to Goleman, humans are wired to connect, neurologically speaking. Holy rapid-fire synapses, Batman! That means you are wired to market and sell! But really, all brain function aside, you've already got the mental crampons to do the steep climbing and naturally scale to the top of your class.

Marvel at this. The news gets even better. Goleman doesn't believe that these competencies (the ability to connect) are necessarily innate, but rather can be learned capabilities, if worked on and developed to achieve outstanding performance. Darn-tootin' right, my sharp, big thinker. There's nothing phantom about your direct outreach success. To perform at your highest level and enhance how you connect to real people in the real world, increase your social intelligence. With diligence, reflection, and the commitment to improve, set aside time to study your:

- *Self-awareness.* The ability to read your own emotions and recognize their impact on others while using gut feelings to guide decisions.
- *Self-management.* Involves controlling your emotions, impulses, and the ability to adapt to changing circumstances.

- *Social awareness*. Your ability to sense, understand, and react to others' emotions while comprehending social networks.
- *Relationship management*. The ability to inspire, influence, and develop others while managing conflict.

While you are at it:

- Toss the trite sales pitch and never formulate another "smart" thought. Develop the keen ability to listen and hear what others truly want and need.
- Tear up the How-to-Get-Anything-You-Want-in-3-Easy-Steps manual and increase your empathy by entering into the realm of others' feelings.
- Step away from the PowerPoint presentation and study your self-presentation so you can foster credibility, trust, and connection confidence.

Social intelligence is defined as a person's competence to comprehend his environment and react appropriately for socially successful conduct. This brand of intelligence is therefore *the* most important component of your direct outreach strategies.

Understanding the concepts people use to make sense of their social relations can help you improve your social awareness, presence, authenticity, clarity, and empathy. Bottom line: you'll be more attuned to the needs and desires of others, which will make you more relevant and influential.

The Book Yourself Solid List of 20

Make a list of 20 people within your industry with whom you'd like to develop professional relationships. These are people whom you do not yet know—influencers within your target market who can help you get booked solid. This is your BYS List of 20. The list never leaves your side.

It sits on your desk. Lives on your computer. And travels with you when you're on the road. Why 20 and why must you keep it with you at all times? Since your success is, in large part, determined by the people within your industry who are willing to refer others to you or to put you in front of your ideal clients or endorse you, you need to keep these people at the top of your mind. Keeping this list by your side will ensure that you're thinking of them and, if you do, you'll begin to notice opportunities to connect with them and get to know them. And 20, because it's a large enough number to keep your focus expansive but narrow enough that you won't be overwhelmed.

4.11.1 Written Exercise: Identify a minimum of three and a maximum of 20 people you'd like to reach out to directly and personally. (These may be prospective clients, decision makers at an organization or association, or the press.) At this moment, you might not think you can fill out your list of 20, but now that you know what you need to do, you'll start to take notice of the people you should add to this list. You'll see in a minute how your list will grow far beyond just 20 people.

In the Book Yourself Solid® marketing software at BookYourselfSolid. com/software, there is a special section for your BYS List of 20. Here's what the software will help you do with you list. (If you're not using the software, make sure you find another way to track this process and create an accountability structure of some sort to make sure you get it done.)

- Each day, the system will prompt you to reach out to the person at the top of the list, giving you options on exactly how to connect with him.
- After you've reached out to this person, the system will place this person in the twentieth spot on the list and prompt you to connect with him again after 20 business days, which is about one month.

- Now that this person has been moved to the end of the list, the person who was Number Two on the list becomes Number One and each other person on the list moves up one spot. This way your list of 20 always stays at 20.

This direct outreach activity occurs every day. You'll reach out to one new person, each and every day, and you'll follow up with people you've already reached out to, each and every day. This is critical. Dedicated, disciplined, and determined action is key to your direct outreach success. Remember, the Book Yourself Solid List of 20 is your wish list. Your list of 20 people who could have a significant impact on your business through their referrals, introductions, and advice. Do this daily and you'll be booked solid in no time flat.

4.11.2 Booked Solid Action Step: Reach out to the first person on your list of 20 and then add her to your follow-up system. Then add a new person to your list of 20.

Making Your Case

When you get to the point in a relationship at which it's time to make your case for something you want, usually after the initial courtship, the next step is to expand upon your reason for contacting her and make your case. To do this, there are three things that others take into account, whether consciously or unconsciously, when they consider a proposal you make:

1. Is it going to be successful?
2. Is it worth doing?
3. Is this person able to do what she says she can?

If you get a resounding "Yes!" for each question, you're in. If your reader raises an eyebrow at even one of the questions, you've probably gone as far as you're going to go with this person. For your direct outreach to be effective, all the questions must be answered in the affirmative. Also, to make sure all your bases are covered, before you make any calls or send out any letters or e-mail, ask yourself the following questions:

- Do I connect with the reader about one of her accomplishments?
- Do I indicate that I will follow up?
- Do I know how I'm going to follow up?
- Am I being direct without pushing?
- Am I being real in the message?
- Am I clear about the next steps?

Whatever-It-Takes Direct Outreach

You can do a lot to grab attention, but attention is only valuable if it shows you off in a light that's flattering. If you're a creative soul with a strong and developed sense of play, you'll have a lot of fun conceiving of and executing no-rules attention-grabbing direct outreach campaigns. Because, yeah, there may be a time when someone you really want to connect with is just not paying attention.

Years ago, when I was a vice president at an entertainment company, I had a boss who swore, literally, every which way till Sunday that I had to get a particular executive at a big cosmetics firm to agree to sponsor one of our programs. The only problem was that the executive wouldn't take my calls. I tried to explain to my boss that I didn't think they were the right fit for us, but he disagreed and directed me to make it happen.

After a few more weeks of trying to get a meeting with the executive, I was about to give up when his assistant, the toughest gatekeeper I'd ever encountered, let slip that the executive was at lunch when I called. Just making pleasant conversation, I asked, "Oh, yeah? What'd he go for today?" "Chinese, it's his favorite . . ." she replied, without thinking much about it. "Okay, thanks. Have a nice day!" I said and hung up.

The next day I had a great big order of Chinese food delivered to him at that exact same time. Inside the order was the proposal for the project. Twenty minutes after the food arrived, I called him. This time I was put right through. I said, "Will you take a look at my proposal now?" "No," he answered. "Why not?" I asked. "Because I don't like any of the dishes you sent over." "What do you like?" I asked. He told me. I said, "If I send these over tomorrow, will you read my proposal and take a meeting with me?" He said, "No, but I will read your proposal. If I like it, then I'll take a meeting with you." I said, "Great. When would you like me to follow up?" He told me and we said goodbye. He did like the proposal and subsequently took a meeting with me, but we never actually made a deal. It turned out that our companies really weren't a good fit, just like I was telling my boss. But we became friendly, and he introduced me to one of my first clients after I left the corporate world and started my own business. You just never know.

One of my clients was trying to connect with a meeting planner at a large multinational corporation and couldn't get the planner to give him the time of day. After all his other direct outreach attempts failed, he sent her a coconut with a note that said, "You're a tough nut to crack. How about it?" She was still laughing when she called him to schedule an appointment.

Think creatively about what kind of fun, outrageous, no-rules attention-grabbing direct outreach strategies would work for you. Really let loose and let the ideas flow freely.

4.11.3 Written Exercise: List five wild, wacky, and unique ways to make a personal connection, especially with anyone you've been unsuccessful connecting with in the more traditional ways.

Direct Outreach Plan

There are many ways to connect with potential clients and customers, but none of the concepts I laid out are effective without a plan. After you identify a person or organization you'd like to reach out to, what do you do? Do you create a plan and then execute the plan? No? Well, that's okay because now you will and you'll be delighted with the success your new plan will bring. Each day, when working with your BYS List of 20, here's how to keep it simple.

1. Identify the individual you're going to reach out to.
2. Choose the steps you'll take to connect with her.
3. Create a schedule for your initiatives.
4. Execute the plan.
5. Evaluate the plan.

Patience and Persistence Pay Off

Remember that there is no *trick* to direct outreach. The magic formula to direct outreach, if there is one, is a consistent and open course of action throughout the life of your business. Direct outreach, like networking and keeping in touch, is something that must become a part of your regular routine. It takes time, but if you're patient and persistent, you *will* book yourself solid.

12

The Book Yourself Solid Referral Strategy

For it is in giving that we receive.

—Saint Francis of Assisi

Imagine enjoying deeper relationships with every client you work with while attracting three or four times as many wonderful new clients as you have right now. It's not only possible but simple and inexpensive. The key lies in generating client referrals. By starting an organized referral program, you can immediately and effortlessly connect with an increasing number of potential new clients.

Because your clients enjoy and respect working with you, they will be eager to recommend your services and products to their friends and family. In fact, the vast majority of your new clients already come to you as a result of word-of-mouth referrals, either directly or indirectly. If I had to, I'd guess that you don't have a program in place to benefit from all the word-of-mouth promotion that you could be receiving.

It is simple to increase your referral quotient exponentially. How many referrals do you get without a referral system right now? Now triple or quadruple that number. That is the potential increase in clients you could be working with as early as next month. Referral-generated clients are often more loyal, consistent, and better suited to you than any other category of potential clients you could find.

Quick Referral Analysis

Let's look at how you've already received referrals. By identifying a situation in the past where a client or colleague, or someone else altogether, referred a client to you, you will recognize patterns that will help you consistently produce the results you desire.

4.12.1 Written Exercise: Start by remembering the last time a quality referral came to you:

1. From whom did the referral come?
2. What was the referral for, specifically?
3. Did the referral need your services immediately?
4. How were you contacted—by the person making the referral or the potential client?
5. Had you educated the referrer about your services before he made the referral?
6. How did you accept the referral and follow up?
7. Is that new referral a continuing client today?

You may have already noticed some of your strengths in generating referrals, or perhaps parts of the process need a little of your attention. Either way, we're creating an easy and profitable process.

Finding Referral Opportunities

Referral opportunities are all around you, and most are slipping through your fingers right now because you either aren't noticing them or you aren't acting on them. Start by choosing one day of the week that you can focus on where and when you could be asking for referrals. Don't get nervous yet! You are simply increasing your awareness of potential referral opportunities. Pay close attention and mentally seek out every possible situation in which you could see yourself asking for referrals.

4.12.2 Written Exercise: Create a referral tracking log based on the seven questions in the preceding written exercise and begin to track daily referral opportunities. Your referral tracking log should focus on the details of your referral interactions. Doing so will help you see what works and what doesn't work in the referral process. If you study these interactions, you can learn from them and adjust your behavior accordingly while significantly increasing your referral quotient. You're going to be pleasantly surprised at the plethora of untapped referral opportunities that are appearing before you every day.

Beginning the Referral Process

Are you ready to begin working with eager new clients who have heard about your expertise and seek the benefits you offer? Never forget how profitable and prosperous your business can be. How committed are you? Are you convinced that this is something you absolutely must do? Yes? Okay, let's continue, you unshakable, committed one, you!

Step 1: Identify Your Clients' Benefits

Keep their benefits in mind when you speak to your clients about referrals. These are the reasons they work with you and why they would want others to do the same.

> **4.12.3 Written Exercise:** Create a list of the benefits your clients will experience by working with you. Keep going until you've exhausted all the possible benefits.

Step 2: Identify Why Others Would Refer Clients to You

What are the emotional, social, and professional benefits that go along with being someone who refers people in need to those who can help?

> **4.12.4 Written Exercise:** Bring to mind your two best clients and list the reasons they would want to refer their friends and family to you. Again, think in terms of benefits. How do they feel after having referred their friends and family?
>
> *Examples:* They feel great helping their friends improve their business or life in a specific way. They feel special having made a positive influence in their friends' lives. They feel important and knowledgeable about something. They feel connected and accepted when they introduce friends and business associates to a high quality professional. They feel confident that they are a valuable resource in their friends' lives and that they sent them to someone who is qualified, committed, and well-liked.

Step 3: Identify the Types of Referrals You Seek

Remember your Red Velvet Rope Policy of working only with ideal clients with whom you do your best work?

> **4.12.5 Written Exercise:** Write down the types of people you want your clients, associates, friends, and family to refer to you. Your friends and family may have no idea whom to refer to you.
>
> *Examples:* Family members, best friends, neighbors, acquaintances, work associates, small business owners, executives, people going through divorce or struggling financially.

Step 4: Identify the Places Where Your Referrers Meet Ideal Referrals

Your goal here is to help your clients and other acquaintances understand who in their lives will benefit most from your services and products and where they cross paths with these people. You are helping them get a clear picture of the people in their lives who must meet you and work with you. With these two things in mind—whom your referrals should be referring and where they will meet them—you have all you need to start on the referral path.

> **4.12.6 Written Exercise:** Write down the places where your referrers would meet or connect with good referrals for you.
>
> *Examples:* At the office, taking the kids to school, neighborhood events, sporting events, lunch appointments, after-work socializing, charity functions, the gym, political events.

Step 5: Clarify and Communicate How Your Referrers Make a Referral

Let's focus on how to help your referrers have a simple conversation with a potential referral that will effectively connect them to you and your offerings. You can't leave this to chance. Being able to articulate what you do in a way that makes you stand out from the crowd and truly connects you to the people you're meant to serve is not only necessary, it's essential for booking yourself solid.

4.12.7 Written Exercise: Write down how you'd like your referrers to refer their contacts to you. What do you want them to say? How do you want them to talk about what you do? What specific words and phrases do you want them to use? Do you want them to say that you are "the best"? Do you want them to mention that you recently received an award for outstanding community service? Get very specific. Think of yourself as a one-person PR firm. You decide how you want people to talk about you.

Step 6: Ask for Referrals

If you want to increase your referral quotient by 50 percent, the best strategy is to ask for referrals. This is the simplest part of the Book Yourself Solid Referral Strategy, as well as the most important. The preceding and following exercises will help you ask effectively. Please make sure to complete these exercises thoughtfully before you run off and just ask for referrals willy-nilly. What you can start with today is seeking out opportunities for referral conversations. Here are a few excellent situations that naturally lead to a referral conversation:

- Your ideal client thanks you for a great session or work well done.
- Your ideal client asks you for more services.
- Your ideal client asks for clarification on a process or concept.
- Your ideal client describes a past problem that you helped fix or goal you helped her achieve.

And here are some obvious situations:

- Your ideal client mentions a friend or business associate who's been facing the same challenges your client has faced.
- Your ideal client mentions she is going to an industry conference for a few days (and you serve businesses or individuals within that industry).

Or you can create the opportunity for a referral conversation by:

- Thanking clients for their energy and enthusiasm during your session or project.
- Clarifying their goals or making a suggestion to work on their own.
- Asking clients how they are feeling about the work you're doing together or about past challenges.
- Complimenting clients on their progress—always.

Once you get clients talking, ask them about the value they get from your sessions. Use this as an open door to have them talk about how your services could benefit other people or organizations they have relationships with.

Step 7: Facilitate the Referral Connection

Offer to meet, consult with, or advise anyone who is important to your clients. Let them know that you want to help educate their friends about the benefits of your services.

Hand out a card or send an e-mail that clients will pass on to friends and family. Or better yet, ask them to make the introduction today. There are times when you can take the burden of calling or sending the e-mail off of your referrer. Not because your referrer doesn't want to make the referral happen but because life gets in the way. People are busy and they can get distracted by other tasks on their to-do list. If *you* actually make the connection and do the follow-up, it's sure to happen.

The same is true any time you personally meet potential clients. They say they're going to call you, and even if they have the best of intentions, things come up that get in the way, and you don't get a call. So I suggest that when you meet someone you really connect with and who has expressed interest in your services, you call him.

Step 8: Follow Up with Referrals and Referrers

Contact new referrals and introduce them to what you have to offer—in a meaningful, connected, and helpful way. This is where your always-have-something-to-invite-people-to offer comes into play. It gives you a really easy way to start a conversation with the potential client and extend a no-risk, no-barrier invitation that is compelling and attractive. All you have to do is make a generous invitation and you've started the Book Yourself Solid Sales Cycle.

When beginning a relationship with potential clients, consider the following:

- Hold private meetings or demonstrations to eliminate any fear or embarrassment they may have about trying something new.
- Learn about any past experience with your type of services or products that they may have had and, most important, what they hope to achieve.
- Tell them what to expect, how you work, and the benefits they will experience.
- Include administrative details too: what to have available, if anything. Help clients feel as comfortable and prepared as possible.
- Provide third-party articles and facts that support your analysis in describing benefits they will achieve.
- Invite clients to work with you, and remember the Book Yourself Solid Super Simple Selling System. Offer a specific date and time that suits their schedule.

Practice Your Referral Presentation

- Speak with lots of expression, get excited, and show the passion you have for the benefits your services can offer.
- Smile.

- Make eye contact.
- Be confident.
- Open your heart.
- When your potential client starts speaking, hush up and listen.

> **4.12.8 Booked Solid Action Step:** Make the commitment to ask for referrals every day for five days straight.

Are you as excited as I am about the dozens of potential clients you're going to meet? Just think about all those potential clients who've been searching and waiting to be introduced to an expert like you. I hope and expect that you will serve your potential clients and community by immediately starting to ask for client referrals. Once you start speaking with your potential clients on a deep and personal level, they will see you as far more than just your title. They will see you with more value, dimension, and a higher level of respect.

This meaningful connection is the key to achieving a greater level of prosperity and personal satisfaction. It's the Book Yourself Solid way.

Who Wants What You Want?

While some of your clients, friends, family, and colleagues may refer others to you without your having to ask, many won't. As I mentioned earlier, it isn't that they don't want to; they're just busy with their own lives and it hasn't occurred to them. While it may feel awkward at first to ask for referrals, give it a try. You'll be surprised at how willing they are to do so once you've brought it to mind. Certainly, if they've worked with you, they'll want their friends, family, and business associates to experience the same great benefits they have. And they'll enjoy being able to help you as well. When someone has a positive effect on one's life, even in small ways, it feels good to give something back, and referrals are a great way to do it.

Other Professionals— The Other Source of Referrals

Other professionals who offer services and products that are complementary to your own, and work with your target market, are ideal sources of referrals. When you operate from a perspective of abundance and cooperation, rather than from scarcity and competition, it becomes easy to reach out to others to develop relationships that can be mutually beneficial.

The more you refer to others, the more they'll be inspired to refer to you.

Many service professionals have a formal referral group with five or six other professionals who serve the same target market but offer complementary services and products. Each member of the group works to send referrals to each other member of the group. If you join a high integrity referral group, you'll greatly extend your referral reach. You'll also build your reputation by having others talk about you and your services.

Affiliate Fees and Rewards Programs

Create rewards for those who refer others to you. A reward could be anything from a formal affiliate program, through which you pay cash for referrals, to coupons for discounts on your services, products, or programs, or a basket of gourmet food.

Some professionals worry about losing money by paying affiliate fees. The numbers tell a different story—that you'll *make* money by paying for referrals. Say you charge $500 per month for your services and you currently have 10 regular clients. You're currently earning $5,000 a month. Now let's say that each one of your 10 clients refers one more client to you at $500 per month. That's another 10 clients for another $5,000 a month. If you give a referral fee of 10 percent, you'll be paying each referrer $50 per referral for a total of $500 in referral fees. Would you spend $500 to make $5,000 for a profit of $4,500 and a new monthly income of $9,500, almost double what you were making? I would. And think about what this means if you are currently making $40,000 or $50,000 per month.

A word to the wise. It's rare that someone will refer simply because you're offering a referral commission or reward. They'll do it because they believe in you and what you stand for. The fee or reward is just a nice bonus that makes them feel all tingly inside.

Strike While the Iron Is Hot

Nurture the relationships you develop with those who refer others to you, and *always* follow up right away on any referrals you get. You'll then create not merely satisfied clients but raving fans by delivering your best work. Before you know it, you'll be booked solid.

13

The Book Yourself Solid Keep-in-Touch Strategy

Be well, do good work, and keep in touch.

—Garrison Keillor

This keep-in-touch strategy may be the most important marketing strategy you'll ever use. You already know that you need to connect with potential clients many times before they feel comfortable hiring you or purchasing your products. If you don't have a systematized and automated keep-in-touch strategy in place, you may, as the saying goes, leave a lot of business on the table. Most important, you'll miss out on the opportunity to serve the people you're meant to serve.

Many businesses fail for lack of a solid keep-in-touch marketing strategy. Either they bombard you with too much information and too many offers that turn you off, or you never hear from them at all, which leaves you feeling unimportant and irrelevant.

Consider the experience of my client Barbara. Within a few short years she had compiled more than 5,000 opt-in names for her database.

The names were captured, but Barbara never really followed up with any of them until one day when she created a promotional offer to send to her list, and she eagerly clicked *Send*. What came back were mostly e-mails from recipients inquiring as to who she was and how they knew each other. Barbara learned a valuable lesson that day: Determine the best approach for using this strategy and build it into your keep-in-touch plans!

Each time I send out my electronic newsletter, which has historically been my primary keep-in-touch strategy, I get new orders for my products and calls about my services. *Every time!* Without my solid keep-in-touch marketing strategy in place, I would not be able to build trust with people over time.

There is an important distinction to be made between following up with potential clients, colleagues, and others on a personal one-to-one level, and developing an automated keep-in-touch strategy through which you broadcast electronic newsletters, send direct mail campaigns, write blog posts, or use other publishing platforms like social media. When you've met someone and exchanged contact information, you have permission to communicate with him, and to start or continue a dialogue that is valuable to both of you. However, this does not equate to having permission to add that person to your mailing list so you can send him your newsletter or other automated or broadcast messages. All of the broadcast follow-up that you do to groups must be based on the principles of permission marketing, offering a potential client the opportunity to volunteer to be marketed to. According to Seth Godin, in his book *Permission Marketing*, "By only talking to volunteers, permission marketing guarantees that consumers pay more attention to the marketing message. It allows marketers to calmly and succinctly tell their story. It serves both consumers and marketers in a symbiotic exchange." Permission marketing is anticipated, personal, and relevant to the potential client.

- *Anticipated*—people look forward to hearing from you.
- *Personal*—the messages are directly related to the individual.
- *Relevant*—the marketing is about something the prospect is interested in.

This is essential because you want to communicate only with someone who is looking forward to hearing from you. When potential customers anticipate your marketing messages, they're more open to them. And, of course, when they have not explicitly asked you to send them things like a newsletter, and you do, it's not just possible spam, it is 100 percent pure spam—no matter how much you think they'll enjoy it.

With that said, once you get to know people, you should ask them if they'd like you to subscribe them to your newsletter. Tell them about it, what's valuable about it, when it's delivered, and any other relevant information. Then, if they accept your invitation to be on your mailing list, you have permission to send it to them along with special offers and other promotions.

Relevant, Interesting, Current, and Valuable Content

It's up to you to ensure that the content you share with your potential clients through your leveraged (one to many) keep-in-touch strategy is relevant, interesting, current, and valuable. There are six basic categories of content that meet those criteria:

1. Industry information
2. Strategies, tips, and techniques
3. Content from other sources (experts)
4. Product and service offerings
5. Cool keep-in-touch
6. Special announcements

Industry Information

Industry information that is relevant to your target market and that may or may not be widely known is excellent content to deliver to your list. You'll position yourself as an expert within your industry while providing constant value to your current and potential clients. What's more, they will appreciate the information and your generosity for sharing it.

Let's say that you certify yoga teachers. Information regarding industry standards, regulations, and laws would be helpful to your target market. Perhaps if you were a project manager, the latest findings and announcements from OSHA would be meaningful, as would information about safety issues.

Including important information in your keep-in-touch strategy also makes it more likely that your potential clients will keep the information and refer back to it, keeping you at the top of their mind for future support.

Strategies, Tips, and Techniques

Strategies, tips, and techniques is probably the most common type of content, especially for service professionals. It's the primary type of information that I deliver to my e-zine subscribers.

Despite the appeal of this content-rich approach, many service professionals fear they will give away too much of their material. "If I provide all these great tips and strategies for free, then why would anyone ever hire me?" they wonder. Of course there are some who will take everything you offer and never hire you or purchase a product, but they wouldn't be hiring you anyway, and you never know—they may be out in the world talking about what you do and how you help. I've received tons of referrals from people who are not clients just because I've helped them for *free*. Most people who eventually do hire you or buy your products will need to receive free advice and support to build the trust they need for them to believe that you can really help them. Furthermore, most people will assume that you know a lot more than what you are giving away. They'll think, "Wow! If she gives away this much great stuff, can you imagine what I'll get if I actually pay her?"

Content from Other Sources

I often provide my current and potential clients with relevant content from other people so that I can overdeliver as much as possible. This gives me a break from continuously creating content, it allows me to offer my contacts more than I can offer by myself, and it allows me to position other professionals who appreciate the promotion. There is a bonus as well: The experts I feature often return the favor by promoting me to the people *they* serve. Isn't that a win for everybody? It's also the easiest way to create great value for the people who have given you permission to serve them when you're first starting out.

Again, if you're concerned that you'll lose customers or clients because you highlight other experts, please recall this Book Yourself Solid principle:

> *There are certain people you're meant to serve and others you're not. If you can help other professionals attract business through you, you're creating more abundance for everyone involved.*

Product and Service Offerings

If you don't make offers to your potential clients, how will they know you can help them? If you aren't doing everything you can to serve the people who need your help, what are you doing? Seriously, I believe you have an obligation to offer your services to those who need them and to those whom you know you can help in a meaningful and connected way.

Here's another way of looking at it: Most of us express our values through the things we buy. We are what we purchase. Think about it. If you didn't know me but came across my personal and business financial statements from the past three months, you'd know a heck of a lot about me, like what I value and how I spend my time. If my financial records showed that I was at the bar every night and spent most of my money playing the slot machines in Vegas, you'd get a sense of what I value. If those records showed that I attend meditation class five times a week, purchase four books a month, and spend thousands of dollars a year on private schooling for my son, you'd see a person with different values.

Most of us want the opportunity to express ourselves through the things we purchase, especially when those things are adding value to our life or work. So *please* give the people you serve the opportunity to express their values by buying what you have to offer.

With that said, making only product and service offerings to your potential clients may not be appreciated very much. Your offers must be accompanied by an overdelivery of free value. My personal goal is to subscribe to the 80/20 rule when it comes to keeping in touch. That means 80 percent of my keep-in-touch marketing is based on giving away free content, opportunities, and resources that will help the people I serve, and 20 percent is made up of offers to purchase services, products, and programs that will also help the people I serve. Remember, the people who have expressed interest in your services want to know how they can work with you, and it's your responsibility to tell them and show them their options.

Cool Keep-in-Touch

You know that I love it when you express yourself. And you also know by now that you will more easily and quickly attract your ideal clients when you do. This category is the cool keep-in-touch category because it can include any fun, different, unique, or exotic method of keeping in touch, some of which may expose your quirks! Please remember that quirky does not mean weird or bizarre. It means unusual, unique, and special. So get creative! Be bold! Dare to stand out from the crowd!

For example, Susan is a hair stylist and dog lover. Each month her keep-in-touch includes a photo shoot of her and her dogs with new fun, wild, and outrageous hairstyles and colors. It is fun, memorable, and totally Susan!

What is your special, unique, and entertaining quirk that can be turned into a cool keep-in-touch strategy? The possibilities are limitless.

Special Announcements

This is a valuable method of keeping in touch if the special announcement is relevant, important, and presented as a learning tool to your target market. But be careful—it's often an overused category and can be irrelevant and annoying when it comes in the *all-about-me* form, like news about your company that is irrelevant to your contacts. How many times have you received announcements telling you about a new development in a company or about a change in management that you really cared about?

4.13.1 Written Exercise: What is the best kind of content to include in your keep-in-touch strategy based on your interests and the needs and desires of your target market?

Choosing Your Keep-in-Touch Tools

Once you've got great content to share with your clients and potential clients, you've got to choose how best to deliver that content to them. These are the most common methods:

- Electronic newsletters (e-zines)
- Printed newsletters
- Phone
- Postcards and mailers
- Social media (Facebook, Twitter, LinkedIn)

Historically (well, at least during the 2000s) e-zines (e-mail newsletters) were the easiest and most cost effective way to keep in touch with large numbers of people. That's been changing, in large part because of consumer behavior—most of us ignore as much e-mail as we possibly can because of the never-ending, mass proliferation of spam and, to a lesser degree, because of the advent and rise of social media as an alternative keep-in-touch tool. Paper newsletters can be effective marketing tools, but they can be costly to print and mail. The phone is a wonderful direct outreach tool but often the most anxiety provoking of them all, so I say stay away from cold calling and wait to get on the phone until you've had at least one positive interaction with your direct outreach subject. Postcards and mailers are great for one-on-one correspondence, but again, they are costly and time-consuming endeavors when attempting to keep in touch with large groups of contacts. When you grow to a multimillion-dollar small business, we'll talk about including a paper newsletter and other mailers in your marketing campaigns to increase your touchpoints with your subscribers and contacts; and we'll talk about how to use social media (Facebook, Twitter, and LinkedIn) to keep in touch with large groups of people in Chapter 16. For now, let's focus on e-zines, which are still an effective marketing tool for:

- Building your mailing list, adding value, and marketing to your subscribers over and over again.
- Selling your products and services while you're delivering great content and adding value.
- Positioning yourself as an expert within your industry or field.
- Keeping in touch with all the people who've expressed interest in your products or services, and reaching them all with the click of a button.
- Creating a viral marketing campaign (it grows exponentially as it's passed along to others) because your subscribers will send it to their friends when they think it will help them.
- Creating ongoing marketing campaigns that cost virtually nothing and reap great rewards.

Ninety percent of my product and service sales are generated from 20 percent of the space in my monthly e-zine as well as through other direct e-mail promotions. Let me be clear about this because it's so important.

I track my sales and know that 90 percent of my online sales are in direct response to my monthly newsletter, not from a new visitor landing on one of my web sites. As you'll learn when we discuss your web strategy, your web site is used most effectively as a vehicle for enticing people to opt in to your subscriber list so that you deliver value and build trust over time. Your follow-up is where you reap the financial and personal rewards of your marketing efforts.

E-Zine Format

There are many ways to format an e-zine. For starters, I recommend whatever is easiest, most cost effective, and aligned with your strengths. If you have a strong desire to learn how to edit HTML, then by all means start right now learning how to edit your own HTML e-zine. However, if you're not interested in learning this skill, farm out the work to a professional or use templates. You'll write the e-zine, send it to the professional, and she'll create the HTML version with graphics, colors, and other pizzazz.

You don't need an HTML newsletter to appear professional, however. Some of the most successful Internet marketers use text-only e-zines, which generally have a higher rate of delivery success because they are less likely to get caught in spam filters. Spam filters tend to detect more HTML than plain text, and the filters block a higher percentage of HTML e-mails.

4.13.2 Written Exercise: What format will you use to send out your e-zine . . . and why?

E-Zine Layout

The layout of the text in your e-zine is just as important as what you have to say. Most of your readers will not actually be reading your e-zine.

First, they'll scan it. Then, if the issue seems relevant and interesting, they'll read it more carefully. To make your e-zine compelling, easy to scan, and easy to read, make the width of your text small, especially if you're using plain text e-mail. There is an industry standard for e-mail that suggests you do a hard carriage return on your text at no more than 65 characters so that your text will be readable in most e-mail programs. If the text line is too long, your reader may have to scroll right and left to read it. And remember, most of your readers won't read—they'll scan. If they can't see all of the text in their screen, from left to right, they won't be able to scan.

Keep your paragraphs to no more than seven lines unless they are testimonials, and shorter paragraphs are just fine, if not better. Large blocks of text are harder to scan. And finally, to make the layout support your content, consider the following criteria when writing any kind of keep-in-touch or promotional content:

- Use headlines to get your readers interested.
- Use case studies and testimonials to add credibility to your claims.
- Write from your reader's point of view.
- Write about benefits, not just features.
- Read your text out loud to make sure it sounds conversational.
- Get a colleague or customer to review your e-zine and make suggestions.
- Write as if you're speaking to one person—the person who's reading the newsletter.
- Be specific.
- Be concise.
- Keep it simple.

E-Zine Frequency

Frequency depends on a lot of factors but should be mostly based on what you're trying to accomplish with your e-zine. Some people send out weekly e-zines, some twice a month, and others monthly or quarterly.

I've even seen some daily e-zines. I suggest you begin with a monthly e-zine. Daily, and even weekly may be a bit much for you and your subscribers when you're starting out, and quarterly probably won't get the visibility you're looking for. That said, I do a weekly e-zine, plus special announcements and promotions. The weekly frequency keeps me plenty busy and is just right for my readers.

To see firsthand how I create connection with—and value for—my newsletter subscribers, go to MichaelPort.com and subscribe to my free e-zine now. It'll continue to help you book yourself solid. Oh, and you'll also get a free chapter from each of my other three books: *Beyond Booked Solid, The Contrarian Effect,* and *The Think Big Manifesto.*

Automating Your Keep-in-Touch Strategy

Creating a monthly e-zine, and whatever other content and offers you plan to provide to those you are keeping in touch with is only the beginning of implementing the strategy. I know I'm repeating myself, but if you don't have a system for automating your keep-in-touch strategy, you don't have a keep-in-touch strategy. It's time to:

- Build and manage your database.
- Follow up with prospects and professional opportunities.

Building and Managing Your Database

I'm sure you've met hundreds, if not thousands of people over your professional life you've not kept in touch with. Now that you're a service professional wanting to attract more clients than you can handle, I'll bet you wish you had kept in touch with all those folks. Well, no matter! You will keep in touch with everyone you meet from this point forward. It is encouraging, however, to reflect on all of the people you have met with whom you did not keep in touch because it shows you how easy it can be to build a database of potential clients and networking contacts.

Now that you'll put your focus on building your database, you'll be booked solid in no time.

Choosing a Database Program   To have an effective keep-in-touch strategy, you'll need a reliable and comprehensive database program. There are many database programs from which you can choose, and more than I can list here, but I'll give you a few examples and important criteria to consider as you make your choice.

There are two important differentiators that I want you to consider: sales management versus contact management. CRM (customer relationship management) systems like the Infusionsoft®, Salesforce®, Goldmine®, or Act® are all designed to manage not only contacts but also the sales process, to turn leads into opportunities and opportunities into clients. Whereas, contact management systems, like Microsoft Outlook® or Apple® Contacts, typically provide a way to organize your company and personal contacts, some of which may be sales opportunities. Others may be networking or referral opportunities but have a very limited functionality related to the tracking and managing of sales leads and sales opportunities. Contact management systems may provide a way to take notes on a record, but they don't provide a good way to track the sales process, what might be the most critical process in your business.

You see where I come down on this issue: you need to start using a CRM system to manage, not only your contacts but also your sales process, from lead generation to opportunity management to sales conversion.

Using a CRM system you'll be able to:

- Track performance of lead sources—it's likely that a small amount of lead generation efforts will drive the bulk of your sales.
- Create a consistent sales process—if you have even one person working with you—it will help you see what is driving results.
- Increase the speed of your sales conversion—respond to new leads quickly, follow up frequently with e-mails and calls, and nurture leads that don't convert immediately.

- Keep track of activities—get things done when you need to and when you say you will.
- Report on past performance—if you don't know what you've done, how are you going to know what you need to do.
- Forecast future sales—if you don't know where you're going, how are you going to get there?

Remember, the key isn't purchasing the program to help you manage your keep-in-touch strategy, it's actually using the program to keep in touch with potential clients, current clients, and past clients. Bottom line: CRM is about managing these relationships—better.

Entering Data   You certainly have to get a new lead's contact information, but that's not where most people fall short. It's that they don't actually do anything with it. You must enter and store it in the system and then continue to connect with the lead, building trust over time. The size of your database, but most importantly the *quality* of the relationships you have with the people in your database, is directly proportional to the financial health of your business.

Back Up Your Data   Back up your data daily. Your database is the foundation of your business. If you lose that integral support structure, you can't replace it; you're essentially starting over, which could cost you many hours, if not months, of time and money.

Getting and Following Up with Prospects and Professional Opportunities

Following up with prospects and professional opportunities is a major key to your success. It's an investment that will deliver huge returns.

Your Book Yourself Solid Sales Cycle is based on the success of your keep-in-touch strategy and requires you to deliver great value. Please, I implore you to make this a top priority.

4.13.3 Written Exercise: How are you going to automate your keep-in-touch strategy?

The Book Yourself Solid Keep-in-Touch Strategy is the key to ensuring that your marketing efforts are effective and successful. Keeping in touch with your potential clients is critical to developing trust and credibility, and keeping in touch will keep you foremost in the minds of your potential clients when they need you, your services, or the products and programs you offer.

14

The Book Yourself Solid Speaking Strategy

It usually takes me more than three weeks to prepare a good impromptu speech.

—Mark Twain

The Book Yourself Solid Speaking Strategy can be used by virtually any service professional to get in front of potential ideal clients based on your knowledge, talents, and strengths.

The wonderful thing about sharing your knowledge is that it's rewarding for both you and your audience. They will leave your presentation or event a little smarter, thinking bigger, and with an action plan that will help them implement what you've taught them. You will benefit because you'll know you've helped others, which is the reason you do what you do. And at the same time, you'll increase awareness for your services and products.

To get in front of your target market you can promote yourself or have others promote you. When you promote yourself, you're inviting your target market to something that is going to help them solve their problems and move them toward their compelling desires. When you are promoted by others, they put you in front of your target market. You may want to travel both routes. I do. Using the Book Yourself Solid Speaking Strategy, I have been able to speak to more than 100,000 service professionals over the last two years alone. You, too, can see these kinds of results using speaking and demonstrating to get your message out to the people you're meant to serve.

Self-Promotion

Of course, all of the Book Yourself Solid 7 Core Self-Promotion Strategies require that you promote yourself in one way or another. Even using the Book Yourself Solid Speaking Strategy to get other people to put you in front of your target market requires that you promote yourself to the person who is going to give you that platform.

First, let's look at pure self-promotion, such as inviting your target market to events that you produce—not necessarily big workshops or conferences but simple, community-building, meaningful, enlightening events at which you can shine, show off your products and services, and build your reputation and credibility in your marketplace. These types of speaking and demonstrating events might fall into the category of an always-have-something-to-invite-people-to offer or they may be one-off events.

Conference Calls

Start a monthly or weekly call for clients to learn the benefits of working with you. Prepare a new, timely, and relevant topic every time. Pick up a magazine in your industry and use one of the articles to inspire your topic, invite guests to discuss their area of expertise, and ask your clients to tell you what they'd most like to hear about. The rest of the call will naturally flow into a Q&A session. Here are a few ideas to get you started and to spark your inspiration and creativity for your own unique ideas:

- Any service professional can offer a monthly or weekly Q&A on his field of expertise. No planning necessary—just show up and shine.

- Accountants can offer quarterly conference calls on updates on tax law along with planning strategies for decreasing tax liability, for example.
- Financial planners can offer weekly conference calls on the best strategies for building wealth using the products they sell.
- Internet marketing consultants can offer web conferences giving updates on search engine optimization and other web traffic generation strategies.
- Personal coaches can offer conference calls on their area of expertise: reducing anxiety, increasing focus, setting boundaries.

If you're doing a conference call, or teleseminar, as it's often called, it won't cost you a dime. There are hundreds of companies that provide these types of services for free, like FreeConference.com and NoCostconference.com, and others that charge nominal fees, but provide additional features, like MaestroConference.com. Record each call and link to it from your web site—all these services have conference recording built in. Those who couldn't make the actual call will still have the opportunity to listen to it and benefit from it. Archiving the calls on your web site or blog is also a wonderful way of immediately establishing trust and credibility with new web visitors.

Demonstrations and Educational Events

These opportunities are similar to conference calls except that they're conducted in person. Demonstrations and educational events are an excellent way to reach potential ideal clients if your services are physical or location-based or if the people you serve are all located in the same town or city. This approach is also a great alternative if you feel that a conference call doesn't speak to your strengths. This format is another opportunity to get creative and express yourself. For example, you could create some excitement with an open house or outdoor demo at a park or at any other venue. Don't just invite your potential clients but also your current clients, friends, or colleagues who know the value of your services and are willing to talk about their experiences.

- Fitness professionals can offer a weekly physical challenge for clients and potential clients. Ask clients to bring a new friend every week. Each week a new type of workout would be planned with a social event afterward.
- Real estate agents can offer weekly real estate investor tours for which they fill a van or tour bus with active real estate investors and scour the neighborhood hotspots.
- Professional organizers can offer a monthly makeover in which they go to a potential or new client's office or home, along with a small group of 10 or 15 people (it's not bad to have a waiting list for these types of offerings), and the professional organizer reorganizes the space and teaches the guests the basics of how to be more productive and effective through an organized office.
- A hair stylist can do something similar with the monthly makeover concept. She could even offer a contest or raffle each month, and the winner would get the makeover.
- Any service professional can host a no-cost or low-cost morning retreat. Be playful and adventurous. It doesn't have to be expensive, just creative. Allow clients to get to know you and meet other people with similar interests and goals. Make it as simple as serving tea, whole fresh fruit, and scones—and share your wealth of knowledge.
- Start a niche club. Consider cool stuff clients would enjoy. Think about activities that you love. Start a creative brainstorming club, weekly play group, or fun family outing.
- Start a product review club. People love sampling products and trying out new solutions. Give clients a taste of your work and introduce them to fun product overviews that will get them connected to your services. Invite other like-minded professionals to join you if you want to add dimension to the event.

Introduce these offerings at the end of your Book Yourself Solid Dialogue. Add, "I'd like to invite you to _____" or "Why don't you join me and my clients for a fun, playful _____." Try out different venues and topics until you discover the one that works for you. Remember, the difference between the typical client-snagging mentality and the Book Yourself Solid way is that the typical client-snagging mentality plays it safe so as not to look foolish. The Book Yourself Solid way asks, "How can I be unconventional and risky so as to create interest and excitement for my services?"

You will never be at a loss for different things to try or experiences to create for your clients and potential clients. You want to invite as many people as possible to these events for three important reasons:

1. You want to leverage your time so you're connecting with as many potential clients as possible in the shortest amount of time.
2. You want to leverage the power of communities. When you bring people together, they create far more energy and excitement than you can on your own. Your guests will also see other people interested in what you have to offer, and that's the best way to build credibility.
3. You'll be viewed as a generous connector. If you're known in your marketplace as someone who brings people together, it will help you build your reputation and increase your likeability.

4.14.1 Written Exercise: Create three ways that you can instantly add value to your potential and current clients by way of an invitation.

Getting Promoted by Others

Now let's address the second approach—getting promoted by others to speak or demonstrate. I won't address the details of being a professional speaker, someone who makes a living speaking to associations and organizations, but rather how you can use public speaking to create awareness for what you have to offer and get booked solid. If you're interested in becoming a professional speaker, pick up a copy of Alan Weiss's book *Money Talks: How to Make a Million as a Speaker* or Robert Bly's *Getting Started in Speaking, Training, or Seminar Consulting.*

If you're speaking for exposure, you probably won't be paid up front for most of the speaking and demonstrating you do, except possibly an honorarium and travel costs. You're doing it for the opportunity to address potential clients and to interest them in your offerings. There's an assumed trade involved. You receive marketing opportunities, and the association or organization that brings you in to speak or demonstrate gets great content that serves their constituents. The key is to balance the two. If you are invited to speak and you spend 90 percent of your time talking about what you have to offer, you won't be well received and you certainly won't be invited back. However, if you don't make any offers at all, you'll be sure to miss great opportunities for booking yourself solid.

Booking Your Way Up

If you would like to be promoted by others, you need to develop trusting relationships with decision makers at associations and organizations that serve your target market. In the business world, these people are often called meeting planners. At your local associations, these people may be called communication or education directors or something different altogether. Bottom line: They are the people who can get you in front of your target audience.

There are thousands of associations and organizations that serve your target market. For example, colleges and universities all across the country sponsor executive extension courses, community learning programs, and all kinds of management and small business seminars and workshops. And to create comprehensive programs, the colleges and universities will often invite guest experts, like you, to make a presentation on their area of expertise. Trade associations and networking groups all need speakers to address their memberships, and this phenomenon has spread into the public sector as well with organizations like The Learning Annex, The Learning Connection, Shared Vision Network, and others, becoming a big part of the local communities they serve. The most potentially rewarding venues will offer:

- Large audiences.
- Audiences that include potential buyers for your products and services.
- Name recognition that is prestigious.
- The opportunity to sell products at the event (books and CDs, for example).

There is a hierarchy of associations and organizations that can sponsor you and your services. I start the list with the lower-level organizations and associations and work up to the highest-level organizations and associations. The lower-level organizations are usually smaller and less prestigious, but don't let the hierarchy fool you. You can fill your practice by speaking in front of members of the lowest-level associations and organizations, but you don't necessarily have to start with the lowest and work your way up. It may help to have previous speaking experience with some of the lower-level associations and organizations for you to get booked with the higher-level associations and organizations.

Level One

Your entry point to speaking and demonstrating is with local not-for-profit community groups or organizations like the community center, churches, YMCA and YMHA, service clubs, or political action groups and chambers of commerce. Some of these groups serve a particular target market, but most are made up of individuals who share similar interests. They're good places to find potential clients and great places to work on your material and practice speaking and demonstrating in front of other people.

4.14.2 Written Exercise: Identify several Level One groups or organizations that you can contact.

Level Two

Seek out local for-profit business groups, learning programs, and schools, including schools of continuing education and networking groups like The Learning Annex, Business Network International, colleges, and others.

These organizations are higher up the value scale for you because they serve more targeted groups of people who are really there to learn what you have to offer. Furthermore, they tend to be slightly more prestigious than the local not-for-profit community groups.

4.14.3 Written Exercise: Identify several Level Two groups or organizations that you can contact.

Level Three

At Level Three, you'll be speaking at local and regional trade associations. There are more local and regional trade associations than you can count or ever speak to in a lifetime. Do a quick search on Google to find associations for everything from home-based businesses, electricians, and computer programmers, to lawyers, and family winemakers. Local and regional trade associations and organizations are excellent opportunities for you to connect with your target market because you know the exact makeup of your audience.

Another avenue to consider, depending on your target market and the kind of services you provide, is businesses, both large and small. I put the smaller businesses on Level Three and the larger corporations on Level Four. Many companies offer educational workshops, programs, and conferences just for their employees. Sometimes they'll bring in a speaker for a lunchtime session. Other times, the setup is more formal, and you'll speak to large groups of people at a conference center. Just be clear on why you're targeting a particular business. Know what you have to offer them that will serve their needs and what opportunities the business or the individuals who make up the business offer you.

4.14.4 Written Exercise: Identify several Level Three local or regional trade associations or businesses that you can contact.

Level Four

From here you're just going to keep moving up the trade association ladder, from local and regional trade associations to national trade associations and then to international trade associations. There's even a Federation of International Trade Associations (FITA).

4.14.5 Written Exercise: Identify several Level Four national or international trade associations that you can contact.

How to Find Your Audiences

Most of the information you'll need about associations and organizations that serve your target market is on the Internet. It can sometimes be difficult to identify from a web site whom to contact, but it's the best and cheapest way to start. If you're serious about using the Book

Yourself Solid Speaking Strategy as your go-to marketing strategy, pick up a copy of the *NTPA: National Trade and Professional Associations of the United States*. It contains the name of every trade association, its president, budget, convention sites, conference themes, membership, and other pertinent information. You might also consider referencing the *Directory of Association Meeting Planners and Conference/Convention Directors* and the *Encyclopedia of Associations* at your local library.

4.14.6 Written Exercise: Identify the decision makers for the organizations you chose in the previous written exercises. Go through your network to see who you know who might be able to connect you with these decision makers or someone else who might know these decision makers. And, yes, this is where your Book Yourself Solid® software comes in handy again. It'll help you identify who you know who might know them, and then, of course, you'll use your BYS List of 20 to reach out to them and manage your follow-up.

4.14.7 Booked Solid Action Step: After reading this chapter, contact these decision makers using your newfound direct outreach strategies and begin getting booked to speak.

Get Booked to Speak

Meeting planners and their respective counterparts get lots of offers from people like you to speak to their constituents. That's why it's critical that you follow the Book Yourself Solid system. If you have a strong foundation and a trust and credibility strategy in place for your business so you understand why people buy what you're selling, know how to talk about what you do, have identified how you want to be known in your market, know how to have a sales conversation, are a likeable expert within your field, and have created brand-building self-expression products, not only will you get all the clients you want but you'll also earn the respect of the decision makers at the associations and organizations for whom you'd like to speak.

Do your homework. If you're going to contact a meeting planner or education director, make sure you know as much as you possibly can about their organization. You'd be surprised at how many people overlook this step and cold-call these meeting planners without having done their homework. The meeting planner knows it within minutes of the conversation.

Talk to organization members first, if possible. Learn about their urgent needs and compelling desires. They know best what they need, so learn it from them and then reach out to the decision makers. You'll get booked a lot faster that way. Even better, have a member or board member refer you. How much do we love it when other people talk about us so we don't have to? So much!

Send an e-mail or appropriate materials first and follow up with a call. And as always, be friendly, be relevant (meaning that you offer your services only if you can really serve the group), have empathy (step into the shoes of the meeting planner), and be real (no big sales pitch).

What You Need to Present to Get Booked

Each meeting planner, depending on the organization and type of event she's planning, will ask you to submit different materials in order to be considered. If you're trying to get booked at the local community center, a simple phone conversation may do the trick. If you're trying to get booked to speak at the largest conference in your industry, more is expected. You may be asked for a video, session description, learning objectives, speaking experience, letters of recommendation, general biography, introduction biography (which is what is used to introduce you right before you present), and more. Even if five organizations ask for the same materials, it's likely each one will ask for them in their own special way. Here's a word to the wise: make sure you follow instructions. People, especially meeting planners, like that.

Your Invitation to Speak

When invited to speak or present a program, a preliminary meeting or phone call usually sets the stage for further interaction with the person responsible for the program. During the initial contact, you and the meeting planner can usually nail down the topic to be covered and the length of time expected for the presentation.

Contact Information

From the time you receive your invitation to the time you write thank you notes, knowing the key players and how to contact them is vital. Things have a way of changing, however. If you stay on top of your follow-up schedule, you won't get blindsided at the last minute.

- Who is in charge of the event.
- Who will introduce you.
- Landline and cell numbers.

Know Your Audience

Start by considering your audience. Do as much research as you can on the people who will be attending your presentation so that your learning objectives can be directed right at their needs and desires. Work to understand the culture of the group you're speaking to so you can understand how to best communicate with them. Your audience will influence your choice of vocabulary (technical jargon) and may even influence how you dress. Knowing your audience well will also help you decide how much background material you need to deliver for you to effectively communicate your message.

Ask if you may have an opportunity to interview some of the leadership personnel (and even more exciting, some of those who will be attending the seminar or conference) to determine who they are along with their personal goals and agendas. Will they allow you to involve them in the presentation?

Setting up for success in advance will remove much of the stress of preparation and it'll give you more confidence when delivering the actual presentation. Once again, a reminder that a strong foundation leads to super performance.

Knowing Your Audience—Questionnaire

Experience has proven that at this point it is appropriate to present a questionnaire that gives you background information specifically tailored to this particular audience. Developing various forms to help you present effectively and evaluate your performance give you the professional edge when talking with the person in charge of the program.

If you'd like free speaking forms, you can get them from Certified Book Yourself Solid Coach Jan Leaton. She's an expert at teaching people just like you how to get booked to speak. Just send her an e-mail at Jan@ BYSCoachResource.com. The kind of forms that you need, and can get from Jan, include:

- Pre-Questionnaire—Know Your Audience in Advance
- Audience Evaluation Forms, Follow-Up Forms
- Testimonial Forms
- Contact Information Forms

Be Prepared

Of course you will find out where your presentation is to be held and what audiovisual equipment will be available to you, if any. You don't need to use slides or any other visual aid if you prefer not to. Clarify how long you'll be speaking and what your audience will be doing before and after your presentation so you can incorporate that information into your planning. It's even a good idea to end a few minutes early. You'll find that, even when you bring down the house, your audience will appreciate a little extra free time.

Don't forget to remind the facilitator of your requirements closer to the presentation date. Remember, he is juggling a lot of information. Your presentation may be a small part of a larger conference.

Know Your Speaking Venue

Ask to visit the speaking site. As a guest speaker, an appointment with the conference chair, facilitator, or meeting planner is important, as you probably will have only one chance to determine several factors:

- Room setup—speaking area—time of access to facility and meeting room.
- Location of restrooms.
- Setup and breakdown time allowed for your presentation—staff help?
- Your technical and physical needs—Who provides what?
- Back-of-room sales—permitted or not?
- Parking—free, reserved, access, permit required?

The Book Yourself Solid Guide to Putting Your Presentation Together

Now that you're going to be booked to speak, you need to put together a presentation that rocks the house. Keep your presentation as simple as possible. To be an effective speaker, you need to either teach your audience something that they don't know or haven't yet fully realized—but will really value learning—or give them an experience that makes them feel good. Ideally, you want to do both.

When putting your program together, start by considering your venue, the primary learning objectives, and the amount of time you have with your audience. I know how much you have to offer, and I know you want to give so much value that you knock people right out of their chairs. Believe it or not, you'll do that by delivering a reasonable amount of content rather than an overwhelming amount of content. It's likely that your audience is going to be rushing from somewhere else and then rushing to somewhere else after you've finished. So simplicity and clarity is a winning approach. Again, it's important to never run overtime—unless, of course, you get a standing ovation and they scream, "Encore! Encore!" Then, by all means, take a bow and carry on.

Develop Your Bio and Introduction

I've heard it said that the two most important ingredients in a good speech are respect *from* the audience and love *for* the audience. I'm sure you've got the love covered so be sure to give yourself adequate time to develop a bio and introduction that says it the way you want it said. Make yourself a superstar—not (just) to boost your ego but because you need the audience to respect you *before* you set foot on the stage. And, of course, make sure the bio articulates what you do for them. From the questionnaire you have sent out and received back, you know the profile of your audience and what they expect of you.

When you begin a presentation, the audience often wonders:

- Why have you been asked to present?
- Who recommended you?
- What is the speaker's reputation in the company or community?
- Do you personally know the recommender?
- What gives you authority to speak to the specific group?
- Are you considered an expert in your field?

Make sure your introduction bio covers all these details. If it does, the audience is much more likely to offer you its respect right from the get-go.

Who will introduce you? Send your introduction in advance but take at least two copies with you, as it will probably have been lost amid all the conference preparation papers. Go over the introduction with the facilitator in advance and explain that you do not want ad libs. Be sure the person introducing you knows how to pronounce your name correctly and that any other information is clearly understood. Writing your name phonically in your introduction and asking the presenter to say it out loud a couple of times is a sensible precaution to take. Take this seriously even if you think you have a name that is easy to pronounce. I've been introduced more than once as Michael Porter, the esteemed author and Harvard Business School professor. The person introducing you may be a sponsor or some other VIP, and until you become better known, may not know you from Adam. My name, by the way, is Michael *Port*.

Plan Your Presentation

I once heard it said that experts don't necessarily know more than others, but their information is better organized. There may be some truth to that. Knowing how to organize your information is the key to success when making any kind of presentation.

Choose Your Role

I've already suggested that one of the steps you take when developing the content for your information product is to choose the role you will play as the author of the information product. The same is true when creating the content for your presentation: Choose the role you're taking as the presenter. Choosing your role can help you shape the way that you prepare and present the content of your presentation.

Define Your Message

To make your speech compelling, you must have something to say. It's rare that everybody in your audience will agree with your message or opinions. However, if you have a strong message—let's call it a *takeaway*—and you are very clear in the delivery of your message, even people who don't agree will listen with interest. Your entire presentation should focus on delivering the takeaway message in a clear and convincing way.

Develop Your Presentation Title

Here's another nugget from Jan Leaton, a Certified Book Yourself Solid Coach. She describes developing a message as follows:

"I like to think of any presentation title as the gift card on a stupendous gift basket I'm presenting to my audience. How I address my gift card and wrap my package is every bit as important as the gift itself. It provides the '*Wow, I can hardly wait to open this present*' moment. Your presentation title has to say it all. It has to personalize, tantalize, build expectation, and motivate action."

Define Your Content by Filling Your Presentation Basket

Writing your script can be a lot easier if you know where you're going before you launch. Still using the basket analogy—the *first* handle on your presentation basket will be your *conclusion*—or takeaway point, which tells the audience where you're going. Next: balance the basket by grabbing the *second* handle that sets your stage and creates interest in exploring the basket content. When you have balanced the basket, you can now fill it with all the motivating goodies, concepts, and tools you have that make your audience want to carry the basket away with them.

Having a well-organized presentation can determine how well you're received. When considering your material, ask yourself, "What are the steps an audience member will need to take in order to understand the information I'm presenting?"

The following six-step guide will help you organize your information so you're well prepared for any speaking or demonstrating situation.

Step One: To design your presentation, start by setting your main objective for the presentation. What would you like your audience to *take away* from the presentation? What idea, concept, or strategy do you want them to learn, understand, or benefit from?

Step Two: Prepare your opening. It should include:

- The purpose of the presentation—your objective.
- The process of the presentation—what you're going to do.
- The payoff of the presentation—what they're going to get.
- The presenter of the presentation—a few words about why you're the one to make this presentation, including your web site and your always-have-something-to-invite-people-to offer.

Step Three: Deliver the content of your presentation by expressing the key points of the presentation in the appropriate order. Keep it simple.

Step Four: Summarize your key points—what you just taught your audience or demonstrated for your audience.

Step Five: Offer Q&A—or mix it throughout, whatever is most appropriate for your situation.

Step Six: Close by thanking them and your host and remind them how they can continue to connect with you through your always-have-something-to-invite-people-to offer.

Deliver Your Message

When preparing your presentation, remember that people basically learn in one of three ways—although, of course, there will be overlap along the way. Some learn by hearing, some by seeing the written word—PowerPoint or white board illustrations, for example, and some by a touchy-feely atmosphere that is more experiential—sensory word pictures that bring in feeling texture, smelling, and tasting. A good speaker will attempt to combine all three ways of learning into a presentation so that at some point the whole audience is engaged in the presentation. Use few, but appropriate, support materials to support your points. And that means no bullets on PowerPoint presentations. Seriously. Over the years I've found that most slide presentations actually detract from your message. For a great guide to Microsoft PowerPoint take a look at either *Beyond Bullet Points* by Cliff Atkinson or *Presentation Zen* by Garr Reynolds.

What do people see when they hear you? The speaker's own body language also sends a message to the audience. (Read: *What Your Body Says [and How to Master the Message]* by Sharon Sayler.) Some speakers make a special study of how body language influences their audience. A speaker who understands this skill also has an advantage when watching the audience.

How to make your presentation sizzle:

- Practice, practice, practice.
- Stage your presentation.
- Love your audience.
- Dressing appropriately—for your audience.
- Market yourself as an expert while staying on topic.
- Use mics, props, and handouts effectively.

Videorecording your presentations so they can be leveraged into information products, marketing tools, and more is essential.

Know Your Material

The best way to give the impression that you know what you're talking about is to really know what you're talking about. You must understand your subject very well and be able to answer related questions. On the other hand, it is impossible for anyone to know everything. If you're asked a question for which you don't know the answer, there is no shame in answering, "I don't know, but I'll find out and get back to you." Or you might ask if someone in the room knows the answer. Very often you'll find that someone will.

In preparing your presentation, take the time to survey friends, clients, and others in your network who represent the kind of people you'll be speaking to. Learn as much as you can about what others are saying about your topic and make sure that your presentation passes the "so what" test. Deliver it to a test audience and make sure they don't say, "So what?" at the end of the presentation.

Wrap-Up and Follow-Up

Be sure those participants have your contact information and that you have contact information for participants where possible. Your follow-up strategy will also include thank-you notes to those who helped make your presentation a success: The person or organization that invited you to speak, the facilitator who introduced you, anyone who helped with room preparation, and so on. Of course, a survey at the end of your presentation that asks for their contact information and permission to e-mail them additional information would be ideal.

You may want to remind the organization of the availability of follow-up materials as part of your keeping-in-touch plan. Make notes of what you learned so that you can apply it to future presentations and particularly to the current organization, should you be asked back again.

To Speak or Not to Speak, That Is the Question

It's important to be aware of what your talents are and to not use the speaking strategy if public speaking isn't one of your strengths. You've got to be clear about that, which isn't to say you can't get better at public speaking and performing—you can. I'm better at giving presentations now than I was when I started. You integrate what you learn by doing your first presentation into your second, and so on. However, I wouldn't suggest using the speaking and demonstrating strategy as one of your primary marketing strategies if you really aren't comfortable speaking in public or just don't want to.

Having said that, I'd like to make a key distinction: Even if you're feeling stage fright at the thought of speaking, that doesn't mean you don't have the ability to be a good speaker. I'm nervous before almost every single speech I make. I'd be worried if I weren't, because it's natural to feel nervous. If you're drawn to speaking and demonstrating and would like to give it a try, then by all means, go for it! Practice in front of a group of supportive friends or associates, or start by giving a telephone seminar, which may feel more comfortable. Then gradually work your way up as your comfort level and confidence increase.

No one likes to be told that one didn't do a good job, and I'm no exception. Early in my career, in spite of receiving positive feedback about my presentation from many who attended, I was mortified, crushed, by the negative feedback from one or two. I ran into my biggest fear—that people would think I was stupid, that they wouldn't like what I had to say. That's my biggest conflicting intention about being a public speaker— that people will think I'm stupid. But I remind myself of the founding principle of the Book Yourself Solid way:

If you feel called to share a message, it's because there are people in the world who are waiting to hear it.

My job is to work hard to find the people who are waiting to hear my message and not to let the naysayers—the people who don't like what I'm doing—deter me from finding those I'm meant to serve. This principle is what drives me and keeps me going, and it's what prompts me to say again to you, if you feel called to speak, to share your message, there are people out there waiting to hear it.

The Book Yourself Solid Speaking Strategy is a great way to get your message out to the world in a bigger way, allowing you to reach more of those you're meant to serve.

The Book Yourself Solid Writing Strategy

Words are the most powerful drug used by mankind.
—Rudyard Kipling

Article writing is such an important way to build your reputation that I've enlisted my good friend and web writing maven, Rozey Gean from Marketing-Seek.com, to collaborate with me in writing this chapter because I have learned some great writing skills and marketing strategies from her. We're eager to share the Five-Part Book Yourself Solid Writing Strategy. You'll learn how to write effective articles and post them online, one of the most effective ways to generate traffic to your web site.

We'll also teach you how to analyze the different offline writing markets and the steps to get editors to publish your articles. Writing articles and publishing them online and offline will help you establish your reputation as an expert while generating interest in your products, programs, and services. By publishing online and offline, you will imprint your position as a category authority as widely as possible.

If you consider yourself a writer, you're going to say, "Yes, this Book Yourself Solid self-promotion strategy is for me and I'm going to jump on this right now!" If you don't picture yourself as a writer, you might be inclined to skip over this chapter, but please don't! Let me tell you a story that demonstrates how even nonwriters can learn to write effective articles:

My fourth-grade teacher said I had the worst spelling she had ever seen in her 25-year career in teaching. Many years later, when I told one of my childhood friends that I had sold a book to a big-time publisher, he questioned how I could do that without his help. He still had an impression of me as the kid who didn't even like to write five paragraphs for a high school essay. But I wound up writing a lot more than five paragraphs—and good ones, too!

The point is that I don't want you to miss out on this important self-promotion strategy simply because you think you can't write. If you can speak, you can write. You're not writing the Great American Novel here. You're writing to educate the people you serve and promote the services you sell. Even if writing isn't one of your natural talents, it's a skill that can be learned well enough for you to master the Book Yourself Solid Writing Strategy and can be improved upon through practice.

How to Get Out of Writing

Does the thought of having to write an article still make you cringe? If so, don't worry. There are two other ways to gain the benefits that article writing provides without going anywhere near a keyboard:

1. Hire a ghostwriter.
2. Collaborate with a writer.

Ghostwriters are professional writers who will custom write an article for you on the subject of your choice for a fee. Your name and business information appear in the byline and in the author's resource box at the end. Sure, it costs a little, but it's still a comparatively inexpensive marketing tool. And once you've got it, you can use it in many different ways:

- Distribute it to online article directories.
- Send it to related web sites and newsletters that accept submissions.
- Publish it in your own electronic newsletter (e-zine).
- Upload it to your own site and announce it to your mailing list.
- Submit it to print publications that cater to your area of expertise.

You can get a lot of mileage out of one article, especially if it's of professional quality.

Collaborating with a writer is another easy way to get the word out about your services. If you know someone who can write well, maybe someone whose articles you've read and admired, consider pitching a joint venture to this person. You provide the expertise, and she provides the writing skills to prepare an article based on your supplied information. Then both of your names and web site addresses appear together in the author's box at the end.

This sort of collaboration is a great way to solve the I-dislike-writing problem while effectively promoting two businesses at once.

The Five-Part Book Yourself Solid Writing Strategy

Article writing is an exciting self-promotion strategy, so let's get right to it!

Part 1: Deciding on the Subject
Part 2: Choosing an Ideal Topic
Part 3: Creating an Attention-Grabbing Title
Part 4: Writing Your Article
Part 5: Getting Your Article Published

Part 1: Deciding on the Subject

What is your subject? A subject is a broad category of knowledge—dancing, boating, fashion, business, society, and recreation are all subjects. It's possible you already know a great deal about the subject of your article, or maybe you're curious about a new subject and want to expand your knowledge of it. To help identify a direction for your writing, ask yourself these questions:

- What am I passionate about?
- What interests me on a personal level?
- What is the scope of my expertise?
- What life lessons have I learned?
- What is my target audience interested in learning?

Answering these questions will help you find good subjects. Of course, you should always remember the golden rule of writing: Write what you know. For example, if you feel stuck, consider choosing a subject that relates to your products, programs, and services, since this is probably what you have the most knowledge about.

Don't forget to explore your personal interests as well. Consider subjects based on hobbies, family, community involvement, or charity work. Your life experiences can provide you with endless ideas for article writing.

4.15.1 Written Exercise: List five subjects you would feel comfortable writing about on the basis of your passions, your personal interests, your areas of expertise, the life lessons you've learned, and what your target market is interested in learning. Once you've chosen one subject area to write about, you're ready to narrow it down to an ideal topic.

Part 2: Choosing an Ideal Topic

A topic is a specific, narrow focus within your subject area. Subjects such as dancing, boating, and fashion are too broad to write about, especially since article pieces are usually between 500 and 3,000 words. Have you ever noticed that most articles and books (other than reference materials) are focused on a narrow topic? The reason is simple—it makes the writing (and reading) more manageable.

Let's say you're writing about dancing. You might choose a topic like how modern dance evolved from folk dance, how dancing contributes to heart health, comfortable clothes to wear while dancing, or the growing interest in a certain style of dance.

The following examples demonstrate how to narrow a broad subject area to reach a focused topic.

From Broad Subjects to Focused Topics

Dancing → Dancing for Women → Fitness Dancing for Grannies

Dancing → Dancing for Men → Smooth Moves for the Dancing Don Juan

Dancing → Dancing for Couples → Ballroom Dancing for Latin Lovers

Boating → Water Sports → Water Skiing Safety Tips

Boating → Angler Fishing → Hot Bait for the Angler Catching Weakfish

Boating → Safety → Preventing Hypothermia

Fashion → Style → Walking in Style and Comfortable Fashion

Fashion → Seasonal Trends → Top 10 Looks for Fall Fashion

Fashion → Teens → Prom Night: Get the Red Carpet Look for Less

---

4.15.2 Written Exercise: List five focused topics you would feel comfortable writing about based on the subjects you chose in Written Exercise 4.15.1.

Determine Your Objective for Writing   Now that you've chosen a focused topic for your article, you need to establish a clear purpose or objective. Are you writing to inform, persuade, explore new territory, or to express your personal opinion? Knowing your objective will help you zero in on the content of your article. Ask yourself these questions:

- What do I want to teach the reader?
- What life experience do I want to share?
- Do I want to venture into new territory?
- How do I want to be known?

Let's examine these questions in more detail. One of the most popular types of article is the how-to article, in which you teach your readers something. This is a great place to start, especially for new writers, because you can simply tap in to an area of expertise you already have, cutting out the need for hours of research. Likewise, sharing an experience that taught you a life lesson is another straightforward way of telling a story that can really affect people.

Or you can do the research on a brand new topic, educating yourself and your readers at the same time. This keeps the writing process fresh and interesting for you.

Articles that encourage readers to take an action, such as clicking on a link for further information, are also very popular with publishers. Providing links within your item to good resources (perhaps pages of your own web site) is a great way to help your readers while establishing yourself as a reliable source of information.

Deciding now what sort of expert you want to be known as will help you determine the objective of your articles. Let's say you have a home-based accounting business. Writing a series of articles on tax tips for people who work at home is a great way to tap in to your existing knowledge base while establishing a reputation for yourself as an accountant who understands the tax challenges of home-based workers. And that kind of credibility can drive new business to your door without spending a cent on advertising.

Understand Your Target Audience   So far you have narrowed your subject to a focused topic and established your purpose for writing the article. Now it is time to consider your reader.

As we discussed in Chapter 2, your target market is a group of clients or prospects with a common interest or need that you can meet. The same is true for the target audience of your article—a group of people united in their common need for the information you have to share.

To zero in on who they are, ask yourself these questions:

- What do I know about my audience—income, age, gender?
- How educated is my audience—specialized, literate, minimal education?
- How much do they already know about my topic?
- What do they need to know that I can teach?
- Are there any misconceptions about my topic that I can clear up for them?
- What is my relationship with my target audience?
- How else can I help my readers?

Digging deep to ponder and answer these questions about your readers will help you develop a mental picture of their lives and their needs. Let's say you decided to run in a marathon, but you've never run in one before. You know there must be thousands of other people out there just like you who would like to run, get fit in the process, and just feel the satisfaction of knowing they can do it. Your target audience in this case would be people who are highly motivated, health conscious, open to challenges, curious, and willing to try something new. Defining them was easy because they are just like you.

If you know that people are out there who need simple information on the topic you want to write about, and you can describe them as we just did, that knowledge will help you to define:

- *What* you will tell them.
- *How* you will tell them: your tone, vocabulary, and style of writing.

Hot Buttons   Another way to understand more about your readers is to study the emotional hot buttons that make all of us tick. Knowing what these buttons are can help you choose topics and write articles to tap in to your audience's basic interests in life. You can visit this web link to get your copy of Rozey's Hot Buttons List so you can use it to inspire your next writing session: http://bys.marketing-seek.com/hotbuttons.php.

Now that you have a topic for your article, it's time to start writing.

Part 3: Creating an Attention-Grabbing Title

I discussed in Chapter 7 how the title of your information product can make a big difference in whether it sells. The same concept is true when creating attention-grabbing article titles. In fact, some writers say it's the most important part because without an arresting title, no one will bother to read the rest of your article. Here are some additional tips to help spark your creativity when writing attention-grabbing titles:

1. Select a few choice words that sum up the main point of the article. Example: *How to Renovate Your Kitchen Without Spending a Fortune*
2. Tell the reader what he will learn. Use specifics: "95 percent of all" or "two out of three." Example: *New Report Shows 54 Percent of School-Age Children Are Couch Potatoes*
3. Hint at the solution your article provides. Example: *Cook Low-Carb Meals That Don't Leave You Craving*
4. Use questions in the title to involve the reader. Example: *Are You Sleep Deprived and Don't Even Know It?*
5. Curiosity is a powerful tool, so consider a teaser title. Example: *What Your Face Shape and Your Choice of Dog Have in Common*
6. Promise results. Explain how your article will solve a problem for the reader. Example: *Get Over Your Fear of Flying in Five Minutes*
7. Promise to teach them something using phrases like "How To" or "Five Steps to Improve." Example: *How to Belly Dance in Three Easy Steps*

Optimize Your Title   If you're writing an article on, say, belly dancing, then you want people who are looking for this type of information on a search engine to be able to find your article. So you would do keyword research first to determine the most likely phrases your readers would use— for example, how to belly dance, belly dancing fitness, belly dancing—and then include one or two of those terms in your article title. If you determined that the keyword term *belly dancing* is searched on more frequently than *how to belly dance*, you might write a title like this: "Belly Dancing for Beginners." Or you might even incorporate two popular search terms into one heading: "Belly Dancing: Fitness Fun for the Healthy-Minded."

Search engines place a lot of emphasis on words they find in headings, so including your keywords here is vitally important to getting your article found on the Web.

Best Title Prompts   The preceding examples were just to whet your appetite. If you're interested in additional title-writing inspiration, guaranteed to get your creative juices flowing, visit this link for a list of 106 of the best, most attention-grabbing title prompts: http://bys.marketing-seek .com/106titles.php.

4.15.3 Written Exercise: Create five titles based on your topic choices. Remember, titles need to summarize in a few words what your article is about and be intriguing enough to make people who are interested in that topic—and even those who aren't!—want to read more. If you can fit in your top keyword phrase, so much the better!

Part 4: Writing Your Article

The Introduction   The introduction contains the nugget of your story, a short capsule that summarizes what's coming in the body of the article. It builds on the topic already presented in the title and explains why that information matters to the reader, which is why it's so important to know who your target audience is.

Some writers tend to back in to their story by dropping their lead nugget down to the third or fourth paragraph, but this is a dangerous tactic. In nearly all cases, the first paragraph of your article should reflect the title, elaborate on it, and hint at all the juicy information to come.

Your introduction is also the place where you set the tone for the entire article, so be sure to speak directly to your readers using the words they use frequently. A casual style will endear you to your readers much more than an academic or technical style of writing. Above all, a strong introduction presents ideas that entice the reader to keep reading.

A compelling introductory paragraph answers everyone's most pertinent question: What's in it for me? Know how your information will benefit your readers and express that in your opening statement to them. If you can't imagine what benefit they will gain from your article, it may be wise to go back and refine your topic.

4.15.4 Written Exercise: Write your lead-in paragraph by presenting the most important information first. Remember to address the topic presented in your title and explain to your readers what they will gain from your article. Here's where you get to appeal personally to the readers by telling them how you can help them learn something new, solve a problem, or simply entertain them for a short while.

The Body The body of your article is where you fulfill the promise made in your title and lead-in paragraph by expanding on your theme. Here are a few tips to make the writing of this, the longest part of your article, easier:

- *Try to stick to one idea in each sentence and two or three sentences in each paragraph.* Concise bits of information are much easier for your readers to handle and are much less intimidating than long blocks of writing.
- *Use subheadings.* These are like mini-titles that explain what's coming next and help break up the writing into manageable sections. Subheadings also help you organize the presentation of your information, somewhat like an outline. Put them in bold text or all capitals to make them stand out.

- *Use lists.* Giving your readers information formatted with bulleted lists, numbered lists, or any other visual device also makes the writing easier to read. The bottom line is that even the people who are very interested in your topic are in a hurry and want to get the goods fast.
- *Be consistent with your layout.* If the first item on your list of bullet points starts with a verb, make sure the first word of every item starts the same way. For example, in this list of five points, each opening sentence—the one in italics—starts with the imperative form of a verb: try, use, be, optimize.
- *Optimize your body copy.* The keyword phrases you selected for your title must also appear throughout the body of your article if you want searchers to have a better chance of finding it. Repeating these phrases just often enough to be effective without going overboard is an art form, so aim for a level of keyword frequency that reads naturally.

Going to the trouble of optimizing your article's body is worth the effort for two reasons:

1. It helps your article get listed higher in the search engine results than other content, especially if other writers don't include relevant keyword phrases in their articles.
2. It will satisfy people doing the search because you've helped them find information that speaks directly to their needs. And people (you) who help other people (your readers) get what they need are often thought of very highly and remembered!

So you can see that adding relevant keyword phrases to the title and body of your article helps both you and your readers.

4.15.5 Written Exercise: It is time to write the body of your article. You need to elaborate on and fulfill the promise made in your introduction by backing up your statements with facts. Refer back to the points listed earlier if you get stuck. And remember that you don't have to get all the words perfect in the first draft. Much of writing is about rewriting and editing. At this point, concentrate on the broad strokes and allow yourself to enjoy the process.

The Conclusion Have you said everything you wanted to say? Then it's time to wrap it all up. The conclusion is easy because it's simply a summing up of everything you just wrote. The point is to leave your readers with an easy-to-remember summary of your main theme so that it is reinforced in their minds.

If you were simply to finish your article on point 9 of a list of tips, your readers would feel they were left hanging. It's human nature to crave a satisfying ending to a story. You can leave them on an even sweeter note if you share with them how they can best use the information to their advantage, and you can offer a few words of encouragement.

Write a conclusion using these guidelines:

- Restate your main points, wrapping them up in a neat summary.
- Encourage readers to try your advice.
- End on a positive note.

4.15.6 Written Exercise: End your article with a strong closing. Write a conclusion by summarizing your key points from the body of the article and tell the readers how they can best use the information you just gave them.

The Author's Resource Box This is where you get to take a bow, share something pertinent about yourself or your business, and invite your readers to take an action. It's also an important opportunity to offer your services.

At the end of every article is a separate paragraph of about five or six lines (this depends on the guidelines of each publication, so check with them before submitting). This resource box or author's bio can be used in several ways. Most authors put the following information in their resource boxes:

- A brief explanation of who they are and their expertise.
- A line or two about their business or the special offer they want to promote.

- A call to action that prompts readers to either phone, click a link, or make contact in some other way.
- *Optional:* The offer of a gift or other incentive to motivate action.

The Key to Writing Your Resource Box   To make sure your resource box is effective, clearly invite action and explain why this action would benefit your readers. This applies to whether it's signing up for a free report, a complimentary consultation, a newsletter subscription, or simply a visit to your web site to learn more about your products, services, and programs or to read more of your scintillating articles!

4.15.7 Written Exercise: Create your author resource box. Remember to include your area of expertise, your business or offer, a specific call to action, and pertinent contact information and links.

Let It Simmer and Proofread   Now take that article you have so carefully and lovingly created—and ignore it. Set it aside for *at least* a day. Return to it later and take the time to read it out loud. This is when any dropped words or weird phrasing will become apparent. Check your grammar and spelling. Polish your work to perfection. Ten rereads are not excessive; each time you'll see something that could be said better, tighter, or more accurately.

A word about spelling checkers: Your word processing program likely has a spelling and grammar checking function. Use it but don't depend on it. You could use a spelling checker and still make spelling errors. For example, you might have typed *here* when you meant to type *hear*. The English language is complicated, and a spelling checker can't comprehend which word you meant to use or should have spelled differently based on how you used it. Also, share your articles with others and accept their help to spot any spelling or grammar problems that you may have overlooked.

4.15.8 Booked Solid Action Step: Compile all the accumulated elements of your research and writing to complete one article of 500 to 750 words on the topic of your choice, including the resource box. When it's polished to your satisfaction, share it with friends, colleagues, or a writing group to gain valuable insight on your writing progress.

Part 5: Getting Your Article Published

This is when the fruits of your writing labor pay off. After you have completed writing your article, you'll want to search for the niche web sites and the publications that will help share your writing with the world.

Getting Published on the Web   The Internet offers a number of unique environments to display your written work, thereby generating traffic to your web site, building your credibility, and increasing visibility for your products, programs, and services. Here are some examples:

- Article directories.
- Article announcement lists.
- Niche web sites.
- Electronic newsletters (e-zines).

Let's take a closer look:

- *Article announcement lists.* The intent of an article announcement list is to send out e-mail announcing your article to web owners and electronic newsletter publishers who are seeking quality content. The announcement times will vary and are set by the list owner. While many announcement lists hold your article for a period of time, they're specifically used to relay the available content at the time it gets posted—not to archive it for the search engines. See http://Groups.Yahoo.com.

- *Niche web sites.* The owner of a niche web site requires quality content written on a specific topic. The web owners' agenda is to keep their web site fresh with articles that cater to their targeted readers; they look to writers like you to supply them with this free content. See WebProNews.com.

- *Electronic newsletters (e-zines).* Electronic newsletters come in all shapes and sizes on varied topics. You write the content, share it with these publishers, and immediately gain access to their readers who are also your target audience. The publisher gains credible content without needing to write the articles, and you reach a larger group of prospective customers. See New-List.com.

Where should you start? Consider your target audience and where they're most likely to spend their time online. These are the hot spots you'll use to display your writing on a consistent basis. However, before you start the submission process, there are a few more details you need to consider:

- *Researching relevant environments.* Locate the specific environments that cater to your target audience, familiarizing yourself with the article submission guidelines.

- *Creating an article summary.* Write a short synopsis of your article.

- *Deciding on the characters per line.* Prepare different file formats for your article: Several article directories require 60 characters per line (60 cpl), while others require longer lengths. If you're unsure which format is preferred, contact the web site owner before submitting your piece.

- *Converting your article to text.* If you use a software program such as Microsoft Word to write your article, you will be required to save it to a text file in preparation for the submission process.

- *Choosing keywords and keyword phrases.* Make a list of your keywords and keyword phrases for the article directories that require them. (These should be the same keywords and keyword phrases you used to prepare your title and article copy for the search engines.)

- *Listing the word count.* Some content sites will require a word count of your article. The total word count usually includes all words plus the title and resource box that make up your entire piece.
- *Checking your spelling and grammar.* Check your article before submission. I agree with Mark Twain, who said: "I don't give a damn for a man that can only spell a word one way." Unfortunately, not everyone agrees. One misspelled word can really turn people off.
- *Preparing an e-mail.* Write a letter to the e-zine publishers detailing what your article is about and why it would benefit the e-zine's readership. Insert a copy of your article into the body of the e-mail correspondence.

4.15.9 Written Exercise: List five article directories that serve your target market.

4.15.10 Booked Solid Action Step: Submit your article to the article directories you identified earlier.

4.15.11 Written Exercise: List five e-zine publications that serve your target market.

4.15.12 Booked Solid Action Step: Submit your article to the e-zine publishers you've identified earlier.

Consistency is the key to writing and publishing articles as a marketing tool. The idea is to saturate your target market so when a potential client is searching for valuable information, your name and articles come up again and again within the search engines' results.

Getting Published in Print   Once you're comfortable with sharing your written work online, you might consider branching out and offering articles to print publications. Writing for the print market is a highly competitive process, but it's also very rewarding.

Plan your print publishing strategy:

1. Think big but start small.
2. Request the writing guidelines.
3. Analyze the contents.
4. Write a query letter.
5. Send a self-addressed stamped envelope (SASE).
6. Follow up with the editor.

Let's examine each step in more detail.

Think big but start small. Rather than going for the large mainstream magazines, shoot for the small, focused publications such as local newspapers and magazines, trade journals, or neighborhood community newsletters. These publications are more likely to accept your work and even help edit your articles for suitability.

Once you've been accepted to write in one of the smaller publications, you can build your portfolio of printed pieces and approach the larger markets. This is important because many large-publication editors won't consider your writing ability unless they can see you have been previously published. It's similar to when you're trying to break into the speaking circuit: You start at the local level, step up to the regional level, then to the national level, and finally to the international level. It's the same concept when you're trying to get your writing in print publications.

Request the writing guidelines. Never submit articles without understanding what the publication is looking for and accepts. You need to be aware of word count, spacing format, style, and the type of information each publication is looking to include. For more detailed information on writing guidelines for thousands of print publications, pick up a copy of *Writer's Market*, by Kathryn S. Brogan.

Analyze the contents. From what I hear, nothing drives editors bonkers more than receiving articles that don't fit into the theme of their publication. Your chances of getting an article accepted for print will greatly improve if you take the time to become familiar with the publication. Either purchase a subscription or several back issues; then analyze the contents by looking at items such as article length, the tone of the writing pieces, the topics covered, the balance of short articles versus long, and how many illustrations or photos were used.

Write a query letter. Now that you know which topics you want to write about and have identified the publications you want to write in, it's time to write a letter. A query letter is basically a one-page proposal that pitches your article idea. You can send a query letter about an article that has already been written or an article that hasn't yet been created, as a way to feel out the publication's enthusiasm for the concept.

Your query letter should follow the rules of a good business letter; it must immediately grab attention and convincingly (soft) sell your article idea. Use your business letterhead. If you don't own business letterhead, use white copy paper. Choose a simple font, point size 12, with single spaces. Use bullets to list key points for easier reading. Above all, be certain you spell the editor's name properly and use the correct address for the publication.

Send a SASE. Always include a self-addressed stamped envelope along with your query letter for a reply from the editor. Have patience; it can take up to six months for an editor to reply.

Follow up with the editor. After sending your query letter and waiting the appropriate time for a response, follow up by telephone. Your objective is to inquire whether the editor is interested in your article and if she requires additional information. If the editor's response is no, don't be pushy and try to change her mind. Instead, ask her if there is a different slant to the article that might interest her or whether she knows someone else who might be interested in your piece.

4.15.13 Written Exercise: List five print publications that serve your target market.

4.15.14 Booked Solid Action Step: Submit your query letter to the print publications you identified in Written Exercise 4.15.13.

Help Editors Help You

Every publication has an insatiable hunger for good content. They're looking for articles that will inform and entertain their readers—pieces that will help them improve their lives, whether it's how to save money, lose weight, build self-esteem, or build a shelving unit.

Most editors need good writers who also happen to be experts in their field—like you. They usually have to pay top dollar to staff writers or freelancers to provide it. So if you can give them good articles at no charge, the publication saves time and money, and you get great exposure.

A solid relationship with an editor can help you gain insight to:

- What type of information is being considered for future publications.
- What kind of story may be needed in the future.
- How to strengthen your chances of being interviewed to write a particular story.

Consideration goes a long way in the print publishing business. You'll discover that the most vital component for building relationships with editors is listening and providing the best information to meet their needs. If you stay in contact with them and consistently work to supply them with good stories, you'll successfully build relationships that will provide publicity for you and your business over time.

4.15.15 Written Exercise: Decide on an ongoing schedule for submitting your articles. This can be weekly, every other week, or monthly.

4.15.16 Booked Solid Action Step: Schedule the time you'll need to write and submit new articles and then do it; or hire a virtual assistant who is experienced in online article submission and have him do it for you.

It's important to learn the art of delayed gratification. While it's natural to want instant results, this is a process, not a magic formula for overnight fame and fortune. One of the greatest mistakes I see service professionals make is giving up too quickly when their initial efforts don't produce immediate results. It's the cumulative effect that will pay off, so be consistent and be tenacious. Don't give up!

16

The Book Yourself Solid Web Strategy

When I took office, only high-energy physicists had ever heard of what is called the World Wide Web. . . . Now even my cat has its own page.

—Bill Clinton

Most very successful service professionals have a web presence. Why? Because the Web is a powerful tool for starting and continuing conversations with potential clients. That said, using web marketing as a primary strategy for promoting your services, is not essential, nor is it necessarily effective for marketing your services. The Web can be *very* effective, but internet marketing is not for everyone and every business. If the Web is not right for you, then it won't be effective.

If you don't want to become an Internet marketing maniac, don't. Mastering tactics like search engine optimization, pay-per-click advertising, and the many other tools, are for those who want to spend their time online. If that's not where your passion lies, you'll quickly become overwhelmed and the last thing you, or I, want is for you to feel overwhelmed.

If you are simply not driven to spend your energy learning a new technology, but you still want to leverage the power of the Internet, hire or partner with others who have the skills, talents, and desires that you do not.

These days working solo does not mean working alone—far from it. I have a team I work with full-time now that my business has grown beyond a one-person operation. But even in the beginning, I outsourced much of the work that I didn't like to do, and frankly, wasn't very good at, to assistants and technical experts. You can do much more with others than you can alone.

There is something for everyone in this chapter—novice and expert alike. In fact, I've pulled together so much information on how to use the Web for marketing and promotion that I've divided this chapter into three parts:

Part 1: Designing Your Web Site
Part 2: Getting Visitors to Your Web Site
Part 3: Building Your Social Media Platform

The Web is an extraordinary vehicle for self-expression. It offers huge opportunities for sharing who you are and what you offer, as well as the privilege of connecting with others. There is a learning curve, but all great opportunities require that we learn something new. Two of the most important rules for doing big things in the world are learning in action and working with others.

You must learn in real time and in action. You cannot afford to wait until everything is perfect to go out and do what you want to do. If you wait for perfection to go out in the world and do big things, you're never going to get there—or get anything done, for that matter. Many people hold themselves back because they think they have to know everything about how to do something before they actually do it. This is not true. You can and should learn while doing.

You cannot learn how to run or become a better runner without actually running. You can certainly read an article about how moving your arms in a particular way can help your stride, but until you put the tip into action, you won't really know or experience its truth. The same is true for Internet marketing or any other new skill you're interested in learning. As you embrace each of these marketing strategies by learning in action and working with others who have more experience than you, you will be pleasantly surprised at what you're able to accomplish in a very short time.

PART 1

DESIGNING YOUR WEB SITE

Design is not just what it looks like and feels like.
Design is how it works.

—Steve Jobs

In this first part, I walk you through the purpose and benefits of having a web site, the biggest mistake most people make online, how to structure the content on your web site, the 10 most effective web site formats for service professionals, and what to look for in a web site designer. And I promise to make it as easy to understand as a day at the beach—or at least a day at the beach with your laptop.

Purpose and Benefits of Having a Web Site

There are numerous purposes and benefits to having a web site and developing a strong web presence, many of which I'm sure you've considered. Your own web site:

- *Positions you as an expert.* Having your own web site increases your visibility, credibility, and trustworthiness.
- *Builds your brand identity.* Your web site represents you and your business in the marketplace.

- *Reaches a global marketplace.* If you have a product available on your web site, you'll expand your geographic marketplace from your local neighborhood to the entire world.

- *Creates a 24/7 passive-revenue profit machine.* The Web never sleeps, which means that you can turn your computer and web site into a cash register around the clock, and many, if not all, of the processes can be automated.

- *Builds your database.* A web site can instantly increase the effectiveness of your sales cycle by building a targeted list of potential clients who have given you permission to follow up with them. A web site with an opt-in allows you to provide value while building your database (by offering something of value in exchange for e-mail addresses). Remember, your visitors must see your offers and your services as opportunities worthy of their investment, even if that investment is as small as an e-mail address.

- *Allows for filtering out unsuitable clients.* All of your marketing materials can guide potential clients to your web site, where you save precious time by allowing them to familiarize themselves with you, your services, your procedures, and your prices before they contact you for more information. They can then determine whether they feel they'd be well-suited to work with you.

- *Provides an opportunity for bold self-expression.* Your web site is a fantastic vehicle through which to express yourself. It is an extension and a representation of you and what you offer.

The Biggest Mistake Most People Make Online

Before we get into the technical aspects of what makes a great web site, consider the biggest mistake most people make online: they don't know what they want their visitors to do when viewing the site and if they do know, they don't know how they're going to get the visitor to do it.

Most people consider a web site to be one thing. It's not. On the contrary, a web site is made up of a collection of pages that live on the same domain and are related to each other. For each page on your site, you should be able to answer the following three questions with complete clarity:

1. Who is coming to the page?
2. What do you want them to do?
3. How are you going to get them to do it?

Knowing the answer to these three questions will ensure that the content on each page of your site is perfectly designed for the type of person who visits the page. Why? Because you will consider what kind of story you're going to tell, and how you're going to tell it, to get your visitor to reach the goal you've set for that page. Your web site can be a remarkably effective tool for attracting and securing clients—if it's done right.

A pretty web site does not necessarily a good web site make. Sure, you may get a few calls because someone visited your site, or sell a few products, but the majority of the people who visit your site will not come back again just for the prettiness. Their behavior is not necessarily because they don't like what you have to offer, but people are busy and most don't even remember how they got to your site in the first place. Pretty is forgettable. Content that answers the needs of the visitor sticks in people's memories. And, ease of use allows them to consume it.

As a successful online marketer, you will focus on attempting to convert the traffic that comes to your site into a potential client, someone who eagerly anticipates your marketing messages. These messages will come in the form of the next great service offering that will help her advance an aspect of her life. You might do this by giving these clients something of value, like a special report, free video lesson, or a big coupon, in exchange for permission to keep in touch with them. Remember how important building trust over time is. If your primary objective is to offer extraordinary value up front in exchange for an e-mail address and permission to follow up, then you can make relevant and proportionate monetized offerings later on, once you've built trust.

Content and Structure

The content and structure of your web site includes the information you wish to convey and how you organize and label it for easy navigation. Just as you can leverage the same content for an information product into several different formats, you can choose a variety of formats to lay out your web site content.

As you consider your content and structure, your focus should be on your target market. It is especially critical when you're working with a designer to think like your target audience. Think like your audience. What do they want? Design to meet their needs.

Your content and structure are key elements in determining whether your web site is effective. The content has to be relevant to your target market and the layout should make it obvious where the visitor needs to go and what the visitor needs to do.

Visitors to your site want information and resources that will assist them in their work and their lives. If they can't find what they need, they'll get frustrated with your site and with you. The result is a lost connection. Make your site easy to navigate and easy to use, and you'll establish an immediate rapport with your visitors because they will feel that you already know and understand them.

4.16.1 Written Exercise: Consider the home page of your web site. Who is coming to this page? (That is, potential client, current client, past client, referral partner, or the press.)

4.16.2 Written Exercise: Consider the home page of your web site. What do you want the visitor to do? (That is, opt in to a newsletter so she can get access to a special report, sign up for a telephone conference that is your always-have-something-to-invite-people-to offer, and so forth.)

4.16.3 Written Exercise: Consider the home page of your web site. Now that you know what you want the visitor to do, how are you going to get him to do it? (That is, with a compelling story in your copywriting or in a video, or maybe an ethical bribe, and so on.)

4.16.4 Written Exercise: Now repeat the previous three steps for each page of your web site (if you have one). If you are in the process of building your web site, complete these exercises for each page of the site as you build it.

Web Site Basics

Your web site can make you look like a superstar, offering valuable content, experiences, and opportunities for your target market. With a professional, up-to-date, modern design, and loads of great content that serves your target market, you will position yourself as an expert and the go-to person in your field.

As challenging as the journey to web site success may seem right now, you might be pleasantly surprised that the work you've already done in the book has secretly set you up for success. Your web site is your opportunity to decide and control how you're known. Your tagline boldly expresses why you do what you do. Your site should speak to the values of your ideal clients and demonstrate how dedicated you are to your target market, their needs and desires, the number one biggest result that you help them get, along with the financial, emotional, physical, and spiritual benefits they will receive from investing their time with you.

Your web site also demonstrates your platform, helps you build trust and credibility. Also, each of the 7 Core Self-Promotion Strategies can be integrated into the way you promote and use your site. Your web site can help you start a conversation with a potential client by offering free information products or experiences for new potential clients, and it's an effective way to introduce them to your sales cycle so you can build trust over time. Your site is an avenue through which you can offer various pricing incentives for your products and services, leading to super simple sales conversations with ideal clients.

Here are some specific ideas of how you can integrate the Book Yourself Solid 7 Core Self-Promotion Strategies right into your site:

- *Networking Strategy:* You can invite people to join you on various social network platforms like Facebook, Twitter, LinkedIn, and so forth. You can also use it to connect with new people every day through your subscriber list, blog posts, and "contact me" forms.
- *Direct Outreach Strategy:* You can use direct outreach to get to know others in your field by commenting on their posts and also asking them if you can reprint some of their blog posts. You can even offer to write posts for them to publish on their blogs. Not only is your web site a great tool for starting conversations with potential clients, it's also a great way to start conversations with influencers in your industry. It's often the first thing a potential business associate will review when they are evaluating you and your relevance to them.
- *Referral Strategy:* You can implement the referral strategy by writing blog posts or articles, which refer to another colleague who can help your clients with a particular problem they may be having for which you are not the expert. Or, you can create a resource page in which you profile various referral partners. Your newsletter is another opportunity to offer referrals.
- *Keep-In-Touch Strategy:* You can build a subscriber list of potential clients and make sales offers through your newsletter by providing valuable content, advice, and inspiration.
- *Speaking Strategy:* You can advertise your teleseminars, classes, and events on your site. You can also do a podcast through your web site.
- *Writing Strategy:* A blog can be integrated into your site and you can have a page with articles that help position you as an expert in your

field. You can submit articles to article banks or directories that will help drive traffic to your site and enhance your status as an expert.

By integrating the core self-promotion strategies into your site, you will attract potential clients with whom you will build trust, and who will ultimately become ideal, life-fulfilling, and career-making clients.

Holly Chantal (HollyChantal.com), one of my outstanding Certified Book Yourself Solid Coaches, specializes in web design and Internet marketing. She helped one of her clients get an average of four more clients each week by working with her on integrating the Book Yourself Solid strategies into her web site. Holly's client, Jessica, who is in the direct sales industry, used her blog to spotlight products, specials, and provide articles that offered useful information to her customers as well as position herself as the go-to person in her niche. Because Jessica doubled the number of clients she received, she was able to tighten her Red Velvet Rope policy and only work with her most ideal clients. She was then able to refer clients who weren't a good fit to other associates for whom they were a good fit. This advanced her status in the organization by increasing the earning power and profits of her team. Thanks to the Book Yourself Solid strategies (and Holly's coaching), Jessica's team has become one of the top 10 earners for the company in the nation.

The 10 Most Effective Web Site Home Page Formats for Service Professionals

The Brochure

A brochure web site is usually about five pages and is the online equivalent of a written brochure. It's the most common format of web site for the service professional. Generally a brochure web site includes information about you and your company, your services, and some resources, for starters.

The risk you take when using this format is that it can appear to be all about you rather than the people you serve, and if you aren't creative,

your web site may not look much different from another service professional's web site.

The E-Mail Converter

The e-mail converter format—aka the squeeze page—is the ultimate
one-step web site. There's only one thing to do on an e-mail converter
web-page—give your e-mail address in exchange for something of
value, like a special report or white paper, a mini-course or coupon,
or access to your always-have-something-to-invite-people-to offer. You
must have a very compelling offer right out front that prompts visitors
to engage because you've got only one shot at getting that all-important
e-mail address.

Just be careful with a site like this. You may capture e-mail addresses
that help you build a list of subscribers, but some people will be put off
by this type of web site. Essentially, you're asking for something before
you give anything. By now, you probably get that the Book Yourself Solid
way is to give first before you ask for something in return. Feel free to test
it out and see how your target market and ideal clients respond. That's the
true indicator of any marketing tactic—how the people you serve respond
to it—what results does it produce and how do those to whom you are
marketing feel about the tactic?

You will need a tool that allows you to capture e-mail addresses and
automatically send customers a confirmation and follow-up with delivery
of the value in exchange. There are many programs that will help you
do this, including ConstantContact.com, AWeber.com, 1shopping.com,
Infusionsoft.com, and others.

The One-Page Sales Letter

A one-page sales letter is designed specifically to encourage buying a
product, program, or service. You may have come across one-page sales
letters that you found hyped up, over the top, and all about the hard sell.

That's not who you are, so your one-page sales letter won't come off that way. Remember, all of your marketing must be designed to speak to your target market. If your target market responds to hyped-up, over-the-top, and hard-sell marketing messages, well then, that's what you'll use. I have a feeling, though, that that's not the case. The reason so many online marketers use the long form one-page sales letter is that when it's done well, it's a good tool for selling products. It is designed to elicit a direct response from the reader. Long form one-page sales letters work well because they're not really meant to be read in their entirety. They're designed to be scanned. That's why they often boast big colorful headlines and bullets and bold text and highlighted text, for example. The important point here is this: know your market and how they'll respond to this type of sales page.

The Menu of Services

A menu of services is a home page that offers a list of scenarios that you provide services for. Your visitors will choose one of the scenarios based on their needs and then they're automatically taken to a more targeted message on another page. Then you can start a virtual conversation through the more targeted page that speaks specifically to them and their situation and how you can help. It allows you to provide customized value and a level of interaction lacking in other formats.

But beware: Using this format puts you at risk for appearing to do too many things rather than serving as an expert in a single area. It's also a less direct line to an opt-in that begins a conversation because they're required to choose another page first.

The Assessment

Offering an assessment that speaks directly to the urgent needs and compelling desires of your target market is a wonderful way to create an immediate connection and help your potential clients assess how much they actually need your services. Assessments can be created in the form of a quiz, survey, or personal profile. They're effective because they're interactive, they engage the client, and they invite a qualifying action; to receive answers to the assessment would require the assessment takers to enter their e-mail address. The entire process can be automated, and you can create new assessments or quizzes to have on your web site to draw repeat visitors back to your site.

The Portal

A portal site typically offers a catalog of web sites, a search engine, large amounts of content about certain subject matter, or all of the above. It's not often used for the service professional, but can be a good choice for you if you have many products, services, and programs that are different from each other or serve different target markets. This format allows you to present your multiple offerings so that visitors can choose which product or service they want to learn more about based on their needs. However, you have to make sure that you don't create a home page that offers too many choices that may potentially confuse your visitors.

The Viral Entertainment Site

Viral entertainment sites are based on the buzz marketing approach—getting other people to spread your messages. A viral entertainment site offers some sort of media that is either emotional, funny, or makes people say "Wow!" It's a great way to make a positive connection with lots of people who don't even know you. Take a look at EntrepreneurIdol.com. It's a hoot.

The Blog

A blog, which is actually short for *weblog*, originated simply as an online diary. It has become so much more than that over the past few years.

The most recent entries appear on the home page of the blog. Older entries, known as archives, are organized by date and often categorized by topic. Most blogs offer the reader the opportunity to post comments, share the post on other social media platforms like Facebook, LinkedIn, and Twitter, as well as rate the post. As opposed to static web sites, blogs are appealing to readers (and search engines alike) because they are instantly updatable from any Internet connection, offering fresh, timely, and relevant content. If you can send an e-mail, you can publish a weblog. Of course, you can integrate a blog into any other of these other types of sites.

The biggest drawback to a blog is that it works only if you post to it regularly. If it doesn't change often, that's worse than having a static regular web site. See my blog at michaelport.com/blog.

The Social Network

Social networking is the grouping of individuals into specific groups, like a political or religious group or men who collect model trains. Certainly, social networking can be, and always has been, organized in person. In the twenty-first century, it has become even easier to organize groups of interested people using the Internet. Hundreds of millions of people are online and they are looking to meet others that share their interests and can offer advice, support, or connections about golf, basket weaving, entrepreneurship, swimming, parenting, addiction, and more. When you want to organize people online you can use a type of web site typically referred to as a social network platform. It functions like a community center with places for discussions, posting of information, pictures, video, and more. When a new person is granted access to the community, they can usually set up a profile and immediately begin to socialize.

The social network web site format is a generous and effective way to stand in the service of the community you wish to serve. See ThinkBigRevolution.com as an example. It's free and allows the people I serve to connect and collaborate. Basically, you can create your own version of Facebook or LinkedIn but specifically for your target audience. Your smaller, but not necessarily less powerful, site will serve the personal and professional needs of your clients—and be an effective tool for you to build relationships with potential clients as the leader of the community. To see a list of services that you can use to build your own social network site go to Wikipedia.com and search on "Social Media Hosting Services."

The Personal Brand Identity Site

If you're promoting your personal brand rather than the brand of a company, you may want to consider this format. I created one for myself at MichaelPort.com. It's one page, by the way, that demonstrates what I do, what I stand for, and who I serve. It's really pretty simple. It's essentially my personal version of a Google Profile page, which, incidentally, everyone should have as well.

4.16.5 Written Exercise: Go online and find three or four web sites you like and three or four that you dislike. List the formats they use and the features you like and dislike, and why. These will be useful as examples of what you want—and don't want—to show your designer. If possible, choose web sites for this exercise that provide services to your target market and note what they're offering and how they present their offering. This will give you a sense of what's already out there and may spark new ideas.

What to Look for in a Web Designer

When I started my business, I spent over $6,000 on a web site with lots of funky animation that I never used—or I should say, I used it for five months to no avail. The site may have looked cool, but it wasn't effective because it was all Flash-based and all about what I did rather than what I could do for my clients. I learned pretty quickly to look for a web designer who is proficient in all three of the critical skills of web design: design, marketing, and programming. I encourage you to do the same. Now, all of my web design is being done by RetinaWebAgency.com.

Now you know how you want to *design* your web site. Next up is how to get people to *land (and stay)* on your web site. You're in the right place. Turn the page and you'll be on your way to traffic school—where you'll learn how to drive traffic, quickly (and safely) to your site.

PART 2

GETTING VISITORS TO YOUR WEB SITE

*I think the Internet is uniquely suited to this free
market idea . . . we all need each other.*
—Pete Ashdown

Here is where we look at how to create a steady flow of traffic to your site and how to convert that traffic into business; a process that's called *generating traffic*. I'll cover the nine most important and easy-to-understand tried-and-true techniques and strategies for generating more traffic to your site, along with the two essential principles of *visitor conversion*, so that, when someone does visit your site, you can get him to give you permission to keep in touch with him (market to him).

9 Book Yourself Solid Web Traffic Strategies

Get Listed in Search Engines and Optimize Your Site

Search engine optimization (SEO) is all about how to get the search engines to notice your site and, ideally, to give you a good ranking. Then, when someone searches for what you're offering, your listing will be displayed in a high position in the search results. SEO is a big topic. Entire books are written about it so I'll touch on the basics and if you choose to make SEO a primary traffic generation strategy, I trust that you'll continue your learning elsewhere.

To get listed with most of these search engines, they must know you exist. So the first thing to do is either submit your site to each search engine or have another site link directly to your site. Doing so will let the search engines know you're up and ready for prime time.

Once you've submitted your site for inclusion in the major search engines, make sure your site is optimized with the best keywords, that is, words or phrases that your target market types into the search engine to find what you provide. Because every search engine has different criteria for ranking web sites, and none of them actually want you to know what these criteria are, the most effective strategy for search engine optimization (SEO) is to build content-rich pages that your visitors want to see, pages that are legitimately filled with the same keywords and phrases they use to search for what you are offering.

How do you determine what keywords and phrases will help you drive the most traffic? You focus on the urgent needs and compelling desires of your target market. What would a potential client type into a search engine to find what they're looking for? It may not be what you think. The best keywords and phrases are the emotional, benefit-filled terms that:

- Have the most number of searches.
- Have the least amount of competition.
- Draw targeted traffic that is ready, willing, and able to invest in your services.

In fact, there are a number of tools that tell you exactly how many people are searching on your chosen keywords and phrases. Google offers a free keyword search tool. To find it, just search on Google for "Google Keyword Tool." When you find the right keywords and phrases for your site, optimize your site using these same words and phrases. Understanding your best keywords is essential for the success of all your online marketing.

> **4.16.6 Written Exercise:** Identify the top five keywords and phrases for your site.

Boost Your Link Popularity

Boosting your link popularity (the number of inbound links) and having quality inbound links (links from sites that have a good ranking and serve the same target market as you or offer related content) pointing to your web site will help you in two ways:

1. It improves your search engine ranking.
2. It provides a way for more quality traffic to find your site.

Please don't even think about fooling around with link exchange software or programs. Boosting your link popularity has to be done legitimately. It's important to know that you need to create relationships with other sites that already have good web traffic and status. Exchanging links with five of your friends—who just built their web sites—is an enterprising idea, but it's not going to do much for your search engine ranking and probably won't help drive any significant traffic to your site. If you don't know many other people who have a strong web presence, here's what you can do:

1. Put together a list of other professionals who serve the same target market and have already created some demand for their services and products.
2. Go to Yahoo.com and enter this text: linkdomain:urlOfOtherProfessional.com.
3. Click the search button and you'll get a listing of all the sites on Yahoo that are linked to the URL you entered. You can then contact those sites, make friends, add value to their life and work, and offer to trade links with them.

4.16.7 Written Exercise: Identify five sites that are popular with lots of traffic and serve the same target market as you serve.

4.16.8 Booked Solid Action Step: Now add the owner or webmaster of each site to your BYS list of 20, make friends, add value to their life and work, and offer to trade links with them (when you've built the proportionate amount of trust necessary for such a request). Make sure that you link to them first so they can see that you're intent on serving them.

Leverage Your E-Mail Signature

One of the most often overlooked methods of promoting your services is through your e-mail signature file. This is the information that you put at the close of your e-mail. It's a simple and effective way to tell people about what you have to offer and to encourage them to sign up for your newsletter or any other no-barrier-to-entry offer that you make.

You could consider asking a question in your signature file and include a link to your site where the answer to the question will be waiting. Here's an example:

Are you booked solid with high-paying clients all day tomorrow? No? Then go to MichaelPort.com. I can help.

Or keep it short and simple with something like this:

Discover How to Get More Clients
MichaelPort.com

4.16.9 Booked Solid Action Step: Create a compelling e-mail signature and begin using it immediately.

Promote Your Site Using Article Directories

An excellent method for building your credibility and driving traffic to your web site is by writing informative articles on topics that are close to your heart and submitting them to niche web sites and article directories for free.

Why does this work? Web surfers, just like search engines, gobble up information, which means the people who manage web sites are desperate for good content to feed them. They understand that people recognize a web site as a valuable resource if there is adequate, timely, and frequently updated content. If the site owners provide quality information not found anywhere else, people will regularly return to their pages to acquire it.

If you're supplying this content, you can catapult your name into the limelight and become known as a category authority. As long as your written information meets the specific needs of these niche web sites and article directories by being relevant, timely, and well-written, most editors will be happy to accept your article and post it on their site.

You may be wondering: "How does that generate traffic to my web site?" By including a brief byline about yourself at the end of your article, with a link to your site, you can generate traffic back to your web site pages. Since readers have already been introduced to your expertise and credible advice, they'll be interested in reading more of your worthy material and learning about your offerings.

The beautiful part about writing articles to share across the Web is that there is no barrier to entry whatsoever. Posting your articles on these niche web sites and in article directories gets your name and web site address in front of untold numbers of viewers. As a bonus, your article appears in search results displayed by engines like Google, MSN, and Yahoo.

Participate in Online Communities

There are hundreds of thousands, if not millions, of groups online discussing the issues of the day: discussion boards, forums, social networks, listserv groups, and others. Getting involved in the communities in which your target market hangs out offers you an opportunity to become a leader of the community by offering advice, support, and any other value. Many of these communities give you the opportunity to create a profile that displays your bio, e-mail address, web site address and more. When you make a (good) name for yourself in a community made up of your target market, members of that community, will be compelled to visit your web site to learn more about you and how you are able to serve them. You find these groups by searching Google. Input the various keywords and key phrases that your target market would use to find communities built around their industry, situation, needs, and so on. I discuss the big three, Facebook, LinkedIn, and Twitter in Part 3 of this chapter.

4.16.10 Booked Solid Action Step: Find the most active online communities that serve your target market and are focused on topics you know a lot about. As a member of the group, you can make intelligent, thoughtful posts that add value to the discussion topic. You might answer other members' questions or you might suggest helpful resources or simply provide your opinions on issues that relate to your industry. And you never know—you may learn a lot by reading what others have to say.

Cross-Promote through Marketing Partners

This is one of my absolute favorite online marketing strategies because it allows me to partner with, and promote, other people I think are fabulous while they do the same for me. We've talked about how important it is to get other people to talk about you so you can quickly build trust with new potential clients. Well, cross-promoting through marketing partners is the best way to do so.

If my colleague sends out an e-mail to her newsletter subscribers endorsing my services, products, or programs, her subscribers are more likely to trust me. When I promote her, the same will be true. It makes it much easier to build relationships with potential clients that way. It's just like meeting a great friend of a great friend of yours. You love your friend and if your friend loves that person, you assume that person is great. The same goes for cross-promoting online (and offline).

You can cross-promote like this on many levels: between you and another service professional who happens to serve the same target market or with larger associations and organizations. If you're an accountant who serves small business owners and you develop a relationship with the membership director for an online small business association that has 75,000 members and she promotes your services to their membership, just think about all of the newsletter sign-ups you're going to get. And just think about all of these new potential clients who turn into clients. The possibilities are limitless. That is why this is my favorite online marketing strategy.

Here are some other strategies to consider:

- Co-produce special promotions you could not afford on your own.
- Have a contest with the prizes contributed by your partners. For the next contest, roles change, and you contribute your product or service as a prize for a partner's contest.
- Give customers a free product or service from a participating partner when they buy something that month from all of the partners listed on a promotional piece.

Online cross-promotion has the potential for a big marketing payoff because partners can successfully expand through one another's client base. Both you and your marketing partners can gain an inexpensive and credible introduction to more potential clients more effectively than with the traditional lone-wolf methods of networking, advertising, or public relations.

4.16.11 Written Exercise: Come up with several of your own unique ideas for cross-promotions and identify who might be a good marketing partner.

4.16.12 Booked Solid Action Step: Reach out, connect with, and share your ideas with the people you identified in the preceding exercise.

Use Tell-a-Friend Forms

A significant percentage of your clients will come from referrals. If your current raving fans are telling others about you offline, don't you think they would like to tell others about you online as well? Well, they can with a tell-a-friend form. Imagine that a visitor to your site likes what she sees and believes she has a friend who could benefit from your services. With a click on your tell-a-friend link, she can refer your site to her friend. You can even customize it so that it automatically sends a personalized e-mail promoting your site and its web address. Facebook allows you to add a "Like" button to any web page for your visitors to click, telling all their friends that they like your page, building your online social platform and status at the same time.

It's an amazingly simple and effective strategy. Again, you're getting others to talk about you and help build trust between you and a potential client. If you are adventurous and would like to code your own tell-a-friend forms, you can find free tell-a-friend scripts by searching online. For we less tech-savvy mortals, asking our web designer to set this up is probably the way to go.

4.16.13 Booked Solid Action Step: Create, or hire someone to create, a tell-a-friend form and begin using it.

Take Advantage of Online Press Releases

The Internet has unleashed so many new opportunities to connect with your target market and get free publicity online. Online press releases are one marketing tactic often underused, yet effective for increasing web traffic. Online publicity opportunities can improve your site's search engine ranking while, at the same time, enhance your credibility and increase exposure to media outlets.

For example, Rachel, a client of Certified Book Yourself Solid Coach Cindy Earl (GetKnownGetClients.com), a social media marketing and online PR expert, wanted to increase her sign-ups for her always-have-something-to-invite-people-to offer. Cindy advised her to send out an online press release. Together, they crafted the release and within a few days of distribution, through PRWeb.com, it received over 200 reads through Google, Yahoo!, and other search and news web sites. And, most important, the registrations to Rachel's event increased by nearly 50 percent.

Consider using online press releases to increase traffic to your web site. Certified Book Yourself Solid Coach Cindy says that doing so will:

- Increase traffic to your web site quickly (usually within 24 to 48 hours).
- Boost your credibility—it increases the know, like, and trust factors.
- Make you stand out from the crowd because it's a marketing tactic that few small business owners use.
- Often converts traffic better than pay-per-click advertising.
- Deliver traffic for months and years to come because online press releases are permanently indexed by search engines.

So, what's the difference between an online press release and an offline press release? When a small business has news, online press releases are the fastest and easiest way for the media to find them. Sites like PRWeb. com and PRNewswire.com take your press release and place your news directly on leading sites like Yahoo! News, Google News, Ask.com, and other sites, which reach hundreds of thousands of news subscribers and media publications, including bloggers, journalists, and consumers. Online press releases increase traffic to your web site almost instantly and increase your search engine rankings. For small business owners, PRWeb.com is by far the most feature-rich and affordable service.

Your press release must be well-written and targeted. To optimize your press release for online distribution, use keywords for your business throughout the body of the press release, so that when someone does a search on your business or topic, your press release shows up prominently in search engines. Keywords should be used in the headline, subtitle, and body of the release.

If you're not a writer, you can easily outsource press release writing to a freelance writer or PR agency. Many sites have press release distribution services (some may require a wait time of 24 to 48 hours), most have a fee, but some offer various free options as well.

Another useful tool is an online press kit. You can add a page to your web site titled "Press Kit" or "Media Resources." The page should include a personal bio, company bio, any press releases written, article placements, and a professional photo of key business personnel. In addition to adding a page to your web site, you can also host your press kit with online press page services. Journalists and bloggers frequently visit these sites for story ideas and interviews.

4.16.14 Booked Solid Action Step: Write a press release about the most impressive result one of your clients achieved and submit it to PRWeb.com. You can get tips at the site on how to craft a solid press release. Or, go to GetKnownGetClients.com for more information on online PR and social media marketing strategies.

Profit from Pay-per-Click Advertising

Using pay-per-click ads on search engines can be an effective marketing tool. Pay-per-click means that you pay a fee for each person who clicks on the ad. You may be surprised to realize that this is the first time I've mentioned spending money on advertising. Until now our other online strategies haven't cost much besides time. You should not be spending much, if any, money online to generate traffic. If you show up in the top eight regular search results for your keywords, you certainly don't need to pay for clicks. But if you're not in that top eight, this is a great way to get targeted exposure for a small investment with the potential for a big return.

Pay-per-click ads allow you to connect with prospective clients as they're searching for services or products like yours. You create an ad and choose keywords that, when entered into the search engine, will bring up your pay-per-click ad along with the regular search results. You pay only when someone clicks through to your site from the pay-per-click ad.

These pay-per-click ads are good for generating traffic to your site and great for testing what keywords and keyword phrases generate a lot of traffic and what percentage of that traffic converts to potential customers and actual customers. When you sign up for Google Adwords (google .com/ads) and Yahoo! (http://searchmarketing.yahoo.com) pay-per-click accounts, you'll receive a code to put on your web site that will allow you to track the data.

The position of your ad (highest to lowest) is determined by your bid price, the amount you're willing to pay for a click (the exception is with Google, where your position is determined by a combination of your bid price and your click-through rate). You really need to be on the first search page for your pay-per-click ads to generate significant traffic. Of course you can affect your position by modifying your bid. But don't worry—you can cap the amount of your daily spending so you don't exceed your mortgage payment in pay-per-click ads. The other great thing about being in the top three positions on Google and Yahoo is that you're then syndicated onto other sites and search engines all over the Internet.

Be careful: Make sure you're converting the traffic you pay for. Keep in mind that a web site is useless if you can't secure the e-mail addresses of visitors to your site and get their permission to follow up with them. Nothing is worse than paying for traffic to your site and not converting any of it. That's like driving a station wagon packed with cash and throwing it out the windows as you aimlessly drive around town. However, if you do convert a good percentage of that traffic to potential clients and a percentage of them become actual clients, well, now you've invested wisely. In fact, if you run the numbers, you can see your exact return on investment.

4.16.15 Booked Solid Action Step: Go to google.com/ads and set up an account. Then create a test ad campaign for one of your products or services. Make sure that you cap your daily spending at a low amount so that you learn how to profit from pay-per-click before you rack up significant fees. Google.com has great tutorials and help pages that can answer your questions. Track your conversion so you know what kind of return on your investment you are getting.

The Two Essential Principles of Visitor Conversion

You want to attract visitors to your web site and turn them into friends, then potential clients, and finally, current clients. You can generate all the traffic you want, but if that traffic does not want to stay or come back and get more information, advice, or resources from you in the future, it's not doing much good.

There are two essential principles of visitor conversion: enticement and consumption. Understand them, implement them, and profit from them, but never abuse them.

Enticement

Your web site is like your home. What's the first thing you do when someone comes to visit? You offer a drink and a bite to eat. You ask, "Are you hungry? Can I get you something to eat? How about a glass of water or some iced tea?" If you know your visitors well, you can offer them their *favorite* snack and beverage. In fact, when family or close friends come to visit, you make an extra trip to the supermarket to get all their favorites.

This is the principle of *enticement*. You offer something of value to your web site visitors as soon as they land on your site in exchange for their e-mail address and permission to follow up. They give it to you because they're interested in your enticement and they believe you'll deliver more good stuff in the days and months to come.

Be careful not to hide your enticing offers in the crevices of your web site. When you have a dinner party, do you hide the food around the house in strange places or set it just out of reach? Of course you don't. You put the hors d'oeuvres and munchies in the most obvious, accessible places possible. And sure enough, the places you put the hors d'oeuvres are exactly where everybody ends up hanging out! Have you ever been at a party where the host skimped on the hors d'oeuvres? Did you find that everybody started hanging around the kitchen as they got hungrier and hungrier? We're always searching for what we want and need, and your web site needs to speak to your visitors' needs and desires. So please, put your opt-in form in the most obvious place possible. I suggest you place it above the fold (the part of your home page that is visible without having to scroll down).

As an experiment, I recently surveyed the web sites of 50 random service professionals, and guess what? Only seven of them had a prominent opt-in form with something offering great and immediate value to their target market. The other 43 either did not have an opt-in form at all or did but put it in some obscure place that was hard to find. I hope that after publishing this book I can do another survey and see very different results.

4.16.16 Booked Solid Action Step: If you don't already have an e-course, special report, or other enticement to offer your visitors, create one using the easy steps I outlined in Chapter 7. Then ensure that you have an opt-in for your offer displayed prominently on your site.

Consumption

The principle of consumption follows the principle of enticement. When your visitors have been enticed and have given you their e-mail address in exchange for a mini-course, white paper, special report, e-book, article, audio recording, coupon, or other free offer, you must follow up to help them consume the valuable information or experience they just received. Most people don't take advantage of all the opportunities available to them. It would probably be impossible to do so. An even smaller number of people follow up on all of the opportunities available to them through the Internet and e-mail, even the ones they've asked for. When someone does opt in to receive your free offer, he may not really consume it—really use it, learn from it, and benefit from it. It's your responsibility to help him do so by following up with an e-mail.

Does it sound like it would be a lot of work? Oh, no, my big-thinking friend, it's not. You can use an automatic e-mail responder system to set up a series of e-mail messages that are automatically sent to a new contact at any frequency you specify. You can send one a day, one a week, or one a month for a year—it's up to you. Your messages will check in with your new friend and begin to deliver the services you provide or other helpful resources.

The principle of consumption should follow the principle of enticement. It's just as you would ask your guest, the one you generously supplied with her favorite snack and beverage, "How is the tea? Is it cold enough? Would you like more ice? Is it helping quench your thirst?" Maybe you'd offer a suggestion, "You know . . . if you squeeze the lemon like so, it tastes even better!" You'll ask your new friends how they're doing with the information you gave them and you'll help them consume it. If you do this well, you'll increase your likeability, and you'll create a more meaningful and lasting connection with your new friends, turning them from new friends into potential clients or maybe even into current clients.

4.16.17 Booked Solid Action Step: If you don't already have an auto-responder system to help potential clients consume your offer, set one up using MailChimp.com or ConstantContact.com.

Okay, take a break. Take a walk. Take it easy. Then, come on back as we move into Part 3 of the Book Yourself Solid Web Strategy, Building Your Social Media Platform.

PART 3

BUILDING YOUR SOCIAL MEDIA PLATFORM

The Internet is becoming the town square for the global village of tomorrow.

—Bill Gates

Social media sites come and go. When I wrote the first edition of *Book Yourself Solid*, Ryze was one of the most popular business networking sites on the Internet. When writing this second edition, Twitter had about 50 million monthly visits and Ryze was wrecked and will not rise again. So, it's important to understand the principles that support successful social networking and personal platform building (how well you're known). To do this, I'm going to give you an overview of the big three—Facebook, LinkedIn, and Twitter. If you understand what makes someone popular on any of these sites, you can transfer and apply that understanding to any other social media site so you can play to your heart's delight. I'm also going to give you a great primer on online video and how to use it to build your online platform, earn credibility, and ultimately get clients. I think online video is a social media platform in and of itself and it's just going to get more popular as it gets easier and easier for the non-techie to shoot, edit, and upload video.

Like all relationship and platform development, when it comes to social media or online social networking, you must be willing to make a long-term commitment to the cause. And, contrary to some expert advice, you should not outsource your social media marketing to an assistant or outside firm. Sure, get help with the technical aspects of organizing a Facebook Fan page, if you need it, but if you really want to build your social network online, you've got to show up to do it. I mean *social* is the operative word, here. And, really . . . how hard is that? You don't even need to leave your house! You just need to make the time for it. And, as you know, we need to make the time to do our marketing to earn clients.

When you do build a large platform of fans on Facebook or followers on Twitter, or whatever other social media platform is the site du jour while you're reading this, over time, you'll be able to turn your networking efforts into marketing initiatives that drive sales. And, if you're interested in increasing your search engine ranking, your social media platform will help with that too. According to a recent social media study by the TheWritePaperSource.com, 88 percent of companies indicated that they're using social media for marketing purposes and, as a result, over half of them saw a rise in search engine rankings and traffic to their web sites.

Your return on investment in social media networking is both quantitative and qualitative. You are likely to see more leads for new clients and increased profit and, at the same time, enhance your brand identity through positive, professional, and valuable interaction with and service to your community, industry, or field.

Historically, traditional media was driven by professional news organizations and their advertisers. As you know, online media, along with social media, is more democratized. Issues, ideas, and discussions are driven by the public more than they have been in the past. I think the cream rises to the top, so if you're putting out great products and services, your marketing will take hold and you'll book business. But, put out a crappy product and the word will spread like a brush fire through the social media forest.

Social Media Sites and How to Use Them

The Booked Solid Facebook Strategy

For this section on Facebook, I'm assuming two things. First, that you have already done the work on building your foundation; and second, I am assuming that you have a basic knowledge of Facebook and have a profile on the site.

As the most-visited site on the Internet, Facebook is one of the most powerful marketing platforms available. With over 550 million active users, of which half log on daily, Facebook, like most social media, levels the playing field for the small business marketer.

What makes Facebook so appealing is that it is a feature-rich interactive environment accessible to all. Facebook has multiple ways of keeping in touch, including built-in e-mail-like messaging and real-time chat. It enables a savvy businessperson to zero in on a target market through Facebook's ability to let special interest groups gather together in Groups and on Pages.

Facebook makes it possible for you to reach out to the most prominent figures in your field. It allows a small businessperson to make a large presence within a very short span of time. This accelerates the process of gaining credibility and trust—all for little or no cost.

Facebook also smoothly interfaces with your web site, blog, and other social media platforms such as Twitter. Your blog posts can be instantly pushed onto your Facebook Page and your Facebook posts can be automatically tweeted to all your followers on Twitter. (Don't worry if you don't yet have followers on Twitter. If you want 'em, I'll show you how to get 'em later in this section.)

For now, I am going to show you how to get started on Facebook with marketing in mind. While it would take a whole book to cover all aspects of Facebook marketing, here you'll learn not only how to get started, but also how to build your Facebook platform and advance your Internet presence.

Why Use Facebook?

- It is a powerful networking platform that allows you to stay in touch with your clients, prospects, and networking partners.
- It puts whatever you have to say in front of whoever is following you as soon as you post it.
- It allows extremely targeted marketing to any special interest group imaginable.
- It integrates smoothly with your web site, blog, Twitter, and YouTube accounts, as well as many other social sites.
- It increases your trust and credibility with potential clients and referral partners.
- It gives you access to people who otherwise would not be accessible, not only in written messages, but also in real-time chat.
- It provides the ability to directly build your e-mail list through the use of the same opt-in forms you may be using on your web site.

Using Facebook for Business—The Basics   When using Facebook for your business presence, it is important to first understand the difference between your *personal* presence, your *Profile;* and your *business* presence, your *Page.* Each one has features that the other does not. Because of this, to most effectively use Facebook, you want to use your Profile and Page in conjunction with each other. First, it's important to understand the differences between the two. Then, I can show you the different tools that are available to you for marketing on Facebook. You may also have heard someone make reference to Facebook Groups and Community pages, neither of which is particularly appropriate for business use, but I'll touch on them briefly so you understand what they're for.

1. *Profile.* When you first signed up for Facebook, your Profile was created automatically; that's your personal presence. It's made up of two parts: the Profile and the home page (also called the news feed). The news feed is where your friends' postings are made visible to you. The Profile is where you, as an individual, are seen

on Facebook. It has several tabs, of which the two most important are the Wall tab and the Info tab. Your Wall is where your posts appear, as well as any posts directly from a friend to you. Your Info tab contains all your Profile information. *The biggest advantage of a Profile over a Page is that you can see the Info tab of friends and you can only become friends with someone through your Profile.* The Info tab contains much valuable information. While some people may have their privacy settings set to allow any visitors to see their Info tab, most people allow only their friends to see it. The biggest limitation to the Profile is that you are allowed to have no more than 5,000 friends. I know that seems like a lot but you'll be surprised how quickly you can make friends on Facebook if you use it as a primary marketing strategy. It is important to note that you may have only one Profile. Those who create more than one Profile risk being kicked off Facebook and losing everything they've built.

2. *Page.* Also known as Fan Pages, they are your business presence. There are many advanced features available on Pages, including the ability to embed code (such as your e-newsletter opt-in box) into the Page. You can have unlimited followers, who "like" your Page, but can only invite as followers those who are already your friends. This is the main reason why you want to work both together. Until you reach the 5,000 mark with your friends, the best way to get followers of your business presence is with your Facebook friends. Therefore, you will want to target as your friends those who are in your target market. Therefore, you do not want to say or do anything on your Profile that you would not want to be seen by those you do business with.

3. *Groups.* Primarily for special interests, they are very much like private clubs for those who share that interest. They are limited in size, as are Profiles, to 5,000 people. Because they do not permit the use of apps, one cannot put such things as opt-in boxes on Groups.

4. *Community Pages.* These are like Pages in function, but like groups, are for causes and common interests rather than business building.

Tools

- *Messaging*. Facebook messaging is much like e-mail. You have the ability to send a message to anyone on Facebook, not just your friends. Therefore, it is important that you are respectful of others and have a purpose for messaging them that will be of interest or of value to them. With messages, like e-mail, you can send the same message to more than one person. When anyone receives a message, they will get a flag on the top of their Facebook screen that notifies them of it.

- *Chat*. Facebook Chat enables you to have a real-time conversation with anyone you are friends with when they are online. Facebook gives you a list of those friends who are online.

- *Lists*. You are able to create lists of friends based on any criteria you desire. For example, you are able to make a list of family members, and then post something that only family members will see. This can be very helpful for your business. You can create a list of all the people that you recently contacted, and then easily see when an individual on this list is online.

- *Events*. Facebook allows you to announce events that you are holding, and to mass-invite people to the event. All your friends will see your event listed on the right side of their home page. Also listed with events are your friends' birthdays.

- *Posts*. Users can post up to 420 characters to their wall on their Profile or Pages that they administer. Also, users can post to the walls of their friends, and to the walls of Pages, depending on the permissions that are set up for that Page or Profile.

- *Comments*. Users can comment on a post if they have permission to do so. This allows for interaction on posted topics.

- *Likes*. Users can indicate that they like a post, just by clicking the *like* button. Also, where before one would become a *fan* of a Page, users now *like* a Page to follow it.

- *Invites*. Invites are used in various places throughout Facebook. One can invite a user to be a friend. One can also invite others to an event. You can also invite people to like a Page.

- *Discussion boards*. Pages allow you to have a *Discussion* tab, through which you or allowed users can start a discussion, much like a message board.
- *Ads*. You can advertise your Page, your offerings, and your web site. Facebook advertising gives you many ways to target the ad, including geographical and demographic targeting.
- *Links*. You can post links to web sites in your Wall posts, your comments, event listings, and in notes.
- *Notes*. These are extended postings that have their own unique URL, much like a blog post.

What Is Your Goal for Using Facebook? There are many things that businesses could use Facebook for. Here are some of them:

- Finding clients.
- Finding networking partners.
- Cross-promoting with strategic alliance partners.
- Earning credibility.
- Creating visibility.
- Announcing events.
- Promoting your products and services.
- Driving traffic to your site.
- Driving traffic to your blog.
- Building your e-mail list.
- Having sales conversations.
- Creating a base of raving fans.

How to Use the Book Yourself Solid System on Facebook Almost every aspect of the Book Yourself Solid System can be used on Facebook, once you have done the work on your Foundation.

1. *Who Knows What You Know and Do They Like You?* One of the most powerful uses of Facebook is to showcase your expertise

in your field. You are able to list all your qualifications in your Profile. By making frequent valuable posts on your Page, people get to know what you know. Facebook has the ability to accelerate the process of gaining credibility. As an example, you should see what Certified Book Yourself Solid Coach Woody Haiken has accomplished through Facebook. He specializes in teaching massage therapists how to get booked solid and has created a Facebook Fan page to serve this group, facebook.com/TheGrowingPractice. He's done an outstanding job. Also, take a look at his web site, TheGrowingPractice.com, to see how he has integrated his Facebook Strategy into his general site.

2. *Book Yourself Solid Sales Cycle Process.* By being actively engaged with prospective and active clients on Facebook, they know that they can find you there and what you can do for them. Since you know who is online among your friends, you can connect through a real-time chat conversation. By having information that is salient to your target market, you can make your Page "sticky" through content-rich, informative, interesting posts that invite interaction. Facebook provides many ways that you can enhance relationships over time, and also provides the platform for sales conversations (when the time is right) for those who are following you. You can also announce your, "always-have-something-to-invite-people-to" event on Facebook.

3. *The Power of Information Products.* It is very easy to promote your Information Products on Facebook. Since you can place an opt-in box on your Page, you can offer a free information product in exchange for someone's contact information.

4. *Super Simple Selling.* Facebook allows you to have many interactions with people, and gives them easy access to you when they want to reach you. Because you can connect in Facebook Chat in real time, you are able to have sales conversations right on Facebook.

5. *Networking Strategy.* Facebook makes it easy to share your network, knowledge, and compassion with others.

6. *Direct Outreach*. Because social media enables so many connections, it can be easier through Facebook to meet people you wish to get to know. You simply invite the person to become your friend. However, it is very important to note that if you do, you must do it with a message that introduces yourself and recognizes the person for his accomplishments. Never send a message to someone you do not know asking him to do something for you. I know I've said it before.

7. *Referral Strategy*. Facebook makes it easy to not only give referrals to others, but to promote others' efforts. One of the best ways to get others to help you promote your business is for you to promote their business.

8. *Keep-in-Touch*. Facebook makes it easy to stay in touch. You can easily send Messages, or engage in a chat. It is very easy to make it personal on Facebook.

9. *Speaking and Demonstrating*. You can hold teleseminars and announce and promote them on Facebook. You can also use recordings of teleseminars as an info product that you promote on Facebook to build your list.

10. *Writing*. Facebook gives you a phenomenal platform for writing. Not only can you write short posts that inform your audience of what you do, but you can also provide information of value and write posts that encourage interaction. You can write longer posts through Facebook Notes, and also feed your blog to your page. Facebook gives you many avenues for your writing, which will enhance your credibility and help position you as an expert in your field.

11. *Web Strategy*. Facebook easily interfaces with your web site by posting Links with your Wall posts, comments, ads, and notes. Also, by importing your blog into your page using NetworkedBlogs, a Facebook app, you are able to drive traffic to your blog.

Facebook Done Wrong Facebook's power can be a double-edged sword. For example, the Events feature allows you to not only schedule and make public your "always-have-something-to-invite-people-to" event, but it also permits you to send out invitations. Be careful, one of the easiest ways to lose credibility, likeability, and trust is to send out invitations to everyone you are friends with on Facebook. This is a big pet peeve of mine . . . nothing looks sillier to someone on the East Coast than being invited to an event in California that afternoon. I've even been invited to an acrobatic yoga event in Brazil. Think before you invite!

Points to keep in mind when you invite people to events:

- Only invite people to events if they've given you permission to invite them to events. How do you get permission? Ask them and then make lists in Facebook—those who want invitations and those who don't.

If you are given permission to send event invitations:

- Make sure that the person can conveniently attend. If it is an in-person event, make sure you invite only those who are local to the event.
- Make sure that the event would be of interest to the person you are inviting.
- When possible, invite people with a personal message rather than a broadcasted message.

Facebook applications (or *apps*) enable third-party programmers to add to Facebook's functionality. Some of these applications are very useful for your marketing needs. Others, however, can destroy your credibility. Among these are such games as Mafia Wars and Farmville. It is best to refrain from playing games on Facebook if you intend to build a strong business presence. There are apps that will post annoying things to your friends' walls, including inappropriate quizzes and silly gifts. Resist the temptation. Not only do you not want your Wall littered with these frivolous distractions, but you also don't want to litter the walls of those you hope to do business with.

Facebook Done Right Through the use of Facebook, Certified Book Yourself Solid Coach Woody Haiken was able to earn trust and credibility in his field, at an accelerated rate, connect with many influential people in the massage profession, and gain many cross-promotion opportunities. He attributes his success to the application of the Book Yourself Solid system to the Facebook platform. Within a month of rolling out his Facebook marketing plan, Woody was able to accomplish the following:

- Earn membership in a group of the most influential people in his industry dedicated to cross-promoting one another.
- Land 1,400 fans, most of whom are massage therapists, his target market.
- Soar from zero newsletter subscribers to more than 500.
- Gain more than 500 blog followers.
- Book more than 20 new clients.

Woody earned these results by engaging his target market in personalized messages and chats. He regularly posts useful information on his Page's wall, asks provocative questions, and compels readers to respond. He then writes personal notes to those who participate, acknowledging their contribution and thanking them for it. Facebook done right is no different from any other marketing done right: it is about creating relationships over time.

If you'd like to see Woody's fan page, go to facebook.com/ TheGrowingPractice. You can also take a look at my Fan page at facebook .com/authormichaelport. See if you think I did it right. . . .

The Booked Solid LinkedIn Strategy

Compared to Facebook and Twitter, LinkedIn offers a more corporate, professional feel. It is a well-established social network and is a great place to make professional connections and get known among potential customers and clients, especially the corporate market. It has also become a useful job search site, where companies can post job openings and job seekers can market themselves to potential employers.

The mission of LinkedIn, according to its founders, is to "Connect the world's professionals to make them more productive and successful." LinkedIn works similarly to Facebook, with just a little less functionality. One of my favorite aspects of LinkedIn, however, is the ability to give and get recommendations from colleagues or employers, which serve as very effective testimonials.

Why Use LinkedIn?   Here are some of the reasons why LinkedIn is a good tool to add to your booked solid promotion strategy:

- A professional network that allows you to highlight your skills and past work experience.
- A robust environment to find corporate and professional prospects.
- An easy way to keep up with information and trends in your industry.
- Manages your professional identity online.
- Builds your "know, like, and trust factors." By sharing relevant content and knowledge through your updates you become known as an expert in your field.
- A powerful communication platform that allows you to stay in touch with your clients, prospects, and networking partners.
- Offers communication tools for direct messaging and group and event coordination.

Business Uses for LinkedIn—The Basics   How does LinkedIn work?

Now that you've seen some of the compelling reasons *why* you should be using LinkedIn, let's look at *how* it actually works.

- *Profile.* Your profile page on LinkedIn looks much like a resume because you have the opportunity to list your skills and past work experience. The first part of your profile is the *headline*, a brief statement about who you are and what you do—a great place to use your *who and do what* statement and maybe even a written version of your Book Yourself Solid Dialogue.

  - Your profile also includes your industry, regional network, experience, education, web site, and interests. It's important to fill in your profile completely. The more information you share, the more likely people will find and connect with you. Also, using relevant keywords throughout your profile will help the search engines associate the page with you and your other profiles online.

  - Below your web site listing, you can include your Twitter user name to link your account to Twitter. At the bottom of the page, you can choose options for private or public information sharing and indicate your availability for things like projects, new ventures, job inquiries, reconnecting, and so on.

  - LinkedIn also allows you to create a separate profile for your company or business, which can help build your brand on LinkedIn.

- *Network and Degrees of Connection.* One of the unique features of LinkedIn is the *degree of connection* feature that indicates if a person in your network is a first, second, or third degree connection. You will notice this indicated in a circle symbol with a number 1, 2, or 3 inside. If you are connected to someone directly as, say, the Certified Book Yourself Solid Coaches are to me, that connection would receive a 1. A second-degree connection is someone in your network who is not a direct connection, but a connection of one of your direct connections—a friend of a friend, so to speak. This always brings to mind the 1980s Faberge shampoo commercial in which one woman tells another woman about this great shampoo, then she tells two people, who tell two people, and so on and so on. If you're too young to remember it, search "Faberge Shampoo" on youtube.com.

- LinkedIn also calculates the number of people in your total network, which gives you an idea of the vast access you have to hundreds of people through all the network connections. Just like one-to-one networking, you have to remember that when you add one person to your network, you are also connected to their network as well. That's the power of networking.

- *Recommendations.* Another unique feature of LinkedIn is recommendations. You can give and receive written recommendations from colleagues. For example, you may ask a former employer or co-worker to write a brief recommendation for you by sending him a link that says, *"Will you write me a recommendation on LinkedIn?"* Obviously, being recommended is a big credibility booster to anyone who is viewing your profile. Recommendations can help boost your visibility, build your reputation and brand and help you get new clients or business opportunities. You can give and receive unlimited recommendations, which are listed right on your profile page.

LinkedIn Tools   Most of the features on LinkedIn are very similar to those on Facebook; for example:

- *Events.* You can list your own events on LinkedIn and invite your contacts to attend.
- *Applications.* LinkedIn applications function just like the applications in Facebook. You can link to your blog and import your blog postings. You can also link your Twitter account so that your tweets show up on your LinkedIn profile.
- *Search.* You have the ability to search for individuals and companies on LinkedIn and you can import your contacts from popular e-mail programs.
- *Groups.* You can create your own special interest group in LinkedIn focused on a hobby, or more likely, a topic related to your business (that is, your always-have-something-to-invite-people-to event).

- *Answers.* LinkedIn provides a forum to ask questions and get immediate feedback from your network. This is a really great tool for market research and to test the sentiment of your target market around a particular topic. As well as demonstrating your knowledge by answering questions posted by others.

Finding People through LinkedIn There are several ways to find people through LinkedIn:

- Search for people through the "Search" link at the top of your home page.
- Use your current e-mail contact lists on Gmail, AOL, and Yahoo!.
- Invite others to follow you by e-mail. LinkedIn will create an e-mail form that automatically sends a message to your imported contacts with a direct link to your LinkedIn profile.
- Search groups to find people with common interests or those in your target market.

What Are Your Goals for Using LinkedIn? As with any self-promotion strategy, first consider what you want to accomplish. Your objectives for using LinkedIn, just as with Facebook, may include one or more of the following:

- Finding clients.
- Finding networking partners.
- Cross-promoting with strategic alliance partners.
- Earning credibility.
- Creating visibility.
- Announcing events.
- Promoting your products and services.
- Driving traffic to your site.
- Driving traffic to your blog.
- Building your e-mail list.
- Having sales conversations.
- Creating a base of raving fans.

LinkedIn Done Right   Lewis Howes is a social media and LinkedIn consultant and co-author of *LinkedWorking*. He teaches entrepreneurs what they need to do to generate success on LinkedIn, and he should know. Lewis has built his entire business through LinkedIn.

I don't know Lewis personally, but I was excited to see that one of his biggest successes is his creative always-have-something-to-invite-people-to offer. Lewis hosts networking events in different cities around the country called LinkedIn Network Events. He markets them as a networking event and brings professionals together to connect and he gets to promote his business to hundreds of prequalified prospects. The events bring in hundreds of people at a time and generally cost only $10. Not to mention he's providing the community with his valuable service—connecting business professionals.

He gets maximum usage from his LinkedIn profile by posting regular updates, listing his events, showing photos of smiling, happy people having a great time at his events, and leveraging his profile information and past experience. He also imports his WordPress.com blog, has links to slide presentations on SlideShare.com and has tons of great recommendations from his clients and colleagues.

The Book Yourself Solid Twitter Strategy

Twitter is a little bit different from other social networking sites in that it's basically a community-driven microblogging site that allows you to build relationships and promote your products and services. Twitter has none of the other functionality to help execute your business strategies that Facebook and LinkedIn have.

Twitter users post updates to the question "What's happening?" in 140 characters or less. These short updates are called *tweets*. When you follow someone's tweets, you get a live feed of their updates in real time. Tweeters can restrict delivery to those in their circle of friends or by default allow open access to all followers.

Why Use Twitter? Here's why Twitter is such a powerful component of your Book Yourself Solid Web Strategy:

- It helps drive traffic to your web site.
- It's an effective marketing tool for SEO (search engine optimization). Each tweet that you send through Twitter has its own URL, which means each tweet is its own web page, which means that each individual tweet is indexed by Google.
- It builds your "know, like, and trust factors." By sharing relevant content and knowledge freely through your updates you become known as an expert in your field.
- It's a great way to create a strong, personal connection to your clients and potential clients.
- It has robust communication tools that include real-time chat and direct messaging.
- It allows permission-based marketing—the people who follow you have chosen to connect with you and will be open to a certain amount of promotion.
- It allows you to listen in on the conversations of a diverse community and provides an opportunity for excellent, real-time market research.

Business Uses for Twitter—The Basics Now that you've considered the compelling reasons *why* you should be using Twitter marketing, let's look at *how* Twitter actually works.

- *Profile.* Just like Facebook, Twitter users set up a personal profile (use your full name as your profile name, if it's available, and if it's not too long, because that is what people will connect to when searching for you). The profile includes your user name, a photo or logo, and a short bio. You have a very limited space for your bio, so be sure to include your location, web site, and primary keywords for your business in your description. You can also choose a background theme for your profile. Generic backgrounds are provided by Twitter, but you can also have a custom background designed using photos, colors, and your company logo to represent your brand. You should use a professional graphic designer to create your background so your visual brand identity stays consistent with your general web site.

- *Following.* When you join Twitter you are able to follow other people, meaning that you subscribe to their updates or tweets just as you subscribe to a blog. You can follow others on Twitter only if you have your own profile. The updates of people you are following will appear on your home page. Once you have a Twitter profile set up, other people can follow you as well and your tweets will show up on their home pages; and this is how you share your ideas, content, promotions, and more.

- *Twitter Stream.* This term refers to the stream of content (or tweets) from all the people you follow that appear on your Twitter home page.

Twitter Tools   Twitter works in three primary ways. You can tweet by sending a short message to a bunch of people publicly (tweet), you can send a short message to a specific person publicly (reply) or you can send a short message to a specific person privately (direct message).

- *Direct Messaging.* Direct messages are private messages to another Twitter user, which do not appear in the public timeline (or Twitter stream). You can only send a direct message to someone who is already following you.

- *Reply.* The @ symbol refers to a tweet directed to a specific username or a reply to a tweet that that person has posted. It could also refer to your name in someone else's tweet. Replies are not private and do show up live in the Twitter stream. For example, if someone wants to send a reply to Certified Book Yourself Solid Coach Cindy Earl, he would write @CindyEarl in the text of his tweet. You can also view all of your replies and mentions by clicking on the @ link on the right side of your Twitter home page.

- *Re-tweet.* A *re-tweet* (abbreviated RT) is simply resending someone else's tweet out to your followers. It's basically the Twitter way of quoting someone. This is an easy way to share valuable, relevant content posted by someone else with your followers.
- *Lists.* Twitter Lists are used to categorize or group several Twitter users together by creating a common twitter stream. This is a great way to follow your BYS list of 20.
- *Hash tags (#).* The hash tag is used to group tweets around a particular topic. You can see popular topics grouped by hash tags on your Twitter home page under "Trending Topics." Using hash tags is useful to find and interact with others who have similar interests or some commonality, such as attending the same conference or workshop.

Using Twitter to Book Yourself Solid

Building Your Followers   So, how do you use Twitter to grow your business? A big part of your Twitter strategy is building a following of qualified, targeted people who are interested in the content you share through your tweets, just like you would with a newsletter. People who follow you (or subscribe to your Twitter stream) get all of your current updates in real time on their home page. It allows you to stay in front of your target audience on a regular basis.

How often you tweet is up to you, but if you are really looking to build your following quickly, I recommend tweeting (The word really is ridiculous, isn't it?) a minimum of three times per day. If you're going to make Twitter a major part of your marketing strategy, you'll tweet more often. Consistency and frequency is the key to success in social media.

Finding People through Twitter   There are several ways to find people to follow through Twitter:

- Search for people through the Find People link at the top of your Twitter home page.

- Use your current e-mail contact lists on Gmail, AOL, and Yahoo.
- Invite others to follow you by e-mail. Twitter's e-mail form automatically sends a message to your imported contacts with a direct link to your Twitter profile.
- Directories, such as Twello.com, which function like the Yellow Pages of Twitter.

To build your own following, start by following the leaders in your field and then follow the people that are following them. In return, many will follow you and your Twitter list will build quickly.

You may also want to follow competitors or others who serve your target market, not to steal customers or clients, but in following them you may find people who may also be interested in products or services that you offer. If you follow the Book Yourself Solid philosophy, there really is no competition. We all are our own brand with different qualities, which attract different people to us. Always remember, there are certain people we're meant to serve and others whom we are not. Our job is to work hard to find the people we are meant to serve.

What Are Your Goals for Using Twitter?   As with any self-promotion strategy, first consider what you want to accomplish. Your objectives for using Twitter, just as with Facebook and LinkedIn may include one or more of the following:

- Finding clients.
- Finding networking partners.
- Cross-promoting with strategic alliance partners.
- Earning credibility.
- Creating visibility.
- Announcing events.
- Promoting your products and services.
- Driving traffic to your site.
- Driving traffic to your blog.
- Building your e-mail list.

- Having sales conversations.
- Creating a base of raving fans.

What Is Your Message? In other words, what exactly should you be tweeting about? You can apply the 80/20 Rule for developing social media content. Eighty percent of the content you share on Twitter (or any social network) should be educational or thought-provoking in nature and 20 percent can be promotional.

Share tips, strategies, articles, online press releases, links, and retweet content that is relevant to your target market. You can also import your blog posts directly into Twitter by using tweetfeed.com. If the content you provide is compelling, your followers will be interested in your more promotional tweets. As you know by now, social networks are about building relationships first and establishing yourself as an expert by communicating relevant educational content to your followers over time.

Automation Outside developers (called Twitter clients) have created hundreds of applications you can use with Twitter to automate and leverage your time. Here are some of the most common uses of automation tools:

- Automate content and preschedule Tweets. For example, you can write out your tweets for an entire week using a Twitter automation tool to preschedule tweets to go out at certain times during the week. Just remember, you should automate things like tips, strategies, quotes and other promotional content, but you cannot automate things like personal updates throughout your day.
- Send a welcome message by direct message to new followers.
- Manage multiple Twitter accounts.
- View multiple columns to see @replies, direct messages, keyword tracking, and other social network accounts at one time.
- Track statistics of clicks to links posted in your Twitter stream.
- Create groups of friends and lists.
- Post audio or video content to Twitter.
- Cell phone and handheld applications so you can tweet from anywhere.

For an up-to-date list of Twitter applications, go to Certified Book Yourself Solid Coach Cindy Earl's site, GetKnownGetClients.com. She publishes a list of great Twitter apps on her site for your reading and using pleasure.

Twitter Done Right   Chris Brogan is president of Human Business Works, a media and education company and co-author of *Trust Agents*, a *New York Times* best-selling book about the vital importance of establishing trust and credibility with your clients and customers.

Chris is a master at using Twitter for business. At the time this chapter was written, he had more than 150,000 followers on Twitter and had posted over 65,000 tweets. His tweets are fun, interesting, and all related to social media marketing. He has a distinct, casual Twitter style, effectively combining tweets about everyday life with relevant, high-value content. If you follow Chris, you'll notice that he follows the 80/20 Rule. Most of his content is educational (how to do social networking) or personal (what he feels and thinks about various social issues) in nature. Very few of his tweets are outwardly self-promotional.

One of the things I like about Chris is his unique style. His Twitter home page is custom designed with graphics that represent him as a brand. His *who and do what* statement is immediately apparent with just a quick glance at his page. He also uses Twitter to communicate with his followers directly through frequent direct messages and replies. If you want a great example of Twitter done right, plus some really useful social media content, make sure to follow Chris at @chrisbrogan.

Be sure to follow me, too, @michaelport.

The Book Yourself Solid Video Marketing Strategy

The use of online video as a marketing and promotion tool has exploded over the last few years, and with good reason. The emergence of YouTube and other no or low-cost video resources has made it possible for small businesses and entrepreneurs to reach potential customers quickly, easily, and affordably.

YouTube is now the fourth-most-visited site on the Internet, and—surprise—the second most popular search engine, right behind Google. Video gives you new opportunities to increase your visibility and credibility within your market.

Using video can be one of your most powerful tools in getting booked solid. Just like the other social media strategies I've discussed, video marketing could easily take up a book of its own so here I'll focus just on what you need to get started—without getting bogged down by the technology. I'll also point out several ways to use video marketing to your advantage, and we'll look at a few entrepreneurs who are using online video successfully.

Why Use Online Video? Here are some reasons why video marketing is such a powerful, new booked solid promotion strategy:

- As mentioned earlier, video has a low barrier to entry. There is very little investment to creating online videos. All you really need to start is a webcam and a free account on YouTube.com.
- Online video is a great way to create a strong, personal connection to your clients and prospects. Like social media, video begins building a personal relationship even if you've never met face to face.
- Video enhances your trustworthiness, credibility and likeability. It's easier for people to relate to you when they can see you on screen and hear your voice.
- Another benefit of video is that it can significantly improve your search engine rankings. SEO experts agree that Google loves video, and a Forrester Research study found that video has a *50 times better* chance than plain text for getting to the top of search rankings!
- All of these strategies work together to create one of online video's biggest strengths—increasing awareness for who you are and what you offer—and it accelerates the sales process.

Business Uses for Video   Now that we've looked at some of the compelling reasons *why* you should be using video marketing, let's look at some of the *how*. Here are eight suggested business uses for video:

- *Web site*. You can create a welcome video for your home page, perhaps sharing your *who and do what* and *why you do it* statements with your web visitors.
- *Blog*. Turn your blog into a vlog, or video blog, with which you can provide expert tips, product reviews, and news about your programs and services.
- *Sales Page*. Video sales messages are becoming more common online, and you can get in on the act by adding a video to your sales page.
- *Client testimonials through video*. Create video testimonials for clients or colleagues, and ask them to do the same for you.
- *Video e-mail*. Add video (or a link to a video) in your e-mail, turning your message into a video postcard.
- *Video coaching*. You can also use video to enhance the delivery of your services by making your sessions or meetings with your clients more personal, interactive, and dynamic. Check out online tools such as Skype.com, Ustream.tv, or Dimdim.com.
- *Video tutorials and screen captures*. You need not be on camera to create videos. Consider creating video tutorials or online demos using tools such as Jingproject.com, Camtasia.com, or ScreenFlow.com for the Mac.

Create Online Video in Four Simple Steps   If any of these video suggestions sound daunting to you, take heart in the knowledge that the entire process of creating online video boils down to four simple steps . . .

1. Your goal.
2. Your message.
3. Your format.
4. Your distribution and promotion.

Let's take a brief look at each . . .

Step 1: Goals for Your Videos   Begin with the end in mind and consider what you want to accomplish with your video. Your objectives may include one or more of the following:

- Increasing online exposure.
- Driving traffic to your web site.
- Enhancing your expert status.
- Building trust and credibility.
- Developing your personal brand.

Consider what video can do for you. Where can video have the most impact on your business? Whatever you decide, be sure it's part of your overall marketing strategy. Video marketing should be integrated with the rest of your marketing plan, and not just as an add-on or afterthought.

Whether your objectives for video include visibility, branding, search engine optimization, web traffic, or client attraction, your goal will determine your path. If your goal is to enhance your expert status, for example, you may consider doing a weekly, live webcast on Ustream.tv. With a free account and a webcam, you can create your own "Ask the Expert" web TV show. If, on the other hand, your goal is to educate or inform with instructional videos, then a Camtasia or Jing screen capture demo may be your best option.

Step 2: Your Message   When it comes to video, content is king. Focus more on your message than on the technology. When crafting your message, keep your target audience at the top of your mind and share something of value with them. Attention spans are short on the Web, so be sure to get to the point and keep your video as brief as possible. Here are a few other tips to consider as you develop your video message:

- Be consistent with your content. Don't confuse your viewers.
- Develop an overall theme for your videos and stay on message.

- Maintain an almost fanatical focus on your core message.
- Your message includes not only what you say, but *how* you say it.

Why is keeping your message consistent so important? If your video message is clear and coherent, people will immediately understand what you do, and that makes it much easier to attract clients. Customers will seek you out because there's no confusion about who you are and who you serve. Do this consistently over time, and your message will become part of your brand.

If you're still not sure about developing your video message, here's a list of different types of video messages you might consider:

- Expert tips series.
- Your backstory—what you stand for—your *why you do it* statement.
- Personal message on your home page.
- Product launch promotion.
- Instructional or how-to demo.
- Editorial—your take, or rant, on an issue or topic.
- Your "Top Ten" list.
- Testimonial or book review.
- Live Q&A "ask the expert."
- Interview format.
- Speaking demo or event video.

Step 3: Your Video Format The third step in creating your video is deciding on the delivery method you will use to share your video. Will you be on camera, or do you prefer to create a screen capture or slide show? Do you want to prerecord a video and edit it later, or would you be more comfortable doing a live webcast? There are a number of options when it comes to the actual format of your video. Choices include:

- *Record directly through a webcam.* Probably the quickest and easiest option.
- *Record live through a webcast.* Using free web sites such as Ustream.tv.

- *Shoot on location.* Usually outdoors using a portable pocket camera like the Flip Video camera.
- *Tape a screen capture or slide show.* Using PowerPoint or Jingproject.com.
- *Create a video or photo montage.* Using web tools such as Animoto.com.

Keep in mind that whatever delivery method you choose, your format also includes your personal style. In other words, consider the tone and attitude of your delivery. Do you want to be humorous or informal, or does a more authoritative and informative approach work better for you?

Obviously, your format is going to dictate your equipment needed, so let's take a brief look at some nuts and bolts. Fortunately, with an inexpensive webcam, pocket video camera, or minicam, you'll be armed with enough to get started. Most digital photo cameras even have a video function, so your existing camera may be all you need. With your camera, your computer, and a free account on YouTube.com, you're ready to create video.

Whether you use a webcam, the popular Flip Video camera or you decide to stay off camera and record a screencast with software from Jingproject.com, the five-step process is the same:

1. Develop your content.
2. Set up your equipment.
3. Record your video.
4. Upload your video to the Web.
5. Share and distribute your video.

If you decide to edit your video—which is not a requirement—you may want to start with editing programs that likely came with your computer or operating system. If you're on a Mac, chances are you already have iMovie. If you're a PC user, Windows Movie Maker comes standard with most Windows-based computers. Both are good starter programs if you choose to add graphics, music, or simple effects to your video.

For more complex editing options, and a lot more on using video for marketing, visit Lou Bortone's site at OnlineVideoBranding.com. Lou is a Certified Book Yourself Solid Coach and an absolute master at teaching people how to get booked solid using video.

What if you are having a bad hair day or you're terribly camera-shy? If you do not want to be on camera, you can still create great online videos to promote your business. There are several software programs and online resources to help you create videos without you having to be on screen.

I mentioned Animoto.com earlier, which is a great web resource for making videos using your own photos and text. Animoto even provides music for your montage. Just plug in your photos and the Animoto software outputs a slick, professional, ready-to-go video. A similar web site with even more bells and whistles is OneTrueMedia.com.

You can also create video tutorials or screen captures using Jing (JingProject.com), Screenr.com (free), or the more expensive and more complex screen capture program, Camtasia.com. Even PowerPoint presentations can be adapted and used as online videos.

Step 4: Distribute and Promote Your Video   The fourth and final element for video creation is your online distribution. It's rarely enough to simply upload your video to YouTube.com and expect instant fame and fortune. Your video must be leveraged and distributed across a number of platforms for maximum impact. Sharing and promoting your video is a vital step in the process. The greater the distribution of your video, the more visibility you'll receive.

One video can serve many purposes and be distributed across multiple sites. Of course, there are dozens of video hosting sites in addition to the big kahuna, YouTube. To simplify the distribution process, I suggest the following:

- Start by uploading your video to YouTube.com.
- Use the embed code that YouTube provides to post the video on your own web site or blog. You can also use the link YouTube provides to send out in an e-mail or e-zine.
- Use YouTube's one-click share functions to cross post your video from YouTube to Facebook, Twitter, MySpace, and more.

- Once you've got YouTube covered, you can open a free account on TubeMogul.com.
- After you set up your account on TubeMogul.com, you can use that site as a launch pad to blast your videos to more than a dozen other video hosting sites with a single click.

As you can see, YouTube can serve as the foundation for your video distribution. Like most video hosting sites, YouTube makes it easy to share your video across several social media platforms.

There are a few important considerations to keep in mind when you upload your video to YouTube. First, you want to make sure that the title of your video is descriptive and incorporates your keywords. Then, be sure to start the description section of your video with your web site URL. If you include your web address in the first line of the description, it will show up as a live link back to your web site. Finally, be sure you also fill out YouTube's tags section with your keywords.

Get Social   Part of the magic of video marketing is expanding your visibility and exposure through social media. Video is viral by nature, and sharing your video across as many social media platforms as you know of can extend the reach of your video all across the Web.

Once you've created your video, be sure to use social networks like Twitter, Facebook, LinkedIn, and others to get your video in front of as many people as possible. While you can't post your video on Twitter, video-friendly sites such as Tweetube.com and Twiddeo.com make it easy to promote your video on Twitter.

Facebook is also an excellent platform to share your video. You can share your video on Facebook from YouTube, or upload your video directly to Facebook. You can then alert your friends that you've posted a new video. When others comment on your video, the video appears on their page as well. One more thing: While you can tag people who appear in your video to alert them on Facebook, please, please, please, don't randomly tag people who have nothing to do with your video. It's more than annoying—it's spam.

Before we look at a couple of examples of video marketing done right, let's review a few takeaways for your Book Yourself Solid Video Marketing strategy:

- Focus on content over quality.
- Be consistent. . . . Quantity counts.
- Develop a plan to integrate video into your marketing efforts.
- *Done* is better than *perfect*. Just get started.
- Keep your videos short and share compelling content.

Video Done Right   One of the benefits of video marketing is that there are so many ways to run with it. In fact, there's no one formula for video marketing success—you're limited only by your imagination. That's why creativity and content are so much more important than what webcam you use, or whether your video lighting is just right. Your clients crave compelling content, and there are plenty of ways to give it to them. Here are just a couple of the ways entrepreneurs are using video marketing successfully.

Monkey Business   What do you do when you own a luxury rental property and the economy tanks, taking most of your market with it? You get creative with online video, of course. That's exactly what Evelyn Gallardo did for her upscale rental homes located in the midst of a nature reserve in Costa Rica.

Evelyn, with her husband David, moved to Costa Rica in 2000, after an adventurous career traveling the world as a wildlife photographer. They built two dream homes in Manuel Antonio, on the Pacific coast of Costa Rica, the Discovery Beach House and the aptly named Monkey House. However, the vacation rental home business can be tricky, especially in a challenging market.

To differentiate her rental properties and keep business booming, Evelyn turned to video. Armed with only a Flip Video camera and her energy and creativity, Evelyn taped a virtual tour of the Discovery Beach House as well as breathtaking footage of the surrounding area.

She had the videos professionally edited and began posting them on her web site (discoverybeachouse.com) and on her YouTube channel (youtube.com/user/DiscoveryBeachHouse). Thousands of people viewed the videos.

In addition to giving potential customers a full video tour of the rental home, Evelyn's videos included the monkeys frolicking by the pool, and local activities and adventures such as the Canopy Safari Zip Line tour. Evelyn's videos gave potential clients an up-close and on-the-spot look at the experience, generating buzz—and bookings—for her vacation home. She also shared and promoted her videos through social media on Twitter and Facebook, giving her Costa Rica rental property exposure to new audiences. Evelyn's video marketing campaign is the perfect example of bringing the product directly to prospective clients through the use of online video.

LouTube! Lou Bortone, the Certified Book Yourself Solid Coach and online video expert I mentioned earlier, has an extensive background in marketing and promotion. Before becoming an online entrepreneur, Lou was a marketing executive for E! Entertainment Television and Fox Broadcasting. Since one of Lou's strengths is video production, it's no surprise that he uses video marketing effectively.

Still, when Lou opened his own business, he was starting from scratch: No clients, no mailing list, and no visibility to speak of. That changed quickly when, on a whim, he created his answer to YouTube, LouTube!

Lou began taping branding tips, but he'd cleverly wrap the video messages in funny or outrageous packaging. One of his first, and my favorite, was "Spam I Am," a rhyming rant on Facebook spam. He followed it up with "The Ten Commandments of Online Video," dressed as Moses—complete with props and sound effects. Other amusing videos and characters followed, and Lou's online presence and notoriety began to build. Once Lou added social media to the mix, his video visibility skyrocketed, attracting the attention of both joint venture partners and new clients. He's my go-to guy for video.

Lou's "LouTube!" videos combined information, humor, and personality, creating the foundation of a compelling and memorable online brand. You can see Lou's hysterical videos at LouBortone.tv.

Whether you follow Lou's example and create your own, unique video presence, create an "ask the expert" web TV show, or follow your own video marketing path, online video can be a powerful Book Yourself Solid Promotion Strategy.

Social Media: Pulling It All Together

If you are serious about adding social media to your self-promotion strategy, you must start with a plan and schedule time in your day to devote to each of these platforms. Effective use of social media requires consistency and commitment. Results are not always apparent right away. Give your social media plan three to six months to start working.

Social media expert Nancy Marmelejo of VivaVisibility.com, suggests that the ROI (return on investment) for social media is threefold:

1. Return on interaction.
2. Return on involvement.
3. Return on investment.

According to Nancy, "Return on interaction and involvement speak directly to the time you put into finding ideally matched followers and turning them into stark, raving fans. These fans are the ones who gladly and voluntarily do your marketing for you. Return on investment starts coming in when your loyal legion of followers start responding to your offers. Your interactions and involvement transform followers into ready to buy."

Start using social media by developing your own daily, weekly, and monthly routine. Certified Book Yourself Solid Coach Cindy Earl, of

GetKnownGetClients.com, also an expert in social media, suggests adding the following tasks to your routine.

Daily

- Post your personal tweets and updates a minimum of two or three times a day.
- Schedule 15 to 20 minutes of time in your calendar each day to post and monitor your social networks.
- Get involved in relevant discussions, conversations, and responding to direct messages, friend invitations, responding to @replies on Twitter, and so on.
- Read your Twitter stream, Facebook wall, and LinkedIn discussions for new, relevant information for you and to share with your social network.

Twice per week

- Write and post a new blog entry two or three times per week. If you are using article writing to promote your business, or doing an e-newsletter, simply reuse the same article in your blog. Blog content can also be used for your business-related posts and updates.
- Visit other industry-related blogs and add to the conversations.

Ongoing

- Add new photos, links to videos you've produced and posted on YouTube, audio from radio interviews (such as Blog Talk Radio), and so forth.

Facebook, LinkedIn, Twitter, and videos—sometimes it can all sound so exhausting. "Do I have to?" a little voice in your head whines, and you want to pull the covers over your head. Actually, no, you don't, as I said at the outset of this chapter. Perhaps you have the kind of business that can flourish without an online strategy. For many of us though, an online strategy is essential, and using the social media platforms to their fullest is one of the surest routes to success. Not only that, as I think you've already seen in each of the three parts of this chapter, it's not nearly as daunting as it might seem at first. Why? Because being social about what you love to do (that is, your business) is not hard. In fact, it can be downright inspiring to connect with others and share what you know. After all, if you love to serve your target audience, what could be better than serving them better, faster, and easier. The Internet is your friend. Use it to make more friends. Oh yes, and to make more money.

Final Thoughts

This is not the end. It is not even the beginning of the end. It is, perhaps, the end of the beginning.

—Sir Winston Churchill

Congratulations! You made it through. The Book Yourself Solid system is provoking, challenging, sometimes scary, often exciting, and always powerful. The rewards you reap as a result of all your hard work will be well worth the time and effort you've devoted to this process. I hope you'll take the time now to acknowledge all that you've done because it's no small task. In fact, it's really big! We've covered a lot of ground, and you stuck with me, step by step, from beginning to end.

You now know who your ideal clients are and how to ensure that you're working only with those who most inspire and energize you. You've identified the target market you feel passionate about serving, as well as what their most urgent needs and compelling desires are, and what investable opportunities to offer to them. You've developed a personal brand that is memorable, has meaning for you, and is uniquely yours, and you know how to articulate whom you serve and how you serve them in a way that is intriguing rather than boring and bland.

You've begun thinking of yourself as the expert you are, and you're continuing to enhance your knowledge to better serve your market, and you understand the importance of your likeability factor. You know how to develop a complete sales cycle that will allow you to build trust with those you want to serve. You've learned how to begin developing the brand-building products and programs that are a key part of that sales cycle, how to price your products and services, and how to have sincere and successful sales conversations with your potential clients.

You are networking with others in a way that is genuine and comfortable, and you've learned how to build a web site that will get results, how to reach out to others in a personal and effective way, how to generate a wealth of referrals, how to use speaking and writing to reach more of your potential clients, and then how to keep in touch with the multitude of potential clients you'll connect with when implementing all of the Book Yourself Solid core self-promotion strategies.

Everything you've learned is important, but even more important is to remember the philosophy that underlies the entire Book Yourself Solid system: There are people you are *meant* to serve, and they are out there waiting for you. When you find them, remember to give so much value that you think you've given too much, and then be sure to give more.

I mentioned at the beginning of our journey that the people who don't book themselves solid either don't know what to do or do know what to do but aren't doing it. You now know exactly what to do. There are no more excuses, no more reasons to procrastinate or drag your feet or hide in your office.

The question now is what are you going to do with what you've learned? Throughout the course of this book I've given you written exercises and Booked Solid Action Steps that can earn you more clients than you can handle. Have you been doing them throughout the book? If you have, fantastic, keep going. If you haven't, are you going to start doing them right now? Your success hinges on your continued action.

To that end, at MichaelPort.com, you can continue to get support and advice about all of the concepts I've laid out in this book. If you want more help, if you want to have your own Certified Book Yourself Solid coach, if you want to work in a structured environment that will inspire you to action and keep you accountable so that you do book yourself solid, then join one of our highly acclaimed online learning programs, watch for a live event near you, or work directly with me in my personal mentoring program.

This may be the end of this book, but that doesn't have to mean the end of our work together. Your business is a generative and iterative process. You will be changing and evolving as you adapt to the ebb and flow of your growing booked-solid business, and I look forward to continuing to serve you in the best and most effective ways I can.

I sincerely thank you for spending this time with me by learning the Book Yourself Solid system. It means so much to me that you've taken the time out of your busy schedule to read my book and follow my advice. I am honored to serve you. I hope these principles, strategies, techniques, and tips make a true difference in your life and in the lives of those you serve.

I hope the Book Yourself Solid path helps you to look in the mirror every morning and have a mad, passionate love affair with yourself, do the work that you love to do, and book yourself solid while standing in the service of others and making a difference in their lives.

I love you very much (and not in a weird way).

Think Big,

Michael Port
MichaelPort.com
questions@michaelport.com

P.S. If there is anything that I can do to serve you, please just ask.

References

Bayan, Richard. 1984. *Words that Sell*. Chicago: McGraw-Hill Contemporary Books.

Bly, Robert. 2000. *Getting Started in Speaking, Training, or Seminar Consulting*. New York: John Wiley & Sons.

Boiler Room. 2000. Directed by Ben Younger. Las Vegas, NV: New Line Cinema.

Brogan, Kathryn S. 2004. *2005 Writer's Market*. Cincinnati: Writer's Digest Books.

Collins, Jim. 2001. *Good to Great: Why Some Companies Make the Leap and Others Don't*. New York: HarperCollins.

Covey, Dr. Stephen. 1989. *The 7 Habits of Highly Successful People*. New York: Simon & Schuster.

Crum, Thomas F. 1987. *The Magic of Conflict: Turning Your Life of Work into a Work of Art*. New York: Touchstone.

Curtis, Dr. Glade B., and Judith Schuler. 2004. *Your Pregnancy Week by Week*. Cambridge, MA: Perseus Book Group, First Da Capo Press.

Gerber, Michael E. 1995. *The E-Myth: Why Most Businesses Don't Work and What to Do About It*. New York: HarperCollins.

Godin, Seth. 1999. *Permission Marketing*. New York: Simon & Schuster.

——. 2004. *Free Prize Inside! The Next Big Marketing Idea*. New York: Penguin Group.

Levinson, Jay Conrad, and David Perry. 2005. *Guerrilla Marketing for Job Hunters*. Hoboken, NJ: John Wiley & Sons.

Mehrabian, Dr. Albert. 1971. *Silent Messages*. Belmont, CA: Wadsworth.

Meyerson, Mitch. 2005. *Success Secrets of the Online Marketing Superstars*. Chicago: Dearborn Trade Publishing.

Peters, Tom. 1999. *The Professional Service Firm 50 (Reinventing Work)*. New York: Knopf.

Pink, Daniel. 2001. *Free Agent Nation*. New York: Warner Books.

Sanders, Tim. 2005. *The Likeability Factor: How to Boost Your L-Factor and Achieve Your Life's Dreams*. New York: Crown Publishers.

———. 2002. *Love Is the Killer App: How to Win Business and Influence Friends*. New York: Crown Publishers.

Weiss, Alan. 1998. *Money Talks: How to Make a Million as a Speaker*. New York: McGraw-Hill.

How to Reach Michael Port

Participate in a Book Yourself Solid Training Course or Mentoring Program or Become a Certified Book Yourself Solid Coach

They're like living, breathing, how-to manuals that will start your engine roaring and send you out the door with a complete system you can use to propel your business, your income, and your life.

Learn more at MichaelPort.com
Follow Michael on Twitter: @michaelport
Join Michael on Facebook: facebook.com/authormichaelport
E-mail Michael at: questions@michaelport.com

Never hesitate to be in touch. We're here to serve you. And it's an honor to do so.

Fulfill Your Destiny

Thousands of others have turned their passion for what they do into an abundant career that profoundly affects others. You can too.

About the Author

Called "an uncommonly honest author" by the *Boston Globe* and a "marketing guru" by the *Wall Street Journal*, Michael Port is the author of four bestselling books, including the first edition of *Book Yourself Solid*, *Beyond Booked Solid*, *The Contrarian Effect*, and the *New York Times* best seller, *The Think Big Manifesto*.

A television personality, Michael can be seen regularly on cable and network TV. He receives the highest overall speaker ratings at conferences around the world and offers inspiring, collaborative, and results-oriented mentoring programs for small business success.

At the end of the day, his most significant accomplishment and responsibility is probably just like yours, the job of being a devoted parent, son, friend, and citizen.

Michael speaks to companies and associations throughout the world on marketing and sales. For availability, please e-mail questions@michaelport.com.

Learn more at MichaelPort.com.

Index